International Cultural Tourism:
management, implications
and cases

International Cultural Tourism: management, implications and cases

Marianna Sigala and David Leslie

ELSEVIER
BUTTERWORTH
HEINEMANN

AMSTERDAM • BOSTON • HEIDELBERG • LONDON • NEW YORK • OXFORD
PARIS • SAN DIEGO • SAN FRANCISCO • SINGAPORE • SYDNEY • TOKYO

Butterworth-Heinemann is an imprint of Elsevier
Linacre House, Jordan Hill, Oxford OX2 8DP, UK
30 Corporate Drive, Suite 400, Burlington, MA 01803, USA

First edition 2005
Reprinted 2006

Notice
No responsibility is assumed by the publisher for any injury and/or damage to persons
or property as a matter of products liability, negligence or otherwise, or from any use
or operation of any methods, products, instructions or ideas contained in the material
herein. Because of rapid advances in the medical sciences, in particular, independent
verification of diagnosis and drug dosages should be made.

British Library Cataloguing in Publication Data
A catalogue record for this book is available from the British Library

Library of Congress Control Number: 2005925256
A catalog record for this book is available from the Library of Congress

ISBN–13: 978-0-7506-6312-X
ISBN–10: 0-7506-6312-X

For information on all Butterworth-Heinemann publications
visit our web site at books.elsevier.com

Printed and bound in Great Britain

06 07 08 09 10   10 9 8 7 6 5 4 3 2

Working together to grow
libraries in developing countries

www.elsevier.com | www.bookaid.org | www.sabre.org

ELSEVIER   BOOK AID International   Sabre Foundation

Contents

Biographies of Contributors

Dagmar Abfalter, Mag (MSc), is a University Assistant at the Department of General and Tourism Management – Centre of Strategic Management and Leadership at the University of Innsbruck, Austria. Dr Abfalter's research fields include arts management, leadership and cultural tourism.

George Anestis is a researcher at the Technical University of Crete and holds a Master's degree in Computer Engineering and a Master's degree in Operational Research. His interests include database modelling, information retrieval, user modelling and information filtering, artificial intelligence and agents, distributed systems and web-based technologies.

Ian Baxter is a lecturer and Associate Director of the Heritage Futures Network based at Glasgow Caledonian University. He trained as an archaeologist, and has spent 15 years working with a variety of heritage and tourism organizations throughout the UK. He plays a leading role in the development of 'State of the Historic Environment Reports' for UK heritage agencies and his research also covers landscape conservation and management, historic visitor attraction development and site interpretation (this includes ongoing major research on Stonehenge). He has a particular research interest in policy and reporting issues within the cultural heritage sector. Ian is a member of a number of professional committees with interests in the field of heritage management, including the ICOMOS-UK Cultural Tourism Committee, and the UK Government agencies' Historic Environment Research Group.

Christine Burton is a Senior Lecturer in the Faculty of Business at the University of Technology, Sydney. She has worked in Australia and in the UK on project evaluation, visitor profiles, business planning and feasibility studies for arts organizations. Her research interests are marketing strategies for museum and impact of museums.

Christopher Chippindale is Reader in Archaeology and curator for British Archaeology in the Cambridge University Museum of Archaeology and Anthropology. His areas of research interest include rock-art, Australian archaeology, and the consequences of the esteem in which fine ancient objects are held. His *Stonehenge Complete* (Thames & Hudson), first published in 1983 and now in its twenty-first anniversary edition, has become the standard account of the later story of Europe's most famous pre-historic place.

Stavros Christodoulakis is Professor of the Department of Electronic and Computer Engineering of the Technical University of Crete, Greece, and Director of the Laboratory of Distributed Multimedia Information Systems and Applications (TUC/MUSIC). He holds a PhD in Computer Science from the Department of Computer Science of the University of Toronto.

Evangelos Christou, PhD, is an active researcher, consultant and academic. He has been awarded the status of Chartered Marketer. He has professional experience from the hospitality industry in Greece and the UK, and has co-ordinated or participated in several research projects in Europe and Africa focusing on tourism. He is Assistant Professor of Marketing at the University of the Aegean, in Greece, and Visiting Professor of Tourism Marketing at the University of Bolzano, in Italy. He is the author of two books focusing on tourism marketing and research and his work of over 30 academic papers has been published in several international referred journals and scientific conferences.

Harry Coccossis holds a PhD from Cornell University and is Professor of Urban–Regional and Environmental Planning, Department of Planning and Regional Development, University of Thessaly, Greece. He has directed national and international interdisciplinary research. He is also a consultant for environmental planning, coastal management, island development, tourism, urban planning and regional policy for Greece, the European Commission, UNEP, the World Bank, OECD and FAO, among others.

Adriana E. Estrada-González graduated in Leisure Management Studies from Universidad Mexicana del Noreste in 1991

(Monterrey, Mexico). She completed the Graduate Master Programme in International Leisure Sciences from WICE (WLRA International Centre of Excellence) in the Netherlands in 1994. She has been widely involved in leisure, recreation and tourism projects locally, as well as internationally. She was in charge of the Secretariat for the WLRA World Congress in Jaipur, India, in 1993. She has been a Board Member of World Leisure and Recreation Association from 1997 to 2003. Currently, she is Head of the Leisure Management Studies Programme and Co-ordinator of the Master Programme on Tourism Management and Development in Universidad Mexicana del Noreste.

Daniela Freund de Klumbis is a Lecturer in ESADE-Escuela Universitaria de Turismo Sant Ignasi, Barcelona, Spain. She is currently the head of Programme IHM Master (Sant Ignasi/ Maastricht Hotel Management School). She holds a Diploma in Hotel Management from Les Roches, SHA, Switzerland, and PDP certificates from the School of Hotel Administration, Cornell University, USA. Her interests are mainly in experiential marketing and she has contributed to several events.

Fotis Kazasis holds a diploma (1990) and an MEng degree (1995) in Computer Engineering. He is a senior researcher at the Technical University of Crete and has been involved in many European RTD projects. His research interests include the design and implementation of multimedia information management systems and applications.

David Leslie is Reader in Tourism at Glasgow Caledonian University, where he was instrumental in the establishment and development of the undergraduate programmes in tourism and later the MBA – Tourism Management, for which he is the Academic Director. He has published extensively in the field, most notably in the context of tourism and the environment but also in cultural/urban tourism, recognition of which saw him acting as a specialist witness on behalf of Glasgow City Council during the Parliamentary Enquiry into the Burrell Collection.

Ian McDonnell is a Senior Lecturer in the Faculty of Business at the University of Technology, Sydney. He teaches subjects involving the marketing and management of leisure and tourism services. He is the author of *Festival and Special Event Management*. His current research interest is the application of ICT to the leisure industry.

Nektarios Moumoutzis graduated from the Computer Science Department, University of Crete. He holds an MEng degree in

Computer Engineering from the Technical University of Crete. He is working at the Technical University of Crete since 1992 and has been involved and currently works in various RTD projects.

Wil Munsters is Associate Professor of Cultural Tourism. He has a strong academic background, including a PhD from the University of Nijmegen focusing on French literature and comparative aesthetics. He is the author of a monograph on cultural tourism and as a member of ATLAS he has contributed to the transnational Cultural Tourism Research Project with case studies on Belgium and Maastricht.

Nancy Nuntsu holds a PhD degree from the University of the North. She is currently employed as the Head of the Centre of Excellence in Leisure and Tourism Research Unit (CELTRU) at Walter Sisulu University (formerly known as Border Technikon) and has published several articles in peer-reviewed journals.

Dorothea Papathanasiou-Zuhrt studied Classics and Germanistics at the National Kapodestrian University of Athens, and History, Ethnology and DaF at the Humboldt University in Berlin. She graduated from the Postgraduate Department for Planning, Management and Policy of Tourism, University of the Aegean, in 2002, since when she has been active in Heritage Interpretation Studies at the University of the Aegean as a PhD student and researcher in various European Heritage Management Programmes.

Harald Pechlaner is Full Professor of Tourism at the Catholic University of Eichstätt-Ingolstadt/Germany and Scientific Director of the Institute of Management and Tourism at the European Academy of Bozen-Bolzano/Italy. He is President of DGT (German Association of Tourism Research) and ICRET (International Centre for Research and Education in Tourism). His research fields include destination management, entrepreneurship and strategic management.

Arvo Peltonen is Professor and Director of the Finnish University Network for Tourism Studies (co-ordinated by the University of Joensuu, Savonlinna Campus). He is an executive board member of the ATLAS and member of the Russian Academy of Tourism. He is Doctor in Human Geography at the University of Helsinki. His specialities in tourism research are educational matters in tourism, rural tourism and tourism planning.

Odysseas Sakellaridis, Associate Professor and current President of the Department of Business Administration at the

University of the Aegean, received his PhD from the École Nationale Supérieure des Mines de Saint-Etienne (EMSE), since when he has taught Computer Science at the University of the Aegean. His research interests include programming languages and applications, ICT applications in distance learning, e-learning systems, tourism, and heritage management and destination information systems.

Marianna Sigala, PhD, is currently a Lecturer in Operations and Production Management, University of the Aegean, Greece, and Visiting Professor of Tourism Management at the University of Bolzano, Italy. Before joining the University of the Aegean, she had been lecturing at the Universities of Strathclyde, Westminster and Surrey in the UK. She has professional experience from the hospitality industry in Greece, while she is involved and contributes to several international research and consultancy projects. Her major research interests and publications are in Information and Communication Technologies applications management and implementation in tourism and education, as well as in quality and productivity management. She currently serves on the editorial board of five international journals and on the Executive Board of the European Council on Hospitality, Restaurant and Institutional Education (EuroCHRIE) (as President) and of the International Federation of Information Technology, Tourism and Travel (IFITT) (as Membership Director).

Dimitri Tassiopoulos, who is currently reading for his doctorate, holds a Masters degree in Business Administration and a BA (Hons) in Political Science from the University of Stellenbosch. Since 1993, he has been involved in various national and international tourism research projects. He specializes in entrepreneurship and strategic management, and is currently an Associate Director at the Centre of Excellence in Leisure and Tourism, Walter Sisulu University (formerly known as Border Technikon).

Introduction: The rationale and need for this book

In most countries, the cultural economy makes up 'perhaps five percent or more of GDP (…) and by any standards, this is significant in economic terms' (Throsby, 2000: 38). In the European Union countries alone, there are approximately 200 000 protected monuments and 2.5 million buildings of historical interest (European Commission, 1998). With the advent of the Internet and the recent creation of the '.museum' Domain Name, a plethora of totally new, virtual and web-based-only cultural institutions have even been created (Sigala, 2003). Such figures underline the increasing centrality of heritage and cultural attractions in modern, technology and knowledge-based societies. Indeed, culture has become a major driver of tourism demand and flows into a country/region, while cultural heritage resources are placed at the centre of urban and rural development and rejuvenation strategies. Thus, it is not surprising that in recent years the cultural heritage sector has gained much political attention owing to its economic potential and its importance for market development in the information society. Yet, to measure the value of culture in economic terms alone is a fundamental flaw since the value that cultural institutions deliver to society is often indirect and non-financial as they primarily strive to provide intellectual enjoyment and raise awareness about the importance of cultural and historical knowledge. In fact, it is these other cultural value characteristics and the 'intellectual exploitation' that represent the true value of cultural heritage. This does not mean that market opportunities are to be ignored, but it implies that cultural institutions and governments need to maintain a realistic view on the exploitability and management of cultural heritage resources, as well as a return on investment in supporting the continuity of these resources.

In this vein, it is the aim of this book to identify and discuss major issues and trends that need to be addressed by the management of cultural resources and attractions. Thus, the overall objective is not to introduce a new management view of cultural resources, but rather to compile into one cover major management issues, trends and challenges facing the cultural tourism sector. These have been categorized in terms of key management themes and presented in four sections: marketing, operations, environmental and sustainable development, and new technologies applications. It is not claimed that in sum the contents are comprehensive and theory building in scope, but rather that they provide experience-based practical management perspectives as well as analytical and comprehensive examples of international best practices of a truly global industry. Contributions and case studies also aim to stimulate debate and provide directions for future research, while additional resources, references and websites are also provided. Therefore, the book is equally valuable to academics, researchers, practitioners and policy makers who want to further their understanding and knowledge regarding current management challenges facing the cultural tourism sector. Overall, the objective is to make a contribution to help cultural stakeholders as they prepare for managing the inevitable changes that will take place in the next five years.

To facilitate the book's aims and accessibility, the text is structured around key management functions, presented in four sections. Each section encompasses an overview chapter and three international case studies. Learning aims and objectives are provided at the beginning of each case study to help to focus and guide the reader. Effective and efficient management requires a clear understanding of the marketplace and thus the first section is focused on analysing and understanding the heritage and cultural tourism product from a marketing perspective. The overview chapter, by Evangelos Christou, presents an analysis of supply and demand factors, and identifies and summarizes the major marketing-focused challenges facing the cultural sector. The importance of understanding the needs and characteristics of the changing profile of the cultural visitors is recognized and addressed through the case study by Ian McDonnell and Christine Burton, which highlights the importance, and analyses the process, of conducting market research before developing and planning cultural marketing strategies. However, it is not only demand but also the supply of cultural tourism that is continually expanding and developing as a result of changing consumer interests and technological advances and applications. The importance and impact of the latter on cultural demand and supply are analysed in the following two case studies in this section. In their case study derived from their Spanish experiences, Wil Munsters and Daniela Freund de Klumbis analyse the importance and impact of lifestyle hotels (i.e. design and heritage hotels) as a major player in the international cultural tourism market. The driving role of new technologies on cultural product innovation is examined by Harald Pechlaner and Dagmar Abfalter. This case study illustrates how smart cards are used for developing cultural packages and customer relationship management strategies in the region of Tyrol.

The second section addresses operational issues introduced in the overview chapter by Harry Coccossis, which draws attention to the substantial diversity of types of cultural tourism destinations, such as location, activity, and patterns of use in time and space, requiring a diversity of responses, i.e. different management regimes. Even so, there are certain key managerial issues that are common; for example, maintaining attraction versus protection of assets, managing visitor flows, managing externalities (congestion, waste, etc.) and environmental management systems. The significance of the characteristics (e.g. design and facilities) of the site itself, and the way these are managed for enhancing the visitor experience are explored. Subsequently, and based on a typology of cultural attractions, the author analyses how the type of attraction influences the management approach. Examples from a diversity of sites, such as historic towns, historic parks and pilgrimage sites, highlight that the priorities vary, thus requiring a different mix of tools such as approach to heritage interpretation, information-communication and handling flows. Irrespective of the site or management approach, the importance of instituting a process of monitoring and evaluation is seen to be essential. The basic stages of such process include identification of conflicts/opportunities, adoption of goals and objectives, development of a strategic plan, implementation, monitoring and evaluation. This diversity in, and management approaches to, cultural tourism is manifest in the following case studies.

First, in recognition of the attention to the internal management and practical operation practices and in response to the environmental agenda and attention to corporate social responsibility, is the case study by David Leslie. This case study examines the environmental performance of cultural attractions and reflects the wider context of sustainability by drawing data and first-hand experience from an extensive research project designed and implemented to assess the environmental performance, including sustainability, of the tourism sector in the Lake District National Park. Finally, in general, the case study clearly demonstrates the significance, principles, management practices and their values involved in addressing the environmental performance of cultural tourism attractions.

The second case is Arvo Peltonen's case study of Helsinki, which is based on the city's year as a Millennium City of Culture, a competitive status designated by the European Union. This study introduces and explores the background to the city's bid for European City of Culture status, in the process identifying the salient factors with particular attention to the rationale for the bid. The overview of the management of the year's programme and distribution of events and activities demonstrates how a balance was achieved between encouraging community participation and promoting tourism. The 'post-event' research findings serve to reinforce the need for effective monitoring and evaluation and in the process raise a number of substantive issues and lessons of particular value to other cities considering applying to be a designated European City of Culture for a year.

Contrasting sharply with cultural cities is Dimitri Tassiopoulos and Nancy Nuntsu's case study, which highlights a range of operational management issues in their analysis of 'cultural villages' in South Africa. A primary objective of the case study is to evaluate cultural tourism in a developing country context. Attention is drawn to sociopolitical factors such as why cultural tourism is seen to address some of the key economic and social priorities of a country such as South Africa. Two Eastern Cape cultural villages, Khaya La Bantu and Mgwali, are used as cases to explore and illustrate the difficulties and challenges faced in the management of cultural attractions such as these. In the process, major and more widely applicable managerial issues are highlighted.

Operational management should not aim at cultural exploitation solely for economic benefits, but rather at a sustainable cultural development aiming to enhance all non-financial value and benefits of the cultural sector. Thus, sustainability and environmental management is the theme of the third section. Clearly, it is not possible to address the diverse range of management issues that are encompassed under such a broad title. Thus, the aim is to raise overarching issues in the context of cultural resources and the wider environment, rather than to focus on environmental management systems. The latter is well covered in an expanding library of publications, ranging from texts on sustainability strategies and corporate social responsibility to guides on 'how to green your business'.

The overview chapter of the third part, by David Leslie, opens with the challenges arising from tourism development of cultural resources and goes on to introduce sustainable development and Local Agenda 21 and the centrality of community involvement. The attention focuses on the tensions that exist between packaging cultural resources as a product for touristic consumption, while sustaining the community's cultural heritage; in effect, managing the balance between sustaining a community's resources and the benefits for the community and wider society that can be gained by improving access (both knowledge and physical) to them as a result of tourism development. Achieving such a balance is recognized as being fraught with difficulties. In the process of promoting tourism, cultural resources may be devalued in the eyes of the community through commodification and in some ways become disengaged or even 'unwitting' actors. Visitor pressures can also lead to damaging such resources. However, because of the perceived economic benefits attributed to tourism development, funding may be available to support conservation and to aid restoration, interpretation and presentation, thereby improving awareness and access – and not just for tourists. There is a line between contributing to sustaining a community's resources, and potentially therefore the community itself, and touristic exploitation. Thus, sustainability and environmental management are not just about cultural resources, but how those resources may be sustained in the most appropriate and equitable way in terms of the needs of the community. The following three cases draw attention to this key facet of international cultural tourism management, highlighting many of the issues and challenges that need to be addressed, aspects of which, as may be expected, are evident in other cases within this text, most notably in Part 2.

The first case study addresses community participation in tourism based on the tourist attraction New Lanark Village in Scotland, within which there is a diverse community, a community that has come to be as a result of the regeneration and development of the site itself. As such, it provides an invaluable opportunity to explore the participation of a community in situ in the development and management of this international cultural tourism attraction. The case study by Adriana Estrada-González provides fascinating insights into Mexico's ancient and historic cultural resources. Our attention is drawn to how centuries past societies have given little attention to this area and the challenges that this creates. Of particular note is the contemporary shift in emphasis towards developing cultural tourism and the issues that have arisen and which still need to be addressed. These challenges serve as the main focus of the case study on Stonehenge by Ian Baxter. This 'cultural icon' has a long history of management and an even longer one of neglect. Major issues relating to the impact of visitors, controlling visitor flows and protecting the monument itself are all encompassed. More significantly, attention is drawn to the wider significance of the site, the varied meanings it has for different stakeholders and the complexities involved in trying to manage access and at the same time satisfy a multiplicity of vested interests.

Being and going digital for many cultural operators is no longer an option but a reality. Many institutions have turned into 'hybrid institutions' that take care of and manage both analogue and digital cultural resources and visitors' experiences. The conversion of all sorts of cultural content into bits and bytes, as well as the enrichment of visitors' experiences by technological tools, open up a completely new dimension of reaching and creating new audiences by providing access to and experiences of cultural heritage resources in hitherto unimaginable ways. Moreover, in the emerging knowledge society, there is an increasing demand for high-quality, enriched digital content, as lifelong learning and continuous education are already a must. In this vein, successful and appropriate management of new technologies and particularly of the Internet will bring the cultural operators in the prime location to deliver to and meet the unique and personalized learning experiences and needs of an increasing varied and wide profile of cultural audience.

These technological trends and management issues are identified and analysed in the final part of the book, namely new technologies and media. The section starts with an overview chapter by Marianna Sigala that identifies and summarizes the major technological applications and impacts in the cultural tourism sector. Special focus is placed on the innovation role and impact of digital technologies on the cultural tourism sector, as they help to extend the supply chains of cultural operators beyond their institutional walls, and ultimately create and foster cultural ecologies among several cultural stakeholders. Moreover, new technologies diffuse within all operations of cultural operators (e.g. marketing, interpretation and visitor management) and impact on all cultural dimensions (e.g. demand, supply and sustainable development goals).

The three case studies that follow also aim to help decision makers on how to best face current and future management challenges related to building and exploiting a digital cultural landscape within modern societies. The case studies also highlight the interconnections between technology cultural management issues and the previously analysed and discussed cultural management issues. The first case study, by Marianna Sigala, examines how Internet tools and capabilities can enhance online interpretation by analysing the case study of eternalegypt.org. Overall, by adopting a post-modern perspective, the case study illustrates the management interconnections between Internet-based interpretation, online management of visitors' learning experiences and enhancement of online authenticity. Following on, Stavros Christodoulakis, Fotis Kazasis, George Anestis and Nektarios Moumouzis analyse how a virtual community-based information system can support the communication between tourists and locals at cultural tourism destinations, by providing practical implications and examples of such a system through their case study on the Campiello system in Chania, Greece. Their study clearly illustrates how technology can be exploited for developing community-based and sustainable tourism development strategies, as well as for creating cultural tourism packages. The third case, based on Venice, Italy, by Dorothea Papathanasiou-Zuhrt and Odysseas Sakellaridis, illustrates how a destination heritage management system can be managed and exploited for enhancing and managing visitor experiences, supporting heritage interpretation practices and overall contributing to sustainable destination development.

The concluding chapter, by the Editors, highlights the major discussions and management issues debated in the text, as well as provide some insights into future trends and developments. Directions and suggestions for future research are also provided.

Overall, we do not claim that this text covers all management issues or functions, for that is beyond the scope of any one book. Neither have we sought to produce a manual of management practices. What we have aimed to do is to identify substantive issues that are relevant to the global marketplace and as such applicable to all involved in the development and management of cultural tourism, irrespective of location or national boundaries.

References

European Commission (1998). *Culture, the Cultural Industries and Employment*. Commission Staff Working Paper SEC (98) 837. Brussels: EC.

Sigala, M. (2003). Internet heritage and cultural tourism under virtual construction: implications for online visitors' experiences and interpretation management. *Tourism Today* (3): 51–67.

Throsby, D. (2000). The economic dimension of culture: an analytic perspective. In: *The International Bank for Reconstruction and Development/The World Bank (2000): Culture Counts. Financing, Resources, and the Economics of Culture in Sustainable Development.* Proceedings of the Conference, Florence, Italy, 4–7 October 2001. Washington, DC, pp. 38–41.

The Book Editors

Marianna Sigala
University of the Aegean

David Leslie
Glasgow Caledonian University

Part One

Heritage and Cultural Tourism and Products

CHAPTER 1

Heritage and cultural tourism: a marketing-focused approach

Evangelos Christou

Introduction

As an industry, tourism is highly service driven. Tourism provides products and services for people participating in activities in places other than their residence. According to Leiper (1979), the tourism industry consists of all those firms, organizations and facilities that are intended to serve the specific needs and wants of tourism. A more explicit way of describing tourism is to consider it as '... representing the sum of those industrial and commercial activities producing goods and services wholly or mainly consumed by foreign visitors or by domestic tourists' (Ritchie and Goeldner, 1994, p. 72). However, tourism has unique characteristics that differentiate it from other industries. Unlike other industries, which have their own distinct products or services, tourism usually contains multiple products or services, and these often involve the co-operation of several suppliers. For example, a vacation package may include services provided by travel agents, airlines, hotels, restaurants and other related services. Although each of these individual businesses contributes to developing the tourism product – namely, a vacation – an individual business could not provide the product on its own. As Seaton and Bennett (1996, p. 4) noted: 'Tourism is not a homogeneous market like that, say, for breakfast cereals, cars or cat food. It is a heterogeneous sector which consists of several product fields, albeit ones which have a degree of linkage'.

The word 'heritage' in its broader meaning is frequently associated with the word 'inheritance', that is, something transferred from one generation to another. The role of heritage as a carrier of historical value from the past means that it is seen as part of the cultural tradition of society. The concept of 'tourism', in contrast, is a form of modern consciousness: 'Tourism's fundamental nature is dynamic, and its interaction with heritage often results in a reinterpretation of heritage. In its essence, the relationship between heritage and tourism parallels the debate that takes place within a society's culture between tradition and modernity' (Nuryanti, 1996, p. 250). During the past three decades, heritage and tourism have become inextricably linked throughout the world. Tourism is used as an economic justification for heritage preservation. Tourism also serves to preserve artefacts found in many parts of the world; indeed, historical artefacts and their associations have always been one of the tourism industry's most marketable commodities (Timothy, 1997). It can be argued that the early twentieth-century's 'grand tour' around historical sites in search of educational or cultural knowledge was, along with the tradition of the religious pilgrimage, one of the oldest motives for travel (Burkhart and Medlik, 1974).

The definition of heritage tourism is by no means a simple and clear issue. Balcar and Pearce (1996, p. 203) suggested that: '... heritage tourism is at present largely characterised by an expanding range of concepts and definitions, by a mix of individual case studies and more general discourses. Little specific agreement exists on what heritage tourism is, if indeed it is a separate phenomenon or how it should best be studied'. As with tourism, there are no widely agreed-upon definitions when referring to heritage tourism or to cultural tourism; in fact, there have been lively discussions (and in some cases strong disagreements) among researchers trying to distinguish cultural tourism from heritage tourism. A review of the best known definitions for heritage tourism and for cultural tourism is presented in the next pages of this chapter. However, for the purpose of this book, and in accordance with other researchers' views (Stewart et al., 1998), it can be stated at this point that the term 'heritage tourism' will be used to refer to historic sites and buildings and the experiences which people seek to have in them. In this context, the quality of the interpretative experience, the site's collection of antiquities, the environment surrounding the site and the site facilities will all be part of the 'heritage tourism' experience.

Overview of heritage and cultural tourism

The term 'heritage and cultural tourism' refers to that segment of the tourism industry that places special emphasis on heritage and cultural attractions. These attractions are varied, and include performances, museums, displays, archaeological sites and the like. In developed areas, heritage and cultural attractions include art museums, plays, and orchestral and other musical performances. Tourists may travel to specific sites to see a famous museum or to hear a special musical performance. In less developed areas, heritage and cultural attractions may include traditional religious practices, handicrafts and cultural performances.

As stated above, there is no single agreed definition of the term 'heritage and cultural tourism'. Masberg and Silverman (1996, p. 20) expressed the problem in the following terms: '... despite the growing interest in heritage tourism, there is a surprising lack of understanding of how visitors define a heritage site and what the activity of visiting a heritage site means to them'. Below follows a summary of definitions found in the current literature on heritage and culture tourism. This review of the various suggested definitions lends support to the definition of heritage tourism as proposed for use in this book (historic sites and buildings and the experiences that people seek to have in them).

Exploring definitions for cultural tourism

The term 'cultural tourism' has been used interchangeably with 'heritage tourism'. However, a number of researchers have tried to define cultural tourism by approaching it through a number of alternative ways. One of the best known conceptual definitions of cultural tourism has been provided by Richards (1997, p. 24), who stated that cultural tourism is 'the movement of persons to cultural attractions away from their normal place of residence, with the intention to gather new information and experiences to satisfy their cultural needs'. However, Richards (1997, p. 24) provided also a technical definition of cultural tourism, stating that cultural tourism includes 'all movements of persons to specific cultural attractions, such as heritage sites, artistic and cultural manifestations, arts and drama outside their normal place of residence'. According to Silberberg (1995, p. 361), cultural tourism is defined as 'visits by persons from outside the host community motivated wholly or in part by interest in the historical, artistic, scientific or lifestyle/heritage offerings of a community, region, group or institution'. Fridgen (1991, p. 221) also described cultural tourism from the visitors' perspective, stating that '... for outsiders, the culture of an area can represent an attraction in and of itself. This is sometimes called cultural tourism'. Therefore, tourists interested in culture may seek exposure to local behaviours and traditions, to different ways of life or to vestiges of a vanishing lifestyle. Yet tourism permits only selective exposure to other cultures. However, Fridgen (1991, p. 221) also identified the partiality that cultural tourists experience and went on to note that '... frequently, an area's culture is displayed through stage presentations often for pay. Because tourists generally stay in an area for a short time, what the tourist actually sees is just a faint reflection of the true culture'.

Tighe (1991) examined three components of cultural tourism: travel, the tourist and the sites. In particular, in terms of travel he stated that 'cultural tourism is travel undertaken with historic sites, museums, the visual arts, and/or the performing arts as significant elements' (Tighe, 1991, p. 387). In relation to the cultural tourist, Tighe (1990, p. 11) argued that he is '... one who experiences historic sites, monuments, and buildings; visits museums and galleries; attends concerts and the performing arts; and is interested in experiencing the culture of the destination'. However, in his earlier work Tighe (1986, p. 2) noted that the term 'cultural tourism' refers to '... historical and heritage sites, arts and crafts fairs and festivals, museums, the performing and visual arts; and is interested in experiencing the culture of the destination'. Hall and Zeppel (1990, p. 54) defined cultural tourism from an experiential approach, stating that cultural tourism is an experience '... based on being involved in and stimulated by the performing arts, visual arts, and festivals'. In addition, Hall and Zeppel (1990) observed a significant common element between cultural tourism and heritage tourism, namely the experiential element, and went on to note that heritage tourism, whether in the form of visiting preferred landscapes, historic sites, buildings or monuments, is also experiential tourism '... in the sense of seeking an encounter with nature or feeling part of the history of the place' (Hall and Zeppel, 1990, p. 54).

Finally, the World Tourism Organization has provided a definition of cultural tourism as well, focusing on the travel motivations of tourist: 'Cultural tourism includes movements of persons for essentially cultural motivations such as study tours, performing arts and other cultural tours, travel to festivals and other cultural events, visit to sites and monuments, travel to study nature, folklore or art or pilgrimages' (World Tourism Organization, 1985, p. 131).

Exploring definitions for heritage tourism

A recent definition of heritage tourism was provided by Poria et al. (2001), focusing primarily on the tourists' motivations and not on the heritage product. According to Poria et al. (2001, p. 1048) 'Heritage tourism is a phenomenon based on tourists' motivations and perceptions rather than on specific site attributes ... Heritage tourism is a subgroup of tourism, in which the main motivation for visiting a site is based on the place's heritage characteristics according to the tourists' perception of their own heritage'.

Another approach, mainly focusing on the past and on nostalgia, has been adopted by some other well-known researchers in heritage tourism; according to this view, heritage tourism is a form of special tourism that offers opportunities to portray the past in the present. Nuryanti (1996, p. 257) suggested that heritage tourism '... is characterized by two seemingly contradictory phenomena: the unique and the universal. Each heritage site has unique attributes; but heritage, although its meaning and significance may be contested, reinterpreted and even recreated, is shared by all'. In the same vein, Peterson (1994, p. 121) stated that 'we think of heritage tourism as visiting areas which make the visitor think of an earlier time'. Zeppel and Hall (1992, p. 78) also supported the concepts of 'nostalgia' and of 'special form of tourism', noting that 'heritage tourism is a broad field of speciality travel, based on nostalgia for the past and the desire to experience diverse cultural landscapes and forms'. In the same vein, Ashworth and Goodall (1990, p. 162) argued that 'heritage tourism is an idea compounded of many different emotions, including nostalgia, romanticism, aesthetic pleasure and a sense of belonging in time and space'. Sharpley (1993, p. 132) provided an earlier (though broader) definition in the same approach, noting that 'heritage is literally defined as what we have inherited from our past. Over the last decade, however, it has become more broadly applied and now the term is used to describe virtually everything associated with a nation's history, culture, wildlife and landscape'. Two years earlier, Yale (1991, p. 21) also adopted the 'inheritance' approach, suggesting that 'heritage tourism is tourism centred on what we have inherited, which can mean anything from historic buildings, to art works, to beautiful scenery'.

A more technocratic approach was adopted by Prentice (1993), who focused on the 'product element' of heritage tourism. Prentice (1993, p. 36) suggested that 'essentially in tourism, the term "heritage" has come to mean not only landscapes, natural history, buildings, artefacts, cultural traditions and the like which are literally or metaphorically passed on from one generation to the other, but those among these things which can be portrayed for promotion as tourism products ... heritage sites should be differentiated in terms of types of heritage: built, natural, and cultural heritage'.

The heritage tourism industry

The emergence of heritage tourism has spawned a large number of studies dedicated to the analysis of the heritage industry phenomenon and the reasons for its spectacular growth (Prentice, 1993; Silberberg, 1995; Richards, 1997; Pritchard and Morgan, 2001). The fundamental assumption is that heritage is an *industry*, in the sense of modern activity, consciously controlled and planned, with the purpose of producing a

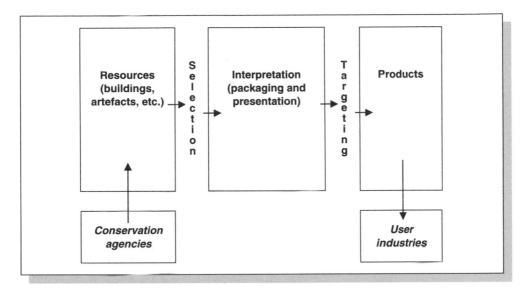

Figure 1.1
Components of the heritage industry (adapted from Ashworth, 1994)

marketable product. The process can be simplified into its basic components (see Figure 1.1). The resources in the model include the raw materials from which the heritage product is derived. These include events, relics, mythologies, artefacts, archaeological sites, legends, and so on. The interpretation process entails the transformation of resources into products through interpretation (Johnson and Thomas, 1995), and involves the selection of the resources and how they are packaged. This is a function of tourism demand, while the heritage product is the end result. This product can differ, based on the market it intends to attract; there is no one set national heritage product. According to Ashworth (1994, p. 27): '... the important point is that different products, for quite different markets can be created from the same set of raw materials by varying the interpretation process'.

The term 'heritage tourism products' refers to institutions, lifestyle-heritage opportunities, artefacts, heritage sites and events. These heritage products can be linked. Indeed, it is possible, and even likely, for heritage institutions located in a heritage or themed district to become the focal point for community festivals and special events (Richards, 1993). According to Silberberg (1995) there is, rather, a continuum of heritage products. The ability of heritage products to attract tourists is related to the eight points listed below (Silberberg, 1995), which serve as a type of 'checklist' to evaluate cultural products:

- perceived quality of the product
- awareness
- customer service attitude
- sustainability
- extent to which product is perceived to be unique or special
- convenience
- community support and involvement
- management commitment and capability.

The characteristics of the visitors of heritage sites are also of great interest both for academics and for researchers in the field. According to Peterson (1994) there are four different types of heritage-tourism visitors. They fall on a continuum, with aficionados being the most involved and casual visitors being the least involved. The following four categories have been defined: (1) 'aficionados' are considered to be preserva- tionists and perhaps very professional in their study of history; (2) 'event visitors' visit sites on special occasions (e.g. festivals); (3) 'tourists' are away from home and visiting historic sites; and (4) 'casual visitors' visit the site because it is a convenient green place (Peterson, 1994). Prentice (1993) stated that her- itage tourists and visitors could be divided into five predomi- nant groups: (1) educated visitors; (2) professionals; (3) families or groups; (4) schoolchildren; and (5) nostalgia seekers. However, Chen's (1996) research found that there was a highly insignificant relationship between educational attainment and reason for visiting a heritage site. Indeed, Chen stated that: '... Prentice's proposition is merely based on value judgements without any support from inferential statistic analyses' (Chen, 1996, p. 134).

Service quality, heritage and cultural tourism experience and visitor satisfaction

Service quality is a major issue in service industries and has become the centre of attention in all sectors of tourism. Service is the essence of services marketing, and service quality is the foundation of services marketing (Berry and Parasuraman, 1991). The main reason for the attention given to improving service quality in all organizations is that service leaders believe that high quality pays off. Zeithaml et al. (1990, p. 9) observed that: '... excellent service pays off because it creates true customers – customers who are glad they selected a firm after the service experience, customers who will use the firm again and sing the firm's praises to others'. In the commercial sectors of tourism, the ultimate goal of a tourism enterprise is to increase profits. As competition increases in the tourism industry, organizations and management have found that mere improvement in the technical aspects of tourist goods and services is no longer enough. Service quality is also an important issue for non-profit organizations and public-sector agencies involved in the tourism industry, despite the fact that they are not profit orientated. Crompton and Lamb (1986) explained that, in the public sector, the ultimate goal is to satisfy the needs and wants of participants. To do so, public organizations and agencies require a marketing orientation. This is because people spend their resources of money, time and energy in the expectation of receiving specific benefits, and not for the delivery of services themselves. In public heritage tourism authorities and organizations, the satisfaction of visitors through high-quality services has been identified as an essential element (MacKay and Crompton, 1988).

Although heritage tourists spend money, time and other resources on a trip or a visit, there is no tangible return on their investment. What tourists receive from their investment is an experience that provides mainly psychological benefits (Kozak, 2001). Hence, the heritage tourist product is not a measurable or quantifiable good. Rather, it is an experience or *un point de vue* ('a point of view') (Mathieson and Wall, 1982). This experience is based on the subjective personal reactions and feelings experienced by consumers when they consume a tourism service (Otto and Ritchie, 1996). Thus, although service quality is important from the perspective of the heritage tourism business, the experience that tourists or visitors derive from interacting with the service is also an important factor. Happy and satisfied customers are more likely to return, and more likely to say positive things about the service they have experienced.

Visitor satisfaction is the goal that both private and public heritage tourism organizations strive to achieve. This means that heritage tourism organizations should pay attention not only to improving the quality of service attributes, but also to improving the emotional and psychological reactions that visitors obtain from the service experience. As Otto and Ritchie (1996, p. 165) noted: '... the intimate, hands-on nature of the service encounter itself affords many opportunities for affective responses; it has long been acknowledged that human interaction itself is an emotionally charged process'. For example, an extended interaction with a tour guide or other service provider can also lead to experiential reactions. In other cases, as in purely recreational activities, the experiential benefits will be ends in themselves. Thus, if a heritage tourism provider ignores the psychological environment of the heritage tourism service experience, the result will be an incomplete understanding of the core tourism experience.

Both service quality and visitor satisfaction are critical aspects of a heritage tourism service. The goal of tourism marketers is therefore to improve both service quality and the level of visitor satisfaction. However, it has been recognized that service quality is an elusive concept for researchers and heritage-tourism practitioners to understand. Crompton and Love (1995, p. 11) argued that '... this elusiveness is manifested in the array of different ways in which it has been conceptualised and operationalised in the tourism, leisure and marketing literatures, and by the continued confusion about its relationship to satisfaction'. Heritage tourism organizations have not been given consistent guidance by the international literature as to the relationship between these two constructs. Although some managers have viewed satisfaction to be a measure of quality and management effectiveness, others have considered satisfaction to be synonymous with benefits. Many practitioners and researchers have treated service quality and satisfaction as being synonymous constructs and have used them interchangeably (Howat et al., 1996). This confusion between service quality and visitor satisfaction originated in the conceptual development of the two constructs. Both are derived from the expectancy–disconfirmation paradigm, and both involve visitors engaging in a comparison between the perceived performance and the visitors' prior expectations of the tourism service. Hence, the relationship between service quality and visitor satisfaction is an important issue in heritage tourism marketing. Understanding the relationship between them is likely to assist heritage tourism organizations in determining those aspects of a service that should be measured, which procedures should be used in such measurement, and which factors are most likely best to predict the behaviours of the visitors of heritage sites.

The case studies

In the following pages three very interesting case studies are presented. These cases provide real-life examples and empirical knowledge focusing on three relevant themes: the marketing of cultural tourism attractions, the examination of culture as a component of the hospitality product, and the use of destination management systems for enhancing cultural tourism packages. The different approaches taken by the authors serve well to illustrate and develop many of the main points made above. In particular, they analyse product marketing strategies or tactics that have been or could be adopted by specific cultural attractions, they present the most important consumer trends observed and outline the major characteristics of cultural tourist behaviour, they describe the relationship between the cultural tourism product and the hospitality product, and they explore potentials and opportunities for the use of smart cards for cultural tourism packaging.

References

Ashworth, G. (1994). From history to heritage – from heritage to identity: in search of concepts and models. In Ashworth, G. and Larkham, P. (eds) *Building a New Heritage*. London: Routledge.

Ashworth, G. and Goodall, B. (1990). Tourist images: marketing considerations. In Goodall, B. and Ashworth, G. (eds) *Marketing in the Tourism Industry*. London: Routledge.

Balcar, M. and Pearce, G. (1996). Heritage tourism on the West Coast of New Zealand. *Tourism Management* 17(1): 203–212.

Berry, L. L. and Parasuraman, A. (1991). *Marketing Services: Competing Through Quality*. New York: The Free Press.

Burkhart, A. and Medlik, S. (1974). *Tourism: Past, Present and Future*. London: Heinemann.

Chen, J. P. (1996). Factors influencing tourists' choices of heritage destinations. Unpublished PhD Dissertation. State College, PA: Pennsylvania State University.

Crompton, J. L. and Lamb, C. W. (1986). *Marketing Government and Social Services*. New York: John Wiley & Sons.

Crompton, J. L. and Love, L. L. (1995). The predictive validity of alternative approaches of valuating quality of a festival. *Journal of Travel Research* 34(1): 11–24.

Fridgen, J. (1991). *Dimensions of Tourism*. East Lansing, MI: Educational Institute.

Hall, M. and Zeppel, H. (1990). History, architecture, environment: cultural heritage and tourism. *Journal of Travel Research* 29(2): 54–55.

Howat, G., Absher, J., Crilley, J. and Milne, I. (1996). Measuring customer service quality in sports and leisure centres. *Managing Leisure* 1(1): 77–89.

Johnson, P. and Thomas, B. (1995). Heritage as Business. In Herbert, D. (ed.) *Heritage, Tourism and Society*. London: Mansell.

Kozak, M. (2001). Comparative assessment of tourist satisfaction with destinations across two nationalities. *Tourism Management* 22(4): 391–401.

Leiper, N. (1979). The framework of tourism: towards a definition of tourism and the tourist industry. *Annals of Tourism Research* 6(4): 390–407.

MacKay, K. J. and Crompton, J. L. (1988). A conceptual model of consumer evaluation of recreation service quality. *Leisure Studies* 7(1): 41–49.

Masberg, B. and Silverman, L. (1996). Visitor experiences at heritage sites: a phenomenological approach. *Journal of Travel Research* 34(4): 20–25.

Mathieson, A. and Wall, G. (1982). *Tourism: Economic, Physical and Social Impacts*. London: Longman.

Nuryanti, W. (1996). Heritage and postmodern tourism. *Annals of Tourism Research* 23(2): 249–260.

Otto, J. E. and Ritchie, J. R. B. (1996). The service experience in tourism. *Tourism Management* 17(3): 165–174.

Peterson, K. (1994). The heritage resource as seen by the tourist: the heritage connection. In Van Harssel, J. (ed.) *Tourism: An Exploration*. Englewood Cliffs, NJ: Prentice Hall.

Poria, Y., Buttler, R. and Airey, D. (2001). Clarifying heritage tourism. *Annals of Tourism Research* 28(4): 1047–1049.

Prentice, K. (1993). *Tourism and Heritage Attractions*. London: Routledge.

Pritchard, A. and Morgan, N. J. (2001). Culture, identity and tourism representation: marketing Wales or Cymru? *Tourism Management* 22(2): 167–179.

Richards, G. (1993). Cultural tourism in Europe. *Progress in Tourism, Recreation & Hospitality Management* 5(2): 99–115.

Richards, G. (1997). The social context of cultural tourism. In Richards, G. (ed.) *Cultural Tourism in Europe*. Wallingford: CAB International.

Ritchie, J. and Goeldner, C. R. (1994). *Travel, Tourism and Hospitality Research: A Handbook for Managers and Researchers*. New York: John Wiley & Sons.

Seaton, A. V. and Bennett, M. M. (1996). *Marketing Tourism Products: Concepts, Issues, Cases*. London: International Thompson Business Press.

Sharpley, R. (1993). *Tourism and Leisure in the Countryside*. Huntington: ELM Publications.

Silberberg, T. (1995). Cultural tourism and business opportunities for museums and heritage sites. *Tourism Management* 16(2): 361–365.

Stewart, E. J., Hayward, B. M. and Devlin, P. J. (1998). The place of interpretation: a new approach to the evaluation of interpretation. *Tourism Management* 19(3): 257–266.

Tighe, A. (1986). The arts/tourism partnership. *Journal of Travel Research* 24(1): 2–5.

Tighe, A. (1990). Cultural tourism in 1989. Paper presented at the 4th Annual Travel Review Conference, Washington, DC, 5 February, 1990.

Tighe, A. (1991). Research on cultural tourism in the United States. *Travel and Tourism Research Association Proceedings*, pp. 387–391.

Timothy, D. J. (1997). Tourism and the personal heritage experience. *Annals of Tourism Research* 24(3): 751–754.

World Tourism Organization (1985). *The Role of Recreation Management in the Development of Active Holidays and Special Interest Tourism and the Consequent Enrichment of the Holiday Experience*. Madrid: World Tourism Organization.

Yale, P. (1991). *From Tourist Attractions to Heritage Tourism*. London: ELM Publications.

Zeithaml, V. A., Parasuraman, A. and Berry, L. (1990). *Delivering Quality Service*. New York: The Free Press.

Zeppel, H. and Hall, M. (1992). Arts and heritage tourism. In Weiler, B. and Hall, C. (eds) *Special Interest Tourism*. London: Belhaven.

The marketing of Australian cultural tourist attractions: a case study from Sydney

Ian McDonnell and Christine Burton

Learning outcomes

- Understand better the process of applying market research in the cultural tourism sector.
- Formulate effective marketing strategies for cultural institutions in order to increase visitation from tourists.

Background and problem identification

A recent study that compared European and Australian cultural institutions under the aegis of the European Association for Tourism and Leisure Studies (ATLAS) was completed to provide data on which management decisions, including marketing decisions, can be based. The gathering and interpretation of these market research data can assist the cultural tourism industry in understanding more accurately market segmentation, information sources accessed by tourists in decision making and the consequent development of appropriate marketing strategies.

These results allow for some comparative analysis between those that may be considered traditional cultural destinations (the Old World) and the relatively new entrants in terms of cultural tourism (the New World). Although Australia has one of the oldest living cultures, it is better known for images associated with hedonistic tourism; tourism that encompasses the 'good life', the outdoors, the beach, adventure and sport. In understanding tourist behaviour within this broader context, it can be better understood how cultural tourist venues might promote and project themselves within this market to develop and maintain a competitive edge. This case study examines the salient elements of these findings to establish marketing strategies that can achieve the objective of increasing international tourist visitation to Sydney's cultural institutions.

ATLAS has suggested a working definition of cultural tourism that, in two parts, covers cultural products and supply as well as conceptual notions based on the behaviour and intention of tourists. This two-part definition is:

Conceptual definition: 'The movement of persons to cultural attractions away from their normal place of residence, with the intention to gather new information and experiences to satisfy their cultural needs.'

Technical definition: 'All movements of persons to specific cultural attractions, such as heritage sites, artistic and cultural manifestations, arts and drama outside their normal place of residence'

(Richards, 1996, p. 24)

Research carried out in Australia by Foo and Rossetto (1998) has also emphasized a more 'practical' approach to defining cultural tourism for the purposes of empirical study. They suggested that the most useful way of measuring a broad definition of cultural tourism effects is to analyse behaviour, motivation and attendance of those seeking cultural experiences.

It is this more practical, empirical approach to measuring tourist behaviour in relation to the consumption of cultural products that has been reflected in the most recent research in Australia. This approach, broadly in line with the ATLAS approach, is a foundation for comparing data within Australia and internationally, and from this developing marketing strategy.

One of the assumptions about cultural tourism has been that in an increasingly globalized and homogenized world, niche marketing and emphasizing the regional and local will become the distinguishing factor in a competitive tourist marketplace.

Reviews of trends in visitor numbers suggest that demand has been declining over a number of years. In Australia, the percentage of the population visiting museums in 1995 was reported as 27.8 per cent and for art galleries 22.3 per cent (ABS, 1997). More recent figures suggest a dramatic downward trend, particularly for museums, which reported attendance in 1999 at 19.9 per cent and art galleries at 21.2 per cent (ABS, 1999). This shift in attendance is not unique to Australia. There is some evidence that suggests an overall downward trend in Britain (de Hahn, 1997), Germany (Kirchberg, 1998) and other parts of Europe (Richards, 1996).

While recent trends suggest that this downward trend had been somewhat arrested, the uncertainty surrounding visitor numbers persists. The reasons for these movements in visitor frequency and numbers are complex and not sufficiently understood. Recent research suggests that an increase on the supply side of cultural attractions has resulted in a thin spread of those who are frequent museum attendees. More speculatively, changes in work patterns and participation rates, perceived rapid 'pace of life', overall leisure competition and the pursuit of depthless pleasure have contributed to the shunning of the search for the authentic and the 'worthwhile', traditionally represented by museums (Rojek, 1995; Lynch et al., 2000).

If cultural tourist product increases, competition for audiences and visitors increases and may result in a reframing of what cultural institutions are for: a fundamental questioning of their core business.

Comparative visitation: Europe and Australia

The ATLAS surveys began in 1991 and were intended to provide comparative data on cultural tourist trends in Europe. Universities carried out surveys in 1992 and 1993 at 26 attractions in several European Union countries, including the UK, Italy, the Netherlands, Ireland, Greece, Germany and France (Richards, 1996).

The general findings from the ATLAS Europe-based research are:

- Cultural tourism itself is not a new entrant in the total tourist portfolio: this sector has been developing for over 20 years and indeed since the end of World War II.
- Specific cultural tourists, whose primary motivation is cultural attractions, are an important part of the sector. However, they are not necessarily a growing niche market. Further study will assess the impact of sustained cultural specialist interest from Italy and Spain (currently the most vigorous special cultural tourists) and emerging cultural consumers from Eastern Europe, which will in itself become a cultural tourist destination for Western Europeans. However, tourists who visit cultural attractions as a secondary motivation are an increasing and important part of the tourist mix.
- Cultural attendances in Europe have declined overall in the past ten years. Richards attributes this to economic factors, but the reasons may be more complex and multifaceted.
- Younger tourists are an important demographic sector of the cultural tourist sector; they are likely to be better educated and more frequent travellers.
- Demand for cultural attractions as such is greater among first-time visitors, while experiencing a 'way of life' is more important for more seasoned travellers.

One of the few available sources of published data on Australian tourist cultural visitation is an Australia Council report by Foo and Rossetto (1998), who indicate that tourist motivation for visiting Australian cultural institutions and attractions focuses on a special or general interest in arts and culture. This report also indicates that visitors from English-speaking countries are more likely to visit Australian cultural attractions than those from non-English-speaking backgrounds, although the research also identifies fluctuations in interest in English-speaking visitors. Friends and relatives tend to play a motivating role in visiting cultural attractions for those from non-English-speaking countries.

Foo and Rossetto's research has been an important step in the direction of understanding motivations and behaviour of cultural tourists as well attempting to differentiate this category of cultural tourists. Importantly, it has highlighted a number of similarities and differences with the ATLAS survey of visitors to European cultural institutions. These are:

- The average age of cultural tourists is younger than that of general tourists in both surveys.
- Not surprisingly, those involved in some form of cultural industry as a professional are more likely to form the core of specific cultural tourists.
- Specific cultural tourists accounted for 28 per cent of overall cultural tourists in Australia compared with 9 per cent in Europe, which implies that tourists to Europe, no matter what their prime motivation for the visit, want to include aspects of culture in their holiday at a much higher level than visitors to Australia.
- Cultural tourists tended to stay longer in Australia than other international tourists. In Europe, cultural tourists tend to stay for shorter periods but take more frequent holidays. The location of Australia relative to Asia, America and Europe is likely to account for these longer stays.
- Many cultural tourists were first-time visitors. Those who had visited before still had a strong desire to visit cultural attractions, unlike in Europe, where repeat visitors were more likely to 'soak up the atmosphere'.

Australia is a relatively new entrant on the cultural tourist trail and may currently be attracting a curiosity value that may not be sustainable in the long term. Given the trends and predictions for cultural tourism in Europe, Australia's cultural institutions cannot afford to be complacent about their cultural tourism prospects.

A comparison of the ATLAS European study, Foo and Rossetto's (1998) report and McDonnell and Burton's (2000) study of 606 touristic visitors to three significant cultural institutions in Sydney gives insights into the demographics, motivations and touristic behaviour of these visitors, from which appropriate marketing strategies can be devised and applied by cultural institutions. The institutions: the Australian Museum, the premier natural history and ethnographic museum in Australia; the National Maritime Museum, the repository of Australia's maritime heritage; and the Powerhouse Museum, a venue for collections of Australian popular culture and social history, are typical of the sorts of cultural institution visited by tourists to Sydney.

The conclusions of McDonnell and Burton's (2002) study were that visitors to Sydney's cultural attractions are more likely to have a reason to visit and are more likely to fall within a traditional profile of cultural omnivores than their European counterparts. That is, they appreciate and consume many types of cultural activity: high culture in the form of music, dance, art, history, ethnography, natural history and literature, and many aspects of popular culture. Cultural tourists to European destinations are less likely to fall within these traditional profiles. They visit cultural attractions because it is a 'must do' activity on the tourist trail: a once in a lifetime opportunity to visit cultural attractions or icons only conceived of formerly in reproduction or by reputation. It is not so much an adherence to cultural capital as an adherence to cultural acquisition. These visitors are less likely to visit for the culture alone and more likely to visit for the multiplicities of both natural and cultural attractions. This is borne out by comparisons between planning for cultural visits: in Europe planning and decisions are more likely to be made before the tour (55 per cent before leaving home), whereas in Australia they are more likely to be made after arrival (30 per cent before leaving home).

McDonnell and Burton's (2002) study found that cultural tourists to attractions in Sydney:

- are evenly spread among age groupings, with a slight concentration in the 20–29 group
- have higher than average household incomes, whereas visitors to European cultural attractions are spread across all income levels
- are well educated: over two-thirds have a university degree or higher, unlike their European counterparts who more reflect the educational levels of their societies
- use family and friends as their principal source of information regarding visiting cultural institutions, or previous experience, with a growing use of the Internet, with only a small (>10 per cent) percentage using other media such as guide books, tour operators' brochures or the electronic media
- are more likely to be motivated to visit to be either entertained or educated on some aspect of Australian life, rather than to discover more about local culture or the history of Australia than visitors to European cultural institutions; conversely, are less likely to be motivated by a need for relaxation than their European counterparts
- are much more likely to decide to visit a cultural attraction after their arrival at the destination than their European counterparts

- are usually independent travellers and are not on a package tour
- are only moderately satisfied by their experience (55 per cent of visitors satisfied or very satisfied compared with 80 per cent of their European counterparts)
- are more likely to visit a performing arts show than their European counterparts, and conversely much less likely to visit a historic house or a heritage centre than their European counterparts
- attach less importance to visiting cultural attraction in their decision to travel than those in Europe.

Marketing strategies

Comparisons between the European and Australian data suggest that a much wider socioeconomic range of people visit European attractions than do Australians and visitors to Australia. This would suggest that managers and marketers of Australian cultural institutions can better achieve their marketing objective of increasing visits from tourists to Australia by broadening their appeal to a wider community than the present well-educated, comfortably off middle class, without dumbing down the quality of their programmes. A programme of product development that enhances the cultural product for visitors without negative consequences for the integrity of the institution can do this.

Product marketing strategies or tactics that have been or could be adopted by these cultural attractions to achieve this include:

- increasing opening hours in high seasons that also coincide with other cultural or sporting events, e.g. during the peak summer season opening hours could be extended to 21.00 h, and the admission price could include a meal at one of the attraction's food and beverage outlets
- joint ticketing between cultural attractions in Sydney that provide value for money and include value-added entertainment, e.g. themed music programmes in museums in collaboration with classical music companies
- talks by Australian celebrities or personalities about the museum collections or aspects of them that appeal to international visitors
- family nights that incorporate family-friendly food, e.g. pizza, and demonstrations, presentations or talks that appeal to both children and adults

- collaborative ventures with tourist operators that present a public face to the scholarship of museums, e.g. the Queensland Museum has offered a special dinosaur dig in the fossil-rich area of Winton in outback Queensland in collaboration with an outback tourist company, the Australian Geographic Society, Land Rover Australia and the Queensland government under the guidance of their palaeontology department, to experience outback conditions and a lifelong learning experience
- joint ventures with transportation companies and non-competing institutions, e.g. the bundling of ferry transportation from Circular Quay (the centre of Sydney's CBD and the place most visited by tourists in Australia) to the entertainment and cultural precinct of Darling Harbour, with entry to the non-competitive Powerhouse Museum and the National Maritime Museum and a meal at the latter's harbourside food outlet
- joint venture packages with non-cultural attractions, e.g. ferry transportation to Darling Harbour, a visit to the National Maritime Museum followed by a visit to the IMAX large-screen-format movie at Darling Harbour about the Great Barrier Reef
- a package performance with a visit, e.g. a concert by the Sydney Symphony at the Sydney Opera House with a visit to the Australian Museum.

As the research shows that a large majority of visitors to Australia do not make decisions about visiting cultural attractions until they arrive at their destination, promotional strategies should focus on promotion at the destination, rather than spend their limited promotion budgets on offshore promotion. This suggests that effective promotional strategies would be:

- making arrangements with hotels, including backpacker hostels, to stock brochures describing the cultural attractions and packages as outlined above
- promotion on http://www.whats-on-in-sydney.com.au/, which also has a paper version that is distributed to hotels
- making arrangements with local tour operators who produce day tours of the Sydney area to promote the cultural attractions to their customers
- promotional messages to emphasize that by attending these cultural attractions visitors will be both entertained and informed on Australian life.

Pricing strategies that flow from this market analysis are:

- as these visitors tend to stay longer than other types of tourist, a bundle of cultural attraction visits discounted from the gross value
- tickets that enable multiple entries for, say, a four-week period would encourage visitors to attend initially, as they would feel that they are getting value for money.

While this provides an opportunity for marketing specialists of cultural attractions to promote their attraction to tourists on arrival, it could still be seen as an afterthought, and is not seen as a 'must do' by a majority of visitors to Australia before arrival, but rather a spur-of-the-moment decision by those 'in the know'. Effective promotion in Sydney of appropriate products is therefore essential if cultural attractions are to improve their market share of visitors to Sydney.

In addition, it appears from McDonnell and Burton's (2000) study that Asian tourists are not particularly interested in the cultural representation developed by significant cultural venues in Sydney. Further research needs to be undertaken to ascertain the reasons for this, as the numbers of tourists from Asia, particularly from China, are increasing rapidly (http://www.industry.gov.au/impact, 2004) and a substantial opportunity exists for Sydney's cultural attractions in this market.

References

ABS (1997). *Cultural Trends in Australia.* Cat. No. 4172.0, DOCA. Canberra: ABS.

ABS (1999). *Attendance at Selected Venues.* Cat. No. 4114.0. Canberra: ABS.

Foo, Lee Mei and Rossetto, A. (1998). *Cultural Tourism in Australia: Characteristics and Motivations, Bureau of Tourism Research.* Canberra: DCITA.

de Hahn, D. (1997). Recipe for success. *Museums Journal* (July): 26–27.

Kirchberg, V. (1998). *The Changing Face of Arts Audiences.* The Kenneth Myer Lecture. Melbourne: Deakin University.

Lynch, R., Burton, C. and Scott, C. (2000). *Leisure and Change: Implications for Museums in the 21st Century.* Sydney: UTS/ Powerhouse Museum.

McDonnell, I. and Burton, C. (2000). North and south: differences and similarities in visitation to cultural attractions in Europe and Australia. In Toiven, T. and Honkanen, A. (eds)

North–South: Contrasts and Connections in Global Tourism. Proceedings of the 7th ATLAS International Conference. Savonlinna: Finnish University Network for Tourism Studies.

Richards, G. (Ed.) (1996). *Cultural Tourism in Europe.* Wallingford: CAB International.

Rojek, C. (Ed.) (1993). *Ways of Escape.* Maryland: Rowman and Littlefield.

Rojek, C. (1995). *Decentring Leisure.* London: Sage.

Websites

http://www.atlas-euro.org
http://www.whats-on-in-sydney.com.au/
http://www.industry.gov.au/impact
http://www.geocities.com/atlasproject2004/

Culture as a component of the hospitality product

Wil Munsters and Daniela Freund de Klumbis

Learning outcomes

- Present the most important consumer trends observed and outline the major characteristics of cultural tourist behaviour.
- Define the cultural tourism product and understand the relationship with the hospitality product.
- Compare the box hotel and the lifestyle hotel as hospitality products.
- Characterize the historic establishment and the design hotel as examples of the lifestyle hotel product.
- Identify the main threats and success issues with regard to the lifestyle hotel product.

Consumer demand and cultural tourist behaviour

The rapid growth that cultural tourism has undergone since 1980 is a direct result of the rising interest in art, culture and history, which can be explained by demographic, social and cultural changes. These changes will be discussed here as far as they influence the choice of the hospitality product as an ingredient of the guest's cultural experience.

With respect to demographic factors, the strong increase in numbers of senior citizens in the Western world has significantly extended the market for historic hotels, since the interest for history and culture grows with age. The 'grey wave' is all the more an interesting target group for the luxury hospitality industry as it consists of a growing number of retired, moneyed and active people in excellent health. These 'whoopees' (wealthy, healthy, older people) have a lot of leisure time at their disposal and more money, which they like to spend on holidays. Thanks to increased life expectancy, they are still active in leisure activities, which make them feel young in spirit: the phenomenon of down-ageing.

Simultaneously, at the bottom of the demographic pyramid, a reverse process is taking place caused by the decrease in birthrate, in the number of households and in the number of persons per household. There are more and more singles and 'dinkies' (double income, no kids). Dinkies use breakout holidays in hotels to escape from their busy professional life and to get charged up again by shopping and cultural activities. This holiday pattern stimulates cultural tourism in historic cities. Because of increasing individualism, there is a need for tailor-made products and services reflecting the guest's personal tastes and requirements, instead of a standardized supply. This explains the growing demand for single rooms without surcharge, as well as the emergence of unique and surprising hospitality products, such as the design hotel.

In social and cultural respects, both the historic and the design hotel benefit from the rising level of education: the more highly people are educated, the more frequently they travel and the wider their interest in art and culture. Being well-informed and critical consumers, familiar with travelling, the post-modern tourists want value for their money. For senior citizens quality and safety matter as choice criteria, while price is of secondary importance. The double-income households, who have less time because of their busy lifestyle, want to be pampered. For both target groups, comfort and convenience are important: post-modern guests expect from holiday accommodation the luxury they have at home, and even more. With regard to the hospital-ity product in general, they desire good quality and appreciate personal service and attention from the hotel employees.

As consumers living in the 'experience economy', tourists are increasingly searching for information that enables them to experience the destination instead of simply obtaining facts about 'how the destination is'. Travellers have become espe-cially concerned not with just 'being there', but with learning, participating and 'experiencing the there' that they visit (Gilmore and Pine, 1999). This trend for tourism suggests that travel has become a means of finding personal fulfilment, iden-tity enhancement and self-expression (Cho and Fesenmaier, 2001). Hotel guests are searching for unique experiences, new challenges and multi-entertainment in the form of action, emo-tion and (aesthetic) adventure. The lifestyle hotel is a hotel product meeting the needs of this special-interest market, and the same goes for 'eatertainment', a combination of eating and entertainment, for example, a medieval banquet livened up by troubadours, dancers and acrobats.

Another relevant trend is the rising interest in local, regional and national history and culture as an expression of its own identity. As far as this search for authenticity is a reaction to the uniformity and large-scale effects of globalization, it can be called localization. Averse to commoditization, the post-modern Western tourist is driven by nostalgia. Not only historic hotels respond to this 'back to the roots' trend, but also the regional gastronomy and the supplanting of fast food by slow food.

The relationship between the cultural tourism product and the hospitality product

General definition of the cultural tourism product

A cultural tourism attraction in itself does not make a tourism product. For that the attraction needs to be embedded in a whole range of services and facilities. On the basis of the elementary definition of the tourism product as an addition of attraction plus accommodation plus transportation, the cultural tourism product can be defined as consisting of:

- the core product: the cultural attraction (monuments, museums, cultural events) plus the related specific cultural tourist services, such as information and education rendered, for example, by museum guides
- the additional product: the general tourism product elements, either apart from or incorporated into the cultural attraction itself, consisting of:
  - general tourist facilities and services rendered by:
    - tourist organizations and travel intermediaries: tourist offices, national tourist organizations, tourist clubs, travel agencies, tour operators
    - primary tourism enterprises (companies that have their core business in the tourism sector and serve primarily tourists as customers): hotels, holiday parks, campsites
    - secondary tourism enterprises (companies that provide their products and services in the first place for the local population, but that are also frequented by tourists): catering industry (restaurants, cafés), retail (shops, banks)
  - transportation infrastructure:
    - accessibility (on their own or public means of transport), signposting, parking facilities
    - private and public transportation facilities: car, coach, train, plane, boat, taxi, city bus, underground (Figure 3.1).

General definition of the hospitality product

Belonging to the category of primary tourism enterprises, the hotel industry is an essential component of the cultural tourism product. Hospitality products need to fulfil customers' needs on several levels (Kotler et al., 2003):

- The core product refers basically to the benefits provided by the hotel to the consumer and not merely its features, e.g. room comfort and convenient location.
- Facilitating products are those services or goods that must be present for the guests to use the core product, e.g. a bellboy in a luxury hotel.
- Supporting products are extra products offered to add value to the core product and help to position it through differentiation from the competitors, e.g. full-service health spa.

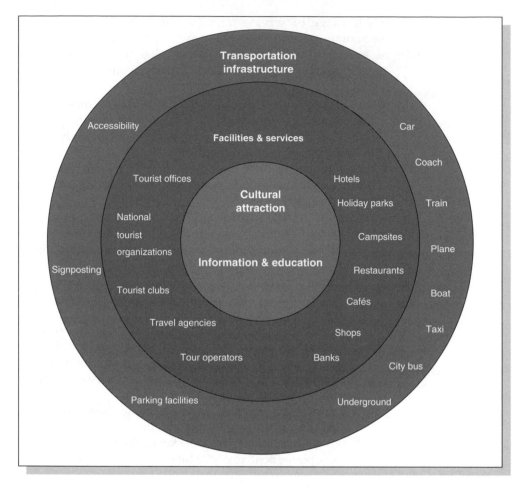

Figure 3.1
The cultural tourism product

- The augmented product includes atmosphere and customers' interaction with the service organization and each other, e.g. lobby socializing. The augmented product is an important concept because it is on this level where the main differences arise between the various hospitality concepts, e.g. atmosphere created by focus on lighting, marriage of textures and colours to please the senses.

The hospitality product as a cultural tourism product

Box hotels versus lifestyle hotels

The expansion of the international hotel chains, in the vast majority, was accompanied and made possible by a process of standardization and commoditization. This process generated the birth of the box hotel concept, characterized by the uniformity of the core and facilitating products. The lack of differentiation between the hospitality products and services resulted finally in a 'McDonaldization' of the global hotel industry. This systematic standardization of the hospitality product provoked a counter-movement inspired by consumers searching for hotels with unique or sophisticated and innovative characteristics, called boutique, design or lifestyle hotels. At the beginning of the 1980s the term boutique hotel swept through the market and was used to describe unique 50–100-room properties, non-chain-operated, with attention to fine detail and individual decoration in European or Asian influenced furnishings (i.e. a boutique as opposed to a department store). Sophistication and innovation explain the growth of the design and lifestyle hotel niches. In order to use a generic term for these new niches, hereafter the boutique, design and lifestyle concepts are referred to as lifestyle hotels.

Being independent enterprises, lifestyle hotels join voluntary groups (membership affiliations, consortia) to benefit from the advantages of chains, especially global marketing and promotion services, common packages and international reservation systems, without having the disadvantages of chain box hotels such as absence of management autonomy, architectural uniformity and standardized operational procedures (Yu, 1996; Andrew, 2001). Examples of these voluntary groups are marketing and sales reservation networks (e.g. SRS World Hotels) and free alliances (e.g. Relais et Châteaux).

The confrontation of box and lifestyle hotels by means of Kotler's product levels shows clear differences between the two concepts. On the core and facilitating product levels, box hotel companies present savings in building and staff costs, owing to standards of performance, as a major advantage to the hotel operator. In the marketing policy, the uniformity of the concept and the strong recognition of the brand are used to influence the consumer's choice. Commoditization generates, within traditional segments, a feeling of security and familiarity. For widely travelling tourists, however, the stay in a box hotel turns into alienation and anonymization. Many of them share the experience of awaking in a hotel room while asking: 'Where am I now?' This negative guest experience, caused by impersonality, predictability and boredom, has led to an important loss of clients and turnover with box hotel companies (Naber, 2002).

Since the supporting and augmented product level make it possible to add a memorable experience to functional lodging, it is especially on these levels that lifestyle hotels can differentiate themselves from box hotels. It is difficult to transmit a memorable experience for a box hotel, where the operations are controlled by standardized manuals and staff procedures are defined to the finest details. Lifestyle hotels, in contrast, seek to offer a fully balanced stay by means of experiential branding, which refers to positioning strategies that promise a certain type of pleasurable experience, encompassing all or part of consumers' interaction with the brand (Dubé et al., 2003). It is possible to manage hotel attributes so as to create pleasurable experiences by applying a matrix including 'hardware' components (the 'what') and 'software' components (the 'how'). Through this matrix, the 'hard' components, on the core and facilitating product levels, are made subservient to the 'soft' elements, the pleasurable experiences belonging to the supporting and augmented level. In order to meet or exceed the customers' expectations, the pleasurable experiences of the guest need to be orchestrated properly. Optical stimulation is achieved, for instance, by the lighting, decoration and presentation. Olfactory stimuli include aromas, freshness and cleanliness. Music, conversation or silence are part of the auditory stimuli (Gretzel and Fesenmaier, 2003). The hotel stay can thus achieve the value of an authentic, surprising and memorable experience for the guest.

Finally, in contrast with box hotels, lifestyle hotels share a strong cultural component and often are cultural attractions in themselves rendering specific cultural tourist services such as brochures on the hotel architecture and guided tours through the building. Since they also offer general tourist services (e.g. the supply of local and regional information) and dispose of their own transportation infrastructure or facilities (e.g. signposting, shuttle buses), lifestyle hotels can even be considered as autonomous cultural tourism products.

Lifestyle hotel products

Historic establishments ● ● ●

The growing interest in art, culture and history is at the origin of the demand for hotels and restaurants offering a historical ambience. The number of historic buildings (castles, farmsteads, houses, churches and even industrial monuments) fulfilling a hospitality function after restoration or renovation is ceaselessly increasing. The guests belong for the greater part to the cultural tourist target groups having a high or average interest in culture and wanting to discover, experience and broaden their knowledge of art and history during their leisure time. That is why they prefer small-scale historic accommodation with a high experience value, personal hosting and regional gastronomy.

An illustrative example of this is Saint-Gerlach, a historic country estate near Maastricht in the extreme south of the Netherlands, consisting of a monumental castle, a convent and a farmstead. It owes its name to a pious hermit who died in 1165 and is still worshipped by pilgrims in the local church next to the estate. Being situated in a river valley rich in natural beauty, the complex constitutes a unique site. In the course of the twentieth century the buildings deteriorated, but in 1997 the estate gained a tourism function, preventing its complete ruin. Camille Oostwegel Holding, a chain of historic hotels and restaurants and a member of the voluntary group Small Luxury Hotels, is the new proprietor of the entirely restored complex, which now offers:

- commercial facilities for the guests
  - a restaurant in the castle and a hotel in the farmstead
  - an apartment complex in the convent and the adjoining buildings. The external architecture has been based on the original style and the number of apartments has been limited to prevent physical pressure on the nearby conservation area
- social and cultural facilities for the parishioners and pilgrims
  - a new presbytery, sacristy and chapel dedicated to Saint-Gerlach, as well as a room for religious education
  - a museum with a treasure-house (Figure 3.2).

The exploitation philosophy is founded on a balance between the commercial, cultural and religious functions of the complex. A stay on the estate provides the guests with an enriching holiday experience in an authentic historical and natural setting. The management is constantly striving for co-operation with the parish when organizing cultural events for the hotel guests, such as organ recitals in the church. To ensure that worshippers are not disturbed, the hotel restaurant has been separated from the religious buildings by means of an intermediate buffer space. In this way cultural tourism can peacefully go hand in hand with religious tourism.

The carefully studied set-up of the Saint-Gerlach project constitutes a sound basis for the public support of the local community. From the point of view of the local authority, the project matches perfectly with the upgrading of the tourism product, involving a shift from mass tourism to quality tourism

Figure 3.2
Château Saint-Gerlach and the local church

that will benefit the well-being of the population. Thanks to the co-operation between the different parties aware of their common interests, the preservation of both the material and the immaterial cultural heritage has been guaranteed, and so Saint-Gerlach can serve as an example of best practice in the sustainable development of cultural tourism (Munsters, 1996).

Design hotels • • •

Having started in the late 1970s with Studio 54, the New York disco club that set the standard for hedonistic excess, Ian Schrager burst on to the hotel scene in 1984 when he opened Hotel Morgans in New York. He brought with him an unconventional approach and outsider mentality that was deeply rooted in the spirit and ethos of the entertainment industry. Design as décor for the hotel experience has always been part of his philosophy. Schrager's Morgans Hotel was the first property to emphasize the experience of hotel design from the inside, giving rise to the terms design hotel and designer hotel. It was the Royalton – the next hotel he opened in New York and the first in close collaboration with Philippe Starck, a renowned French designer – that would provide the blueprint for the Schrager hotel empire.

The most important turning point in the development of interior design trends for hotels was the introduction of the narrative into design brought by Ian Schrager and followed by Jean Nouvel (e.g. The Hotel, Luzern), requiring that the designer views the project more as a film director, theatre set director or author of fiction (e.g. The Park Chennai in India). It is the experience of this overall design concept that guests will identify and carry away as their memory of the hotel (Curtis, 2003).

More and more independent hotel operators embraced a modern approach in styling and equipping their hotels, extending the use of the term design hotel, trademarked by Lebensart Global Networks, the holding company of Design Hotel Inc. Subscribing to the view of design as a measure of living, not as a temporary trend, this company began to co-operate with forward-looking hoteliers and designers who shared a similar vision, such as Matheo Thun from The Side Hotel, Hamburg. For Europe, it is interesting to mention the evolution of the Sorat Group of Hotels, the Berlin group that started with a spectacular design hotel in 1990. This medium-sized company now has twenty-four town hotels all around Germany, becoming the European leader in terms of size in 2003.

Design has become one of the key elements in the evolution of the hotel product, and not only for independent entrepreneurs. With the launch in 1998 of its hotel concept 'W', Starwood is the first example of a traditional box hotel company moving into the design hotel sector. W tries to combine what is popular in contemporary home furnishings with the latest technology.

The cultural tourist target group catered to by the design hotels comprises consumers who want to be associated with other like-minded groups, and their choice of products and services is becoming a statement in itself. The demands from this community are very different from the traditional cultural segment. The typical clientele of design hotels can be described as art interested, early adopters of fashion, media and technology, who share a passion for quality and luxurious living. The latest technology and furniture extravaganza do not, on their own, provide the key elements to appeal to this target group. Instead, these guests feel attracted by the delivery of a total experience combining art, music, entertainment, novel architecture and interesting interiors in an uplifting package to enjoy (Figure 3.3). The design hotel product therefore offers not only quality in its exterior and interior, but also a feel-good element for its customers. This emotional value is achieved by

Figure 3.3
Hotel Omm in Barcelona, designed by architect Juli Capella: a view of its façade

the combination of traditional quality of service and the offering of additional services appreciated by this market segment, such as locality, surprise and originality (Freund de Klumbis, 2002).

The future of the lifestyle hotel product

Competition is fierce on the international hotel market and the imitation of successful concepts is a proven method to attract new target groups. So it is no wonder that many of the ingredients that contribute to the lifestyle hotel experience have been adopted by box hotels. Glocalization, the combination of globalization and localization, has been introduced as a leading principle in marketing policies of chain hotels. In promotional campaigns of box hotels, the role of local culture as a component of the hospitality product is highlighted by means of such slogans as 'Think locally, act globally' (Holiday Inn) and 'International standards, local flavours' (Golden Tulip). Whereas ten years ago design and style were unique selling propositions, nowadays they are minimum requirements to attract the sybaritic post-modern guest. Large hotel groups are even causing lifestyle fatigue through overbranding and, at the same time, the number of low-service stylish concepts is increasing, with design becoming an element adopted by various hospitality products, e.g. Base, the backpacker concept of the Accor group.

In this competitive struggle, the cornerstone of success for the lifestyle hotel product will be to pursue to satisfy the rapidly changing needs and wants of the post-modern consumer by offering an inimitable individuality and a fully balanced hospitality experience. The effective use of customer relationship management databases and one-to-one marketing actions has to be strengthened to be able to personalize products and services, thus increasing satisfaction, retention and loyalty. The quality of the staff will continue to be a key success issue because the lifestyle traveller seeks more than advice or recommendations. Hotel employees should not only be trained to manage the information exchange, but also be required to match guests to experiences. To perform such a consultancy task, they are expected to be informed about the hospitality product itself as well as its cultural environment (Freund de Klumbis, 2002). Furthermore, hospitality employees will be required to possess commercial skills based primarily on making the most out of each customer transaction by creating experiential programmes that push guests to spend the greater part of their money at the hotel.

It should be noted in this respect that consumers see food, accommodation and culture merely as elements of a greater whole relating to a total experience. Because of this, a relevant opportunity for lifestyle hotels, from a marketing perspective, consists of co-branding the property with a leading brand outside the tourism industry, e.g. fashion designers, retail companies, lifestyle brands. As the allocation to an existing brand name enables a quick transfer of the product values and contents to the client, co-branded hotels (e.g. Cerrutti Hotels and Bulgari Hotels) have a competitive edge in penetrating the market. However, co-branding in the hospitality industry requires a profound evaluation of both brand partners' strengths and weaknesses, a strategy for long-term co-operation and, above all, prudent implementation.

At the same time, it remains important to address the role played by the Internet as the most relevant promotional and distribution channel for the lifestyle hospitality products. The Internet still has great potential to link local suppliers to a vast global market of consumers. However, the same Internet and the growth in competition have made travellers increasingly experienced and demanding. Equipped with better knowledge and understanding, tourists will search out trips that conform to their new social awareness. That is why websites have to be designed to convey the types of pleasurable experiences promised by the hotel while ensuring pleasant browsing experiences (Dubé et al., 2003). Despite the high cost level of investment in information and communication technology and the complexity of the global distribution model, further investments and well thought-out planning of the electronic distribution strategy will be of vital importance.

References

Andrew, G. (2001). Evolution of tourist offers: the importance of an individual hotel experience in an independent hotel chain. Lecture given at the Eurhodip Conference 2001, The Hotel and Catering Trades for Employment and Economic Development in Europe, Venice, November 2001.

Cho, Y.-H. and Fesenmaier, D. R. (2001). A new paradigm for tourism and electronic commerce: experience marketing using the virtual tour. In Buhalis, D. and Laws, E. (eds) *Tourism Distribution Channels: Practices, Issues and Transformations.* London: Continuum, pp. 351–369.

Curtis, E. (2003). *Hotel: Interior Structures.* Chichester: Wiley–Academy.

Dubé, L., Le Bel, J. and Sears, D. (2003). From customer value to engineering pleasurable experiences. *Cornell Hotel and Restaurant Administration Quarterly* 44(5/6): 124–130.

Freund de Klumbis, D. (2002). Seeking the ultimate hotel experience. Paper originally presented at the XIIe International Leisure and Tourism Symposium ESADE-Fira de Barcelona, Barcelona, April 2002. *Gestión en H*, No. 11 (May–June): 58–76.

Gilmore, J. H. and Pine, J. B. II (1999). *The Experience Economy*. Boston, MA: Harvard Business School Press.

Gretzel, U. and Fesenmaier, D. R. (2003). Experience-based internet marketing: an exploratory study of sensory experiences associated with pleasure travel to the Midwest United States. In Frew, A., Hitz, M. and O'Connor, P. (eds) *Information and Communication Technologies in Tourism 2003*. Proceedings of the International Conference in Helsinki, Finland, 2003. Vienna: Springer Computer Science, pp. 49–57.

Kotler, P., Bowen, J. and Makens, J. (2003). *Marketing for Hospitality and Tourism*. Englewood Cliffs, NJ: Prentice Hall Pearson Education International.

Munsters, W. (1996). The strategic development of heritage tourism: the Dutch approach. *Managing Leisure. An International Journal* 1(3): 139–151.

Naber, T. (2002). Chain or independent: box hotel or boutique hotel? Lecture given at the Eurhodip Conference 2002, Hospitality Management in Europe: Moving into a New Dimension, Maastricht, May 2002.

Yu, L. (1999). *The International Hospitality Business. Management and Operations*. New York: Haworth Hospitality Press.

Websites

http://www.chateauhotels.nl
http://www.designhotels.com
http://www.hotelomm.es
http://www.overlook.de

Cultural tourism packages: the role of smart cards in the Alps

Harald Pechlaner and Dagmar Abfalter

Learning outcomes

- Understand better how destination cards can be an effective and increasingly used tool by destination management systems.
- Explore potentials and opportunities for the use of smart cards for cultural tourism packaging.

Introduction

While the point is often made that culture and the arts and the tourism sector do not fully comprehend or appreciate each other, recent societal tendencies such as a higher significance of culture and experience and the quest for identity have shown increased interest in cultural tourism. Cultural tourism has experienced a very dynamic development in the past few years, including steady increases in journeys to exhibitions, performances, festivals and other cultural attractions, and culture becoming an ever more important travel motive.

Cultural tourism in this contribution adopts the narrow view of culture which includes visits to cultural activities that are considered 'superior' in some sense, such as heritage tourism or visits to historic buildings and sites (castles, churches, etc.), as well as visits to museums and art galleries and attendances at performing arts events.

In the context of cultural tourism it is important to distinguish whether travel motivation is primarily or only secondarily influenced by the existence of cultural offers. Hughes (2000, p. 5 ff.) differentiates between culture-core tourists and culture-peripheral tourists, the first being a more exclusive audience being primarily motivated by culture, the latter being tourists who visit some aspect of culture during a visit to a destination but do not regard culture as an attraction in its own right. This distinction, also made between generalist and specialist cultural tourists (Richards, 1996, p. 270), is crucial as the market segments may vary significantly. Only a minority of cultural tourists would consider themselves as specialists or culture core.

The segment of the culture-core tourist or specific cultural tourist, in particular, is very attractive to tourism markets, being associated with people with higher levels of income and education, who are middle aged and rarely travel with children. They also seem to be less dependent on tourism seasons and show more respect and sensitivity towards the customs and environments of a destination.

Existing tourism literature provides a wide range of definitions in the field of cultural tourism, but there is no consensus (Weiermair and Pechlaner, 2001, p. 93 ff.). The conceptual definition sees cultural tourism as a journey to cultural attractions outside the familiar surroundings, connected to the purpose of gathering new information and experiences for satisfying cultural motives and needs. To sum up, the market for cultural tourism is in no case homogeneous and the focus is mainly on cultural attractions while consumer behaviour is not treated to the same degree (Sorzabal et al., 1999).

Destination management

Although the factors that attract tourists to a destination in the first place may vary, it is important to note that the actual product they are experiencing is a place, a town, a city or a country.

Destinations are the real competitive factors within the tourism industry (Pechlaner and Weiermair, 1999; Bieger, 2002). The tourism destination comprises a number of elements that combine to attract visitors to stay for a holiday or day visit. According to Laws (1995), there are four core elements that attract guests to spend their holidays in a specific destination: (1) prime attractors, i.e. the main attractors appealing to the visitor and differentiating one destination from another; (2) built environment, i.e. the physical layout of a destination including waterfronts, promenades, historic quarters and commercial zones; major elements of infrastructure such as road and rail networks, plus open spaces and communal facilities; (3) supporting supply services, i.e. essential facilitating services such as accommodation, communications, transport, refreshment and catering, entertainment and amenities; and (4) the sociocultural dimension, i.e. cultural attributes, bridges between past and present, and the mood or atmosphere, ranging from sleepy to vibrant. Destinations are areas where customers benefit from all the services they deem necessary for a stay according to their needs. The size of the guest segment determines the size of the destination areas. The greater the distance from the resident country of the guest, the bigger the destination area has to be defined, and the more specific the interests of the guest, the smaller the destination must be defined.

Destination management and marketing is the consistent orientation of tourist services and service providers towards the needs of potential guests. The concept of destination management has been developed on the basis of recognized industrial economics and management theories (Keller and Koch, 1997; Bieger, 2002) and is generally accepted by the majority of tourism scientists. The decisive factor in this context is the view of the guest, as he or she decides on the destination that fulfils his or her needs the most profoundly (Pechlaner, 2000). A guest's subjective feeling, expectations and experiences during the journey and the stay make his or her satisfaction a vital factor of competence of a destination management: the more expected products and services of a destination correspond to actually experienced products and services, the more likely a guest will be to return to the destination. The guests' needs determine the destination as a competitive unit (Inskeep, 1991). Destination management must be developed to guarantee the quality of the visit, competition on the market and the residents' quality of life. This implies that consensus, co-operation and synergy among destination actors in terms of joint definition and development of strategies, objectives and actions, must be achieved (Murphy, 1988).

The role of a destination management organization (DMO) is to 'act as a facilitator to achieve the strategic objectives of the destination' (Collins and Buhalis, 2003, p. 202). To reach, maintain, defend their competitive position on the global market, tourist destinations need to use methods and tools that guarantee the management of a destination in the future in terms of quality, value and sustainability. In this framework, innovative technologies such as destination management systems (DMS) play a decisive role. DMS stands for a personalized communication between tourism organization, guest and service providers on the spot. A DMS can be described as a collection of computerized information, interactively accessible, about a destination (Buhalis, 1994), and also as the information technology infrastructure of the DMO (Sheldon, 1997). A DMS should act as an enabling mechanism for integrating different services and products from the tourism industry (Collins and Buhalis, 2003). The goal is to cope with the individual wishes and needs of the customer electronically, to care for the guest twenty-four hours a day, and to facilitate booking at very little cost and without the need to visit the travel agency. Whereas in the past guest care was most important on the spot, the Internet now enables providers to take care of guests before they start their holidays, during their stay and when they go back home. A DMS should not only integrate the complete offer of all services provided by a conventional travel agency, it should also increase visitor traffic, attract the right market segment and create more efficient internal and external networks (Fisher, 1998). Electronic destination systems are nothing more than a virtual network of offers of a destination. DMSs also benefit from communication among guests and can be seen as virtual word-of-mouth communication. The co-ordinating body between public service providers and the guest may cope with special needs, wishes and problems of the guests, and take care of them very easily and quickly. Hence, the task of a DMS is to manage the participation of all local actors in the destination, to define standards and to integrate tourist products (Martini, 2000).

Tourists are looking more and more for an extensive offer of experiences providing value added (Pechlaner and Abfalter, 2002). Tourist cards are booming in the tourism sector and a great variety of local and regional cards is at the guest's disposal. Cards may be seen as a support for the destination in the whole process of planning, booking and buying services during or even after the vacation. DMOs primarily use tourist cards as a sales and marketing tool, yet, in the past few years, they have also realized the importance of cards in gathering tourist data as a means of customer relationship management (CRM). According to Fleck (1998), it is a perfect CRM tool for developing an intense and direct relationship as well as loyality among guests. A destination card has a range of advantages: it maximizes liberty of action for customers, grants rapid and cash-free access to services, benefits co-operative marketing among partners and enables network synergies. In the long run a card system may have a positive impact on the attractiveness of the destination. Furthermore, service providers may track the use of services offered in terms of access control, time registration, interrelated services, etc. Card technology provides an efficient way to gather customer information and to develop a pool of information about customers' buying behaviour and lifestyle. In general, cards seem to be a promising tool for the creation of unique value-added product bundles.

Card systems

The first guest card was introduced in Stockholm in the late 1970s and was a forerunner to guest cards in many other cities and regions all over the world. There were 236 000 sales of the Vienna City Card in 2003, and the Kärnten Card reached a market penetration of eight per cent in 2000 (Schmalz, 2000, p. 468). This card is a precursor among electronic bonus cards. With a prepaid card available at €32 for adults, a tourist enjoys free access to more than 100 locations for a period of two weeks. About 300 accommodation venues provide a prolonged card season, from 4 April to 26 October, to their guests. Since 2004 the chip card model, which started in 1996, has broken new ground with the all-inclusive card as an instrument for season prolongation. The 'Kärnten Spring Card' sports some forty destinations and attractions. Those who book a 'Spring inclusive' package receive the card when booking with one of the 140 members. The introduction of a personalized CRM solution is planned for 2005. The personalized Kärtnen Card may then be recharged in the next year (Bulletin, 2004, p. 17 ff.).

Destination cards are usually smart cards valid for a certain time, mostly without a paying function. A smart card is a credit card-sized plastic card containing a smart chip, which delivers e-commerce functionality such as stored value, loyalty and data management. Smart cards have become increasingly common as they provide new levels of customer convenience, knowledge about consumer behaviour and administrative efficiency. A smart card serves as a central tool for invoicing, planning and controlling with an integrated customer management function. Reporting and other functions can also be included in the system.

Different designs are possible; for example, the Bodensee Card, a smart card, is available for three days, one week or a fortnight and uses an all-inclusive concept with a fixed price to ease the calculation of holiday expenses (Kuhn, 2000, p. 450 ff.). The German–Austrian co-operation project 'Allgäu-Walser-Card' has been in use since December 2002. This concept resulted in an electronic chip card functioning as a guest accommodation registration form and at the same time offering a bonus for the guest. The accommodation providers send the guests' registration data online to the local tourism organizations and hand over a personalized chip card to the guest for free. Each community of the region provides a special bonus to the card holder. All 5500 accommodation providers in the region are integrated into the card system.

Each use of a contractual partner's service can be tracked and stored at a central data centre. The data gathered this way allow for an increased understanding of what the guest is really looking for and enable tourism managers to develop customized packages that can exactly meet the guest's expectations. This may be the decisive added value to a tourist destination.

The contractual partners usually receive a fixed amount of money for each destination card sold based on turnover and market size as well as a performance-linked share based on the average revenue and frequency (e.g. Kärnten Card; Schmalz, 2000, p. 466).

Destination card systems for cultural tourism: empirical research

Cultural tourism can capitalize on packaged offers through card systems in several ways and for several players. First, it serves as an important marketing tool for destination and tourism managers, offering options for CRM and market research, as it eases access to valuable information on visitors' needs and leisure attitudes. The packaging of cultural offers in one region, for example, can facilitate targeting culture-core tourists. The available online information allows for pre-voyage information and booking. Secondly, hotels can benefit from the generated awareness as all partners strive towards the same goal of bringing in more visitors. Another advantage is a transregional perception of a destination. Hotels are able to inform their guests and provide a vast leisure offer. Thirdly, participating service providers and attraction operators can attract additional visitors without involving much or any additional cost. Usually the attractions are paid a negotiated rate for each visitor that the card sends through. The attraction of new visitor segments such as cultural tourists plays an important role, especially for cultural institutions that depend on decreasing amounts of public money. Furthermore, participation in such co-operation eases image improvement or changes as well as collaboration with other attraction providers and official bodies. Finally, tourists can benefit from free (or reduced-price) entry to many selected venues with a bonus of special offers, extra facilities and updated information. The aim is to help visitors to make the most of their stay and to devote their trip to events and activities without the inconvenience of booking and buying. Additional costs can be calculated easily. It is important to keep the offer clear, identifiable and authentic when using destination cards. Experience with destination cards reveals high customer satisfaction, better utilization of infrastructure, sustainable customer retention and a clearer awareness of a tourism destination for tourists.

The example of the 'BodenseeErlebniskarte', a transnational and transregional card for Lake Constance, shows that 92 per cent out of 945 users stated that they would not have visited many attractions without use of the card, and 99 per cent supported the statement that the card offer made the region more attractive for a visit (Kuhn, 2000, p. 454). Experiences with the Kärnten Card showed similar results (Schmalz, 2000, p. 466). Cultural offers constitute essential components of probably all of the existing destination and city cards. Destination cards systems try to exploit opportunities to develop, co-ordinate and package the area's cultural and heritage resources to create market-ready cultural tourism experiences that appeal primarily to regional markets and secondarily to more distant markets.

In autumn 2001, the Tyrolean Tourist Board conducted an online feasibility survey via TIScover (Tyrol Information

System) to identify customer profiles, the required offer and design of a prospective Tirol Card, as well as the possible role of the Internet in marketing and supporting an optimal destination card system (DCS) for the destination Tyrol (Pechlaner and Abfalter, 2002). The study dealt with the tourists' level of awareness and information concerning the region, travel motivation and preferences, as well as online attitudes and desires concerning information retrieval, booking and services for such a card. Ninety-five questionnaires had been used for interpretation of the data. One important aspect of this survey was the question of whether there should be one basic card for all or customized options for different interest groups, such as culture, well-being or sports.

Concerning the sample, male and female respondents were similarly represented (58 per cent were male). Most of the respondents came from Germany (36 per cent), Austria (16 per cent) and Switzerland (11 per cent), as well as the Benelux states: Belgium (11 per cent) and the Netherlands (8 per cent). Forty-two per cent of the respondents were aged from thirty-one to forty-five, 29 per cent from forty-six to sixty, and 44 per cent were younger than thirty years old. Only 3 per cent were older than sixty years. The level of education was quite high, the highest level of education usually being vocational/technical training (42 per cent), a university degree (30 per cent) or an A-level education (21 per cent) (Pechlaner and Abfalter, 2002).

A thorough understanding of consumers' motivations for travelling to a certain destination is essential for effective tourism marketing (Fodness, 1994). On a Likert scale ranging from 1 (completely unimportant) to 5 (very important), the most important travel motives were shown to be a search for nature (mean 4.7), fun and new experiences (mean 4.2), sports (3.9) and health (3.8). The motives art and culture (3.6) and visiting historic sites (3.4) rank lower, as does education (2.7), and do not play a decisive role for travelling to the Tyrol. Still, cultural offers in the form of primary sites (57 per cent), museum visits (43 per cent) and historic sites (42 per cent) have been considered absolutely necessary. These results indicate that cultural offers should be more targeted to culture-peripheral visitors and included in overall packages. Nevertheless, 40 per cent of the respondents showed an interest in purchasing a special culture destination card. Cultural motives for a visit to the destination, such as education, cultural interest and interest in visiting historic sights had a significant influence on the interest in purchasing a specified culture card. Willingness to pay for such a tourist card was highest between €20 and

40 (54.6 per cent) for a fortnight; interestingly, this amount corresponded with the projected price. The TirolCard has only been available for one year, as a number of regional cards are already well established. Nevertheless, the example reveals interesting implications for the design of cultural tourism packages and destination cards.

Conclusion

A basic problem in establishing a card system is the free-rider problem; however, this problem is already being considered in the beginning of a card concept. The Allgäu-Walser-Card in the Alps, in the borderland between Germany and Austria, has been able to integrate all accommodation providers in the card by means of guest accommodation registration. Otherwise it would have been much more difficult to offer providers a tangible benefit. Preferably, individual benefit for each provider in the region would form the basis for the conceptualization of a card system. A critical mass of participating service providers is needed to create an attractive offer. Therefore, at least some of the most important attractions and services need to be included in the destination card, as well as a number of other features that allow for a diversified and entertaining holiday. The smart card system requires that unobtrusive, user-friendly smart card reader machines are installed in all of the participating operators. These machines replace the need to collect cash or paper vouchers and record all visits electronically. Still, especially for small providers, first time investment may be important and require assistance from co-operation or public partners. There is a limit to the number of participants in the smart card marketing initiatives, often due to restrictions in the size of the supporting guidebook publications. When demand outweighs the opportunity for inclusion, it may be necessary to limit participation to a representative but manageable number, which helps to control standards subtly. Ultimately, if a single smart card product is developed to market the region's experience and the visitor relies on this product for a quality experience, then it is essential to ensure that all the participants provide a uniform standard. The lasting impression of the visitor at the end of the holiday is only as good as the worst experience in the region.

References

Bieger, T. (2002). *Management von Destinationen*, 5th edn. München: Oldenbourg.

Buhalis, D. (1994). Regional integrated computer information reservation management systems and tourism distribution channels. In Collins, C. and Buhalis, D. (eds) *Information and Communication Technology in Tourism*. Vienna: Springer, pp. 56–72.

Bulletin – Das Fachmagazin der Österreich Werbung, 3/2004, Vienna.

Collins, C. and Buhalis, D. (2003). Destination management system utilisation in England. In Collins, C. and Buhalis, D. (eds) *Information and Communication Technology in Tourism*. Vienna: Springer, pp. 202–211.

Fisher, D. (1998). Virtual enterprise – impact and challenges for destination management. Presentation at ENTER Conference 1998, Istanbul.

Fleck, R. (1998). Electronic payment and additional utilization of smart cards in the tourism industry. In Buhalis, D. (ed.) *Information and Communication Technology in Tourism*. Vienna: Springer, pp. 308–317.

Fodness, D. (1994). Measuring tourist motivation. *Annals of Tourism Research* 21(3): 555–581.

Hughes, H. (2000). *Arts, Entertainment and Tourism*. Oxford: Butterworth-Heinemann.

Inskeep, E. (1991). *Tourism Planning: An Integrated and Sustainable Development Approach*. New York: Van Nostrand Reinhold.

Keller, P. and Koch, K. (1997). New tourism policy: competition, cooperation and innovation. *La Vie économique* (August).

Kuhn, S. (2000). Die BodenseeErlebniskarte als Erfolgsfaktor im Destinationsmanagement. *Tourismus Journal* 4(4): 449–456.

Laws, E. (1995). *Tourist Destination Management: Issues, Analysis and Policies*. New York: Routledge.

Martini, U. (2000). ICTs as competitive drivers for new destination management concept. In Kreilkamp, E. et al. (eds) *Gemachter oder Gelebter Tourismus? Destinationsmanagement und Tourismuspolitik*. Vienna: Linde, pp. 141–166.

Murphy, P. E. (1988). Community-driven tourism planning. *Tourism Management* 9(2): 96–104.

Pechlaner, H. (2000). Managing tourist destinations: why and how. In Manente, M. and Cerato, M. (eds) *From Destination to Destination Marketing and Management – Designing and Repositioning Tourism Products*. P. Padova: CISET, pp. 9–13.

Pechlaner, H. and Abfalter, D. (2002). Effective product bundling with adaptive destination card systems – the case of the TirolCard. In Wöber, K., Hitz, M. and Frew, A. J. (eds) *ENTER – Information and Communication Technologies in Tourism 2002*. Vienna: Springer, pp. 497–506.

Pechlaner, H. and Weiermair, K. (1999). Destinationsmanagement – Führung und Vermarktung von touristischen Zielgebieten, Schriftenreihe der Europäischen Akademie Bozen, Bd. 2, Vienna.

Richards, G. (1996). *Cultural Tourism in Europe*. Wallingford: CAB International.

Schmalz, I. (2000). Die Kärtnen Card – Erfolgsmodell für den Tourismus. *Tourismus Journal* 4(4): 463–469.

Sheldon, P. (1997). *Tourism Information Technology*. New York: CAB International.

Sorzabal, A. A., Hu, Y. -P. and O'Leary, J. T. (1999). International culture and heritage travellers: a multi-country comparison. 1999 European Conference of Travel and Tourism Research Association, Dublin Institute of Technology, Ireland.

Weiermair, K. and Pechlaner, H. (2001). Management von Kulturtourismus im Spannungsfeld von Markt- und Ressourcenorientierung. In Bieger, Th., Pechlaner, H. and Steinecke, A. (eds) *Erfolgskonzepte im Tourismus*. Vienna: Linde, pp. 91–124.

Websites

http://www.tiscover.at
http://www.tirol.gv.at
http://www.sudtirol.com

Part Two

Operations and Facilities Management

CHAPTER 5

Operational management of cultural and heritage sites

Harry Coccossis

Introduction

History, culture and religion constitute significant elements of tourism. Millions of tourists in any one year visit historic centres, temples and places of unique cultural value. Many of these major cultural attractions are located in close proximity to, or within, large urban centres. In general terms, this could be considered 'mass tourism', which reflects the high numbers of visitors to cultural and heritage sites; often for little more than a short stay or brief excursion. This pattern of visitation creates pressures that need to be managed effectively, taking into consideration the visitor experience and the capacity of local systems to support such pressures (Garrod and Fyall, 2000). These two areas are explored below. The constraints of space preclude detailed analysis of the varied forms of cultural tourism and associated sites; to an extent this is well illustrated by the cases encompassed within this text. The approach taken is to focus more on those generic aspects of operational management that may vary according to the type, or more appropriately perhaps, the site, of cultural attraction. In the process, the aim is to highlight key issues and potential management responses, which complement or are developed in the case studies that follow in this section.

Site typology and characteristics

Any typology of cultural tourism destinations or attractions will be both diverse and potentially very extensive depending on the degree of categorization used and the level of detail required. However, in this context, a broad approach is adopted based on three general categories, namely, historic towns and cities, ancient and historic sites, and festivals. In terms of tourism, the operational management of these sites has to address similar opportunities and challenges, but their significance will vary according to the characteristics specific to a particular category and thus the management planning and development of the site will vary in approach.

Historic towns and cities

Tourists are attracted to historic towns and cities for diverse reasons; for example, the built heritage, cultural traditions and events, and the urban amenities. Furthermore, a city may offer widespread attractions and create new ones through urban regeneration to promote tourism and encourage the wider dispersal of tourists. This is well illustrated by Barcelona's Port Vell, where a former 'harbour arm' has been transformed into a tourist destination. Each year they receive a large proportion of the world's tourist flows (Walton, 2000). These visitor destinations are often densely populated, the home of vibrant communities and centres of activity and transport hubs. Major cities may have the infrastructure to absorb high-volume tourism, coupled with transport systems generally able to deliver people into the heart and/or other parts of the city. Conversely, in small historic towns a concentration of tourists can lead to environmental management problems such as congestion, noise and pollution. Tourist flows into these areas can impact on the general day-to-day functions, creating conflicts between tourism and the dynamics of the city, threatening both tourism development and the socioeconomic structure of the settlement (van der Borg et al., 1996). Thus, tourism may engender conflicts between visitors and the local population and impact on urban management capability and urban structure. The management of these conflicts becomes of the utmost importance to ensure the conservation of these sites along with their socioeconomic development, in which tourism can play a significant role (van der Borg, 2004; Russo, 2002).

Archaeological sites, monuments and temples

This type of cultural tourism attraction evidences a diverse range of sites. They may be isolated (e.g. Stonehenge) or within a wider site (e.g. the Acropolis in Athens or Templo Mayor in Mexico), in private or public ownership, and may or may not charge an entrance fee. Visitor numbers vary with their importance and historical recognition as well as in terms of scale and accessibility.

Festivals

Festivals are characterized by the arrival of visitors in a defined period, generally in a restricted area, to participate in an event of a particular nature. They range in scale from a local community gala drawing relatively few visitors, through concerts and theatre festivals, to religious events such as the Maria festival in Coto Doñana, and art festivals e.g. Biennale, Cannes, which may attract many thousands of visitors. They can be one-off events or more regular, e.g. annual. The staging of festivals needs to be compatible with site preservation and protection and with respect for the aesthetic, historical and scientific integrity of the place by following existing regulations for the site or establishing and applying site-specific regulations.

The visitor experience

Visitor satisfaction depends on a diverse range of factors, from the site of interest and the quality of services provided to the facilities available and, indeed, the number of visitors. The visitor experience and satisfaction also depend on personal expectations and the anticipated outcomes of the visit (Vittersø et al., 2000). As such, there are potentially variable visitor needs and requirements, which create different management opportunities; for example, the management of a particular site on the basis of their philosophy and objectives may decide to satisfy the expectations of some particular categories of visitors, while denying satisfying other groups' expectations. Hence, a knowledge and understanding of visitor profiles, preferences and needs is invaluable in the setting of objectives for the infrastructure, staffing needs and education and interpretation programmes of the site (Chaplin, 2003). These aspects, along with the characteristics and assets of the site, will influence the visitor's experience. While the expectations of the visitor are often related to the importance of the site, there are several more widely applicable factors that are generic to all cultural attractions, such as management planning and development, access and assets; all of which can contribute to enriching the visitor's experience or fall short of his or her expectations. Furthermore, the general condition of the site and thus maintenance and cleanliness of the site, facilities and services will contribute to perceptions of the site's management and organization, and to making the visit a more enjoyable experience. The adoption of best practice in these areas is axiomatic. Therefore, the operational aspects attended to here are heritage interpretation and education, facilities and services, followed by a consideration of wider, more general factors.

Heritage interpretation and education

Heritage interpretation and education programmes are an important part of any visitor management plan. These programmes should communicate particular themes and ideas that accord with the aims of the general visitor management plan (Glasson et al., 1995; Moscardo, 1996). To evaluate the success of visitor interpretation and education programmes, visitor surveys should be conducted periodically to assess visitor satisfaction and provide input for readjusting the visitor management plan.

To be highly effective, a variety of media for site interpretation and education should be chosen with the intention of making the visit as enjoyable and informative as possible. Due consideration should be given to the needs of different categories of visitor, e.g. scholars, schoolchildren and the general public, as well as providing information in different languages according to the provenance of the major visitor markets. Signage should be complementary to interpretation, possibly integrated at times where appropriate. It should be well designed and positioned with clear panels (possibly using internationally recognized symbols and colours) and, as necessary, in more than one language. Outdoor panels should also be specifically designed to be weather and vandal resistant. Due consideration should be given to people with special needs in terms of physical access to and around the site, as well as to information and with respect to potential difficulties.

Major cultural attractions often have a reception and visitor orientation centre designed to introduce the visitor to the site, its significance, major aspects and so forth; and what it offers to visitors in terms of experiencing the site. This is usually the first and main point of visitor contact and thus it is vital that staff are polite, informed and willing to help visitors. This is equally applicable to all personnel as they play an important role in influencing impressions of the site's management. Such centres, or reception points, invariably provide promotional material, such as brochures, guidebooks and site maps, and possibly an audiovisual programme and an introductory site exhibit. The lack of availability of such written material can be a cause of frustration to visitors and lead to some dissatisfaction (see Chapter 8). As well illustrated in Part 4, there is a wide range of information communication technology available to provide information to visitors in a captivating way: videotapes, audiotapes, prerecorded station stops, and sound and light shows to interactive programmes. Special exhibits can add value to a visit, enhancing the visitors' experience and their understanding of the attraction. Thus, an exhibit should attract the visitor's attention, avoid tediousness and emphasize the most interesting aspects. Special exhibits for less able persons, for example, poorly sighted and blind people, should be created with more attention to narration to inform and aid their understanding.

Complementary to the above methods is the availability of guides who can enrich the visitor's experience (or conversely make a visit boring and tedious); thus, their knowledge and skills are very important. For this reason they need to be carefully selected, trained, motivated, monitored and regularly evaluated. Guided tours should also be specifically orientated to the needs of different groups, e.g. scholars, schoolchildren and members of local history societies.

In the context of education, the opportunity should be taken to influence visitor behaviour in a positive way, not only regarding the impact of visitors, but also in terms of the cultural norms of the locality or site, e.g. a church may require visitors to cover their heads or maintain silence (Pedersen, 2002).

Facilities and services

It is essential for any site receiving significant numbers of visitors to address their needs through the provision of the necessary facilities and services. The planning and development of facilities and services needs to be well thought through, as undue 'commercialization' will detract from the conservation/preservation and presentation of the site features and overall aesthetics. The conservation of the historic fabric and character and authenticity of the site (the locale) are thus seen as influences on visitors' expectations.

Operational plans should therefore aim to anticipate and pre-empt problems. In many cases these services, such as hospitality operations, provide invaluable revenue flows; therefore, to maximize the benefits they should be of good quality with attentive customer service. Within this context, the management should adopt and promote environmentally friendly practices and encourage visitors to act accordingly. Thus, there should be a clear environmental policy and environmental management system in place (see Chapter 6), an approach that could also be part of the marketing strategy.

Wider factors

All sites attractive to cultural tourists, irrespective of type of location, will be influenced by the degree of access, the quality of the surroundings and the general environment. These wider factors should be carefully considered by the management team and, as necessary, through liaison with the appropriate authorities.

Accessibility should be carefully planned to avoid traffic and pollution problems in areas around the site, ensuring comfortable access but with due regard to the impact of infrastructural developments on the visual amenity of the location. The use of well-planned 'park and ride' facilities may be advantageous in avoiding congestion around the site, on major routes or in urban centres. Such an approach may help to ameliorate traffic problems during peak visitor periods, at which point members of the local community may become annoyed by the extensive presence of visitors using 'their resources', potentially leading to hostility towards visitors. The volume and diversity of visitors that many sites attract require attention to be paid to the quantity and type of accommodation and hospitality services available, the actual and potential demand with regard to the capacity of the locale and environment and, overall, the visual impact.

Attention must be paid to public amenities such as toilets, drinking water, environmental health and safety, and emergency medical services. Consideration should be given to availability and capacity levels in the context of visitor numbers and duration of stay and in the case of litter disposal, for example, strategically positioned collection points, which are not unduly invasive.

Problems arising from visitors to the site

The actual and potential problems arising from visitors can be broadly categorized into the following three areas. However, it should be noted that despite such problems, it is generally recognized that tourism also has a positive impact on the local economy and employment.

Urban management capability

One of the most common problems around or at cultural sites attracting many visitors arriving by car or coach is traffic, congestion and associated problems, e.g. noise and air pollution. Furthermore, the local infrastructure and amenities may not have the capacity to deal with high visitor numbers, such as found during peak periods. This can lead to dysfunction of those systems, creating environmental problems and conflicts with local users that can be especially evident with events attracting many people. This can also lead to associated problems such as litter and damage to the physical environment and overload on public amenities. Allied with this is the impact on the visual amenity of historic towns and the setting of individual sites through the uncontrolled development of tourism services and facilities that may be visually intrusive. This may lead to the alteration of urban fabric and the architectural character of a site or historic town or city, damaging in this way the identity of the locale – the sense of place.

Conversely, a tourism development policy may lead to improvements in infrastructure and services to deal with increased numbers of people due to tourist arrivals.

The site

Too many visitors at any one time can lead to queues at access points or bottlenecks at interpretation displays, overwhelm exhibitions, and block the flow of visitors or the view of smaller groups or individuals, thereby negatively influencing the visitor experience (Lee and Graefe, 2003). Visitors cause wear and tear on buildings and monuments through intensive use and are also associated with vandalism, leading to further damage of the site and environment, and overall to potential deterioration of the site. This can be especially evident in enclosed interior places, where major humidity and temperature fluctuations related to tourist flows may damage irreversibly materials and finishes. Archaeological sites and historic buildings are particularly vulnerable to souvenir collectors, who remove bits and pieces of historic fabric as first-hand souvenirs of their visit. At Westminster Abbey, for example, where there are as many as 16 000 visitors at peak times, pieces of statues have been removed and fragments taken from mosaics (ICOMOS, 1993).

Local community

Pressure arising from visitors may negatively affect the quality of life of residents, owing to pollution, noise and litter, and/or increased costs of living and property prices (Curtis, 1998). Furthermore, tourists may compete with residents for the use of facilities and infrastructure, and increase crowding, inducing irritation of the local population, which may affect the visitor experience, possibly damaging the destination's image and consequently tourism in the longer term.

Social conflicts also arise as a result of the crowding-out phenomenon leading to a tourism monoculture: witness Venice or Bruges. In such situations tourism may come to dominate urban society, leading to higher prices for centrally located land, diminishing the attractiveness of the city for families and firms because of congestion and pollution, and thereby causing the displacement of other activities and functions from the centre to the outskirts.

Within the context of the scale of the festival, visitor flows may create overcrowding, overwhelm services and the infrastructure, causing conflicts with the local community. However, it is recognized that these events can bring positive economic benefits (e.g. supply of goods, employment opportunities) and make a contribution to revitalizing small, isolated and declining communities. On a larger scale, they can serve to promote cultural events to and for the community whilst also acting as a promotional tool for a city (see Chapter 7).

Management responses

To facilitate discussion and aid clarification the following management responses to actual and potential problems identified are presented in the context of the three broad categories of site used earlier. However, this is not to be taken that the responses presented are mutually exclusive.

Historic towns and cities

The management of historic towns and cities is often fragmented among various local and national agencies that control the various aspects of their functions: public services, utilities, etc. (Bryon and Russo, 2003). The only adequate methodology for managing tourism in such destinations is through a planning process that seeks to ensure co-operation and co-ordination among all involved agencies. To be effective this process should encompass the following fundamental elements.

Integration in planning process and institutional context • • •

The process of planning for tourism can provide a general framework to guide the local community, planners and decision makers. This framework consists of principles, goals, objectives and policy measures in regard to tourist development in an area on the basis of the area's distinctive characteristics and features, respecting local capacities to sustain tourism. Setting limits for sustaining tourism activity in a place involves a vision about local development and decisions about managing tourism, which should be made with the participation of all major actors and the community at large.

Establishing a process of concerted action • • •

Any tourism management programme should work in concert with all stakeholders and interested parties, including government agencies, local communities, non-governmental organizations, developers and tourism businesses. Their participation in the planning and management process is of utmost importance to identify common interests. An agreement on the goals of tourism development will be necessary. Through dialogue and collaboration, site managers and planners may better understand various stakeholders' positions regarding tourism issues and activities that could have an impact on a site. Stakeholders can inform managers about easily misunderstood local cultural differences, help to identify problem areas that may have been overlooked by experts, or provide useful inputs regarding desired conditions at a site, and may better support the implementation of envisaged measures.

Archaeological sites, monuments and temples

In comparison with historic town and cities, owing to the complexity of their urban situation, site-specific cultural attractions, in general, are more easily managed as they cover a limited and well-defined area. The site itself may be the responsibility of a single management agency and thus under more direct control (Pedersen, 2002). Potentially, the major problem for popular sites is that of too many arrivals at the same time or too many visitors in one period. Visitor management tools that can be applied in response to such potential problems primarily aim at reducing congestion and peak time demand.

A booking system limiting the number of visitors accessing the site, or a policy aiming at spreading the visitors over space and time, may help to reduce crowding level at a site. Reducing potential queuing at entry points may also be aided by introducing an advanced reservation system to enable groups, in particular, to pre-book, e.g. as practised for the exhibitions at Palazzo Grassi in Venice. Subject to a well-defined entrance to the site, it is potentially possible to limit the number of visitors admitted in any given period. However, this can create problems elsewhere if not carefully managed and promoted. A more appropriate method, where practical, is to scale entrance fees on the basis of temporal demand (by time of day, by day and by week/month), thereby aiming to smooth peaks and troughs while seeking to maximize revenues and at the same time visitor satisfaction.

As regards crowd behaviour, suitably designed educational programmes, presented within the context of interpretation and presentation of the site, can mitigate visitor impacts by informing visitors on how best to conduct themselves both at the site and with respect to other visitors present.

Festivals

Apart from the specific tasks relating to concept, design and delivery of a festival, the management needs to address all the potential problems that may arise in terms of visitors as noted above. Thus, the specific hours of access and departure, projected visitor numbers, crowd control procedures, security and sanitation provisions, insurance requirements, restrictions on the types and locations of temporary structures (e.g. stands and tents), and allowance for placement of sponsor and advertising signs associated with the event all need to be planned. The site itself may require additional attention to safety standards, pathways and so forth depending on anticipated demand and weather conditions. Subject to projected demand, the necessary amenities (rubbish bins, toilets, seating, etc.) will need to be in place.

Possibly the most useful tool available to the event management is that of information management. Ensuring public awareness and forewarning the local community of actual and potential problems, such as along routes to the site, travel times and availability of public transport, any special arrangements and the possibility of noise, e.g. music or fireworks, will all contribute to pre-empting problems.

At large festivals and events, crowding represents a characteristic element; many visitors may well expect this in advance of their visit and thus do not experience the same feeling of being crowded as they might in other situations (Lee and Graefe, 2003). Even so, management planning should aim to reduce the associated problems likely to arise, such as long queues and access to facilities.

Conclusion

Overall, a variety of management tools and policies can be used to minimize or reduce the impact and pressure of visitors while conserving heritage, cultural assets and resources, which should all be used as part of a strategic plan of action with clear goals and objectives, including:

- regulatory (land-use planning and zoning to control development, restrictions to accessibility, restrictions to activities, etc.)
- economic (pricing and fees, charges, taxes, incentives, etc.)
- organizational (reservation systems, information, education, marketing, etc.).

Such a strategic plan must also take into consideration broader issues that cut across sectoral or problem specific issues and offer a broader framework to ensure co-ordination and synergy of action. Thus, there is a need for spatial planning, community participation, monitoring and evaluation (Coccossis and Nijkamp, 1995).

- *Spatial planning.* The concentration or dispersion of development pressures and tourist flows are two different and opposite strategies and the decision to apply them should reflect policy goals and management objectives. Concentration facilitates a higher level of control and protection for sensitive areas, by limiting access to selected areas within the site, which are more resistant to visitor pressures or have been chosen to confine potential external disturbance, e.g. noise. Although a concentration strategy may contribute to limiting the spread of environmental impacts throughout the site, it may also involve creating an artificial environment designed to satisfy tourists' needs and which pushes out, for example, local community shops and businesses to other areas, as exemplified in Bruges (Curtis, 1998). A dispersion strategy aims to reduce pressure on an area by dispersing visitors to different areas and at the same time potentially spreading the social and economic impacts to the wider community. This approach may involve extending the season, providing facilities in other areas and directing visitors to other areas through promotional campaigns.
- *Community involvement.* This is a necessary prerequisite for any public policy targeted at raising support and developing concerted action among key stakeholders/actors (local and national authorities, academia/scientists, artists, performance and tourism industry, sponsors). For example, local businesses, particularly hospitality operations, may be willing to help implement educational programmes or distribute information on low-impact practices to customers.
- *Monitoring and evaluation.* Managers need to know when desired conditions are being threatened and whether policies implemented have the expected results. A well-developed and regular monitoring system can provide managers with invaluable data regarding the impacts of tourism at the site, the effectiveness of actions already taken and visitors' experience. These data can then feed into the review process involved in evaluating, and revising as appropriate, the management policies and planning.

References

van der Borg, J. (2004). Tourism management and carrying capacity in heritage cities and sites. In Coccossis, H. and Mexa, A. (eds) *The Challenge of Tourism Carrying Capacity Assessment: Theory and Practice.* London: Ashgate, pp. 163–179.

van der Borg, J., Costa, P. and Gotti, G. (1996). Tourism in European heritage cities. *Annals of Tourism Research* 23(2): 306–321.

Bryon, J. and Russo, A. P. (2003). The tourist historic city. *Annals of Tourism Research* 30(2): 492–494.

Chaplin, I. (2003). Cultural Tourism: the partnership between tourism and cultural heritage management. *Annals of Tourism Research* 30(2): 508–509.

Coccossis, H. and Nijkamp, P. (1995). *Planning for our Heritage*. Avebury: Aldershot.

Curtis, S. (1998). Visitor management in small historic cities. *Travel and Tourism Analyst* (3): 75–89.

Garrod, B. and Fyall, A. (2000). Managing heritage tourism. *Annals of Tourism Research* 27(3): 682–706.

Glasson, J., Godfrey, K., Goodey, B., Absalom, H. and Borg, J. (1995). *Towards Visitor Impact Management: Visitors' Impacts*. Avebury: Aldershot.

International Scientific Committee on Cultural Tourism (1993). *Tourism at World Heritage Cultural Sites: The Site Manager's Hand Book*. Paris, ICOMOS.

Lee, H. and Graefe, A. R. (2003). Crowding at an arts festival: extending crowding models to the frontcountry. *Tourism Management* 24(1): 1–11.

Moscardo, G. (1996). Mindful visitors: Heritage and tourism. *Annals of Tourism Research* 23(2): 376–397.

Pedersen, A. (2002). *Managing Tourism at World Heritage Sites: A Practical Manual for World Heritage Site Managers*. World Heritage Series 1. Paris, UNESCO.

Russo, A. P. (2002). The 'vicious circle' of tourism development in heritage cities. *Annals of Tourism Research* 29(1): 165–182.

Vitterso, J., Vorkinn, M., Vistad, O. I. and Vaagland, J. (2000). Tourist experiences and attractions. *Annals of Tourism Research* 27(2): 432–450.

Walton, M. (2000). Managing tourism in cities. *Annals of Tourism Research* 27(2): 540–542.

Websites

ICOMOS: http://www.international.icomos.org/publications/index.html

Journal of the Association for Heritage Interpretation: http://www.heritageinterpretation.org.uk/jouridx.html

UNESCO library: //unesdoc.unesco.org/

Cultural tourism attractions and environmental performance

David Leslie

Learning outcomes

- Develop an appreciation of the background and underpinnings to the need to address environmental performance.
- Recognize the importance of the actual and potential impacts arising from the operational practices of cultural tourism attractions.
- Understand the principles and practices involved in addressing the environmental performance of cultural tourism attractions.
- Appreciate the significance of management values and attitudes to the adoption of environmental performance appraisal and related management systems.

Introduction

The latter part of the twentieth century witnessed rising international concerns over the quality of the environment causing pressure on industry: '… to address the actual and potential contribution of their operations in contributing to environmental degradation and develop systems to assess the environmental performance of individual operations – enterprises' (Welford and Starkey, 1996, p. xi). The tourism sector is no less susceptible than any other sector of the economy to this environmental agenda and thus enterprises should recognize and accept that they have a responsibility for the impacts of their operations, including their customers, i.e. visitors (Butler, 1993, p. 5). Furthermore, '… private interests, as they benefit from visitor spending, should invest in protecting and enhancing the local environment …' (Countryside Commission, 1993, p. 6). In combination, this requires the examination of tourism in terms of three key elements: local economy, local people and local environment. Thus, there is a need for a more holistic approach within which the resource consumption of tourism enterprises and their environmental performance is addressed. In effect, this aims for progress towards sustainable development, any achievement towards which requires a substantial reduction in the consumption of resources (Erdmenger et al., 2000). This view is recognized in the need to: '… promote better understanding among operators of the business benefits available from programmes to reduce energy consumption, waste production and water use' (Department of Culture, Media and Sport, 1999, p. 59).

Essentially, cultural tourism attractions need to operate within the natural capacity of the destination, i.e. to adopt the principles of sustainable development. A key to this is careful and considered planning within which cultural tourism is not treated in isolation from the rest of the local economy, and particularly from the community. Furthermore, 'The environment may also be under greater protection when the economy springs from the community rather than being dislocated from the community or imposed upon it' (Department of Environment, Transport and the Regions, 2000, p. 9). In effect, this is to adopt contemporary environmentalism, which most simply expressed means 'going green' – an approach that reflects much greater awareness of the interconnectedness of the economic, the physical and social dimensions of the environment. This '... linking of environmental concerns with tourism has become an increasing global element of tourism promotion ...' (Jersey Policy and Resources Committee, 1998, p. 32), a factor that reflects changing public attitudes and the potential to influence their choice of destination on the basis of environmental performance (Moore et al., 2003). Thus, cultural tourism should not be considered solely in terms of the specific resources on which it is based, but in the wider context of its external environment, an approach recognized by the European Union (EU) (European Commission, 2003).

Environmental performance

The environmental performance of heritage- and culture-based tourism attractions is very much a part of today's agenda. Many of these developments draw on local resources and through the production and delivery of services return pollution and waste back into the locality. Pressure rises on the locality to handle these by-products, hence the need for 'environmentally friendly' management and operational practices. This 'greening' of cultural tourism management and operations is essentially no more than the positioning of the sector to respond to the emerging environmental challenge that will be a key issue in the twenty-first century. Yet this is all too often absent from debate on the management of attractions (Fyall et al., 2003), festivals and events (Yeoman et al., 2004), despite its promotion for over a decade. Over the past fifteen years, leading national and international organizations have been involved through their policies in promoting initiatives designed to address aspects of environmental performance, e.g. energy consumption, waste reduction and local purchasing. In addition, there have been schemes designed to promote environmental management systems (EMS) and/or related practices by national tourist organizations and local authorities

(Font and Buckley, 2001; Leslie, 2005). A comprehensive collection is encompassed in the report on the progress of tourism towards sustainable development (United Nations Environment Programme, 2002). Overarching all such schemes is the publication of extensive and detailed guidance on developing tourism destinations in a more sustainable way (English Tourism Council/Tourism Management Institute, 2003), which includes attention to the World Tourism Organization's 'sustainability indicators' for destinations and is more than complementary to more general destination management systems (Ritchie and Crouch, 2003).

The question therefore arises as to what extent management is addressing the environmental performance of their operations, and therefore whether they will be able to establish insights as to the current position regarding progress towards sustainable development. In the wider arena, this need has led to the emergence of 'sustainability indicators' (Bell and Morse, 2000; Ceron and Dubois, 2003; United Nations Environment Programme, 2003), with particular progress being made in the context of Local Agenda 21 planning (LA21). This recognition of LA21, together with a plethora of non-sectoral specific promotions and initiatives across the world, and sustainability indicators, not only reinforces the advocacy of EMS but also pre-empts the potential argument that the management of heritage and cultural attractions may be unaware of the promotion of EMS if it was just in the tourism domain. Basically, an EMS is all about 'managing an organisation's activities that give rise to impacts upon the environment ...' and essentially therefore '... the interaction between the organisation and the environment ... . It is the environmental aspects (as opposed to the financial or quality aspects) of an organisation's activities, products and services that are subject to management' (Sheldon and Toxon, 1999, p. 2). The starting point is the recognition that the organization does have environmental impacts and that, for example, energy consumption and waste could be reduced. A preliminary review of the operation and identification of ways through which the consumption of resources could be reduced is the first step in the formulation of an environmental policy, which is: 'The company's [or enterprise's] overall aims and principles of action with respect to the environment including compliance with all relevant regulatory requirements regarding the environment' (Hillary, 1994, p. 18), e.g. example, BS7750, EMAS or ISO 14001 (Barrow, 1999). To illustrate: BS7750 basically is a formalized method of demonstrating how an enterprise complies with environmental legislation and regulations, e.g. '... that their products or services are produced, delivered and disposed of in an environmentally friendly manner, minimizing any adverse effects on the environment ...' (Jersey Policy and Resources Committee, 1998, p. 103). But also that '... planning for future investment and growth reflects market needs and the environment' (Jersey Policy and Resources Committee, 1998, p. 103). Although the standard does not dictate performance benchmarks, its adoption does require external verification. Potentially, the most appealing aspect to management adopting such auditing practice is that it can '... enhance the organisation's competitive advantage through the effective environmental management backed by independent certification.' (British Standards Institute, 1997, p. 2).

The case study

This case study of cultural attractions and environmental performance is drawn from an extensive research project designed and implemented to assess the environmental performance, including sustainability, of the tourism sector in the Lake District National Park (LDNP). The LDNP is a part of Cumbria, a rural area in north-west England with a population of 440 000 people, and is less than half of the area of the county. Approximately 10 per cent of Cumbria's population live in the LDNP. Tourism is the major economic activity in the area; the latest estimates indicate some ten million excursionists and five million tourists generating a £1 billion industry (Global Tourism Solutions UK, 2004). The significance of these figures is manifest in the estimated number of jobs supported by tourism in Cumbria, which has been cited as approximately 10 per cent of the population at 42 000, 50 per cent of which are located in the LDNP, compared with about 6 per cent nationally (Leslie, 2005). The LDNP is thus a particularly appropriate area to investigate progress in addressing the environmental performance of tourism businesses, especially given that it has been nationally recognized for promoting 'sustainable tourism', its designated status as a 'Green Globe Destination' and its international recognition. The extensive methodology formulated included surveying cultural tourism attractions and more detailed investigations, in effect environmental audits based on an extensive set of sustainability indicators specifically derived for the study. Thus, the extent to which policies advocating 'the greening of tourism' and related initiatives have been realized was encompassed in the aims, i.e. to identify and evaluate the level of awareness, attitudes and perceptions of green issues, and associated practices, of owners and managers of cultural tourism attractions, and, in the process, to establish those factors influential to the adoption of such practices.

Findings

The LDNP has a range of cultural attractions; indeed, most of the area's built attractions are based on heritage or contemporary cultural products, e.g. Muncaster Castle, Brantwood – the home of Ruskin, the Pencil Museum and the Wordsworth Centre. Not surprisingly therefore, 'heritage/cultural' attractions were predominant in the attractions survey, with historic buildings (and grounds) and museums accounting for some 50 per cent, and art centres/art galleries and craft centres accounting for over 25 per cent; 'Other' heritage/cultural attractions included a historic passenger boat operation and a working water mill. Recognition of the quality of some of these attractions is manifest in national awards, e.g. Heritage Award for Best Property for Families, Interpret Britain Award, Outstanding Museum design and Awards for Visitor Services and disabled access.

The majority of these attractions receive fewer than 100 000 visitors (25 per cent less than 50 000). Annual turnover ranges from less than £100 000 (45 per cent) to over 200 000 (30 per cent). Some of the attractions, mainly the smaller ones, close during the winter. A further indication of their size is reflected in the range of visitor facilities: one-third have no toilet facilities, one-third have a catering operation of some form and approximately three-quarters have a retail operation. Many have been established for over twenty years, although one in five for less than five years (mainly craft-based operations). Compared with the rest of the supply side in tourism, they are less likely to be owner managed and more likely to be part of a local or national group and have charitable status, e.g. the National Trust. Overall employment is limited: 80 per cent are 'micro-enterprises', i.e. employ fewer than ten staff, including part-time staff, but although they are micro-businesses they are significant given that their '... actions impact daily upon sustainability issues' (Becker et al., 1999).

Awareness, perceptions and attitudes of management

The general levels of awareness of 'green' initiatives are low, at less than 25 per cent, across a range of possibilities, e.g. LA21, ecolabelling, EMS and Green Business Schemes. However, two local initiatives gained substantially higher recognition, namely 'Made in Cumbria', a scheme designed to promote Cumbrian products, and the 'Tourism and Conservation Partnership' (TCP), an LDNP organization established by tourism enterprises that introduced and manages a renowned 'visitor payback scheme', which funds repairs to designated areas, e.g. walkways. However, all too evident is the fact that being aware of an environmental management (or allied) initiative does not mean adoption or participation. For example, of those managers aware of the two local initiatives, one in four does not participate in Made in Cumbria and one in three does not participate in the TCP.

Apart from membership of the Cumbria Tourist Board, few respondents were members of a tourism or environmental group, which partly accounts for their lack of awareness of national and, indeed, international campaigns in this field.

To investigate what has influenced or would be likely to influence the introduction of practices considered to be more environmentally friendly, respondents were invited to rate a defined range of factors on a scale of $1 = $ 'least important' to $5 = $ 'most important'. The findings are presented in Table 6.1 in rank order on the basis of the mean response, and suggest a degree of cynicism and a large amount of ambivalence.

Table 6.1   Perceived influence of factors on 'greening operations'

Factor	Mean response
Care for the environment	3.80
Cost savings	3.55
Customer care	3.50
Customer demand	3.45
Health and safety	3.40
Personal beliefs	3.35
Public relations	3.25
Quality management	3.25
In a national park	2.75
Potential legislation	2.70
Industry standards	2.10
Competitors' actions	2.05

Table 6.2 Perception of the impact of cultural tourism attractions and related aspects

Statement	Mean response
The attractions sector has an impact on the environment	3.85
The attractions sector's impact on the environment is significantly less than the manufacturing sector	3.60
Operators who claim to be 'green' are using it as a marketing ploy	3.00
Most owners/managers do not have time to worry about the environment	2.60
Customers are not interested in whether an operation is environmentally friendly	2.60
It is not possible to be profitable and be environmentally friendly	2.00

Perceptions of the sector's impact and related aspects

To investigate further the respondents' views and perceptions, the participants were invited to grade a range of statements, on the basis of 1 = 'strongly disagree' to 5 = 'strongly agree'. The findings are presented in Table 6.2 in rank order on the basis of the mean response. It is perceived quite strongly that the sector has an impact (less than manufacturing); however, again there is a level of ambivalence in most areas.

Resource management and operations

Approximately one in ten of the organizations have a written environmental policy. Although the absence of such a formalized environmental policy does not preclude the possibility of environmental auditing, few managers do this in any formal way.

There are several operational practices that show some degree of attention to resource use. For example, reducing energy consumption is a key factor and potentially one of the most beneficial in terms of immediate cost benefits. Limited attention to this was found, mainly in the use of low-energy light bulbs, which were more likely to be used than is the case for tourism enterprises per se. Reuse of resources was limited, although reusing paper was found to be comparatively high. Overall, little evidence of recycling was found, and the use of recycled paper products was also found to be very limited. 'Open questions' in the survey drew a number of responses on recycling: 'We recycle as much as possible' and, conversely, 'Transportation to recycling sites is time consuming and uses fuel'. Other factors identified included the lack of infrastructure for recycling and a recurrent theme was time: 'Do not have time – cost is prohibitive for very small businesses' and 'I work a 16-hour day and don't have time to deliver these articles to appropriate centres'.

The convenience of the purchaser is often the main consideration in purchasing decisions and, as such, local suppliers are often overlooked owing to competition from, for example, supermarkets and wholesalers where the actual benefits of purchasing are more evident. Purchasers may be less inclined to look at the longer term value and benefit of buying locally in terms of supporting the local community, and may favour short-term gain.

As regards general purchasing, management practices tended to be the same, with few signs of a bias towards supporting local enterprises and local produce. However, those attractions with retail operations were likely to sell local pottery, paintings and wooden crafts; one participant noted that the sale of local products was limited by price and restricted display space. In contrast, almost all of those operations with food services purchased prepacked portioned products that are not made within the county, let alone the LDNP. However, several operations do use local products in food production and locally produced products such as jams and pickles, notably more so than that found in most tourism enterprises. The following comments from respondents offer valuable insights into the attitudes and practices of a number of the organizations involved:

- 'People visiting the area like to sample local produce'.
- 'We cook everything on the premises; we do not use prepared food from large companies'.
- 'We specialize in using as much local produce as possible'.
- 'Moving towards a more consistent "buy local" policy'.
- 'We don't compete with small businesses that depend on catering for their livelihoods'.

Factors identified as militating against the purchase of local produce are cost, availability and quality. An important factor influencing purchasing decisions is cost. If the cost of locally produced or supplied food or non-food items is comparatively high then it is quite likely that the purchaser will favour alternative, non-local suppliers. Any such decision is understandable in part, in that there may be a reluctance to pass on greater costs to the buyer owing to a fear of reducing competitiveness.

Visitor access and education

This area of the study was concerned with those issues that directly involve visitors, e.g. access, the needs of less able people and the promotion of an environmental message. This may be taken as an indication of the level of attention by the enterprises to promoting more environmentally friendly practices.

About half of the enterprises are not 'easily accessible by public transport', which reinforces the general need for a car, particularly so for people with young children and older or less physically fit people. Furthermore, the majority of these attractions did not seek to promote how to access the site by public transport or how to move around the LDNP by public transport. However, and notably so in comparison with accommodation and hospitality outlets, the cultural attractions evidenced far better progress in facilitating access for less able people. One attraction that promotes the use of public transport has a bin for used tickets placed by the door, so not adding to litter.

Practices that were promoted to encourage attention and care for the environment included litter bins, 'no litter' signs and educational interpretative material, mainly on local flora and fauna. A number of these organizations also promoted environmentally friendly activities to visitors, such as walking and cycling (14 per cent) and the use of public transport (10 per cent).

Factors discouraging progress

The most frequently cited reasons discouraging the introduction of environmentally friendly practices were 'cost' and 'time'. Other factors highlighted by respondents included:

- lack of awareness/availability of information on what is possible and also successful practices
- lack of visitor interest and market research into up-to-date visitor opinions, attitude and behaviour
- disruption to everyday running of the business.

Conclusion

As the growth in demand for and worldwide expansion of cultural tourism continue, so too do the related consumption of resources and the generation of waste. The management of such attractions must respond effectively and efficiently to meet these twin challenges of worldwide competition and the environmental agenda. Part of this response means the management of cultural tourism attractions addressing their environmental performance and introducing an EMS. However, this has gained limited attention at best, partly because, as the indicative results presented here show, the awareness specifically of leading government policy on tourism in this area, the promotion of 'green' initiatives and EMS is very low. However, it could be argued that as many of these initiatives are presented within the context of tourism, this may not be considered by the management of heritage/culture sites to be applicable to them or, possibly, they may be outside the loop and therefore potentially even less aware. Indeed, the management may consider that they are not really part of tourism, especially as employment in this sector is not enumerated in terms of EU statistics on tourism (Middleton, 2001). This is disingenuous as they are also predominantly unaware of wider, more general initiatives, knowledge of which may have been gained through membership of environmental organizations and professional associations. However, such membership was also found to be low.

Significantly, it was identified that 'being aware' is not a strong indicator of subsequent positive action, as the even lower levels of involvement in a range of initiatives and activities demonstrated. This may be considered surprising given that these organizations are based on heritage and culture and as such one might expect comparatively greater appreciation of the wider environment within which such resources are being conserved. Quintessentially, organizations are managed by people and it may be argued that it is values and attitudes that lead to environmental performance appraisal. Thus, the gap between awareness and action is seen as a function of the perceptions and attitudes of the management of these organizations and as such a key factor in the introduction of EMS. However, as the findings from the attitudinal questions indicate, there is evidence of a degree of cynicism and a large amount of ambivalence towards addressing their environmental performance. As such, the managers are unlikely to go out of their way to obtain information. Thus, the findings perhaps are not unexpected and bring into question the efficacy of national policies. They effectively demonstrate that the policies presented by the leading bodies involved are often little more than rhetoric on 'good practice'. That more progress has not been made serves to reinforce the view that the availability of literature and/or advice is not in itself sufficient to assume awareness and to engender positive action. Clearly, obvious and more direct encouragement and promotion are needed.

Overall, the significance of this study lies in the fact that it primarily serves to provide invaluable insights into the management and environmental performance, and incorporated wider dimensions of sustainable development, of cultural tourism attractions. The findings thus serve to establish a foundation range of benchmarks on which to base assessment in the future of progress in this area, and contribute to the development of policy and actions to influence such progress in the operational practices and management of cultural tourism at any site or in any destination.

Further, it is vital that if cultural tourism is to develop its environmental performance and more significantly become more sustainable, then the organizations involved need to operate in a more sustainable way by developing more extensive and stronger links with the area's economy, and with the community more generally, and to provide more support for environmental and conservation initiatives. Through such an approach, any cultural tourism development will be far better positioned to withstand fluctuations in demand and a shift in fashion, as well as addressing any opportunities and threats that may arise.

References

Barrow, C. J. (1999). *Environmental Management – Principles and Practice*. London: Routledge.

Becker, H., Dunn, S. and Middleton, V. T. C. (1999). *Think Small – Think Local – Think Micro-Businesses: A First Report for Consultation and Endorsement* (August). London: DCMS.

Bell, S. and Morse, S. (2000). *Sustainability Indicators: Measuring the Immeasurable*. London: Earthscan.

British Standards Institute (1997). *Draft British Standard: Revision of BS7750: 1992 – Specification for Environmental Management Systems*. Milton Keynes: BSI.

Butler, R. (1993). Introduction. In Butler, R. and Pearce, D. (eds) *Change in Tourism: People, Places and Processes*. London: Routledge, pp. 1–11.

Ceron, J.-P. and Dubois, G. (2003). Tourism and sustainable development indicators: the gap between theoretical demands and practical achievements. *Current Issues in Tourism* 6(1): 54–75.

Countryside Commission (1993). *Wise Growth; The Actions Collectively of Micro-businesses will Affect Most Other Businesses in Tourism*. Cheltenham: Countryside Commission.

Department of Culture, Media and Sport (1999). *Tomorrow's Tourism: A Growth Industry for the New Millennium*. London: DCMS.

Department of Environment, Transport and the Regions (2000). *Indicators of Sustainable Development, UK Round Table on Sustainable Development*. London: DETR (July).

English Tourism Council and TMI Tourism Management Institute (2003). *Destination Management Handbook – A Sustainable Approach*. London: ETC/TMI.

Erdmenger, C., Burzacchini, A. and Levett, R. (2000). *Local Loops – How Environmental Management Cycles Contribute to Local Sustainability*. Proceedings of the European Commission Advanced Study Course on Local Instruments. Brussels: European Commission.

European Commission (2003). *Basic Orientations for the Sustainability of European Tourism*. Brussels: Enterprise Directorate-General, EC.

Font, X. and Buckley, R. C. (eds) (2001). *Tourism Ecolabelling: Certification and Promotion of Sustainable Management*. Wallingford: CABI.

Fyall, A., Garrod, B. and Leask, A. (eds) (2003). *Managing Visitor Attractions – New Directions*. Oxford, Butterworth-Heinemann.

Global Tourism Solutions UK (2004). *The Economic Impact of Tourism in Cumbria*. GTSUK. Report for Cumbria Tourist Board, Kendal.

Hillary (1994). *The Eco-Management and Audit Scheme: A Practical Guide*. Letchworth: Technical Communications Ltd.

Jersey Policy and Resources Committee (1998). *Jersey in the New Millennium: A Sustainable Future Framework Consultation Document*. States of Jersey: Jersey Policy and Resources Committee (October).

Leslie, D. (2005). Rural tourism businesses and environmental management systems. In Hall, D., Kirkpatrick, I. M. and Mitchell, M. (eds) *Rural Tourism and Sustainable Business*. Clevedon: Channel View Publications, pp. 249–267.

Middleton, V. T. C. (2001). The Importance of micro-businesses in European Tourism. In Roberts, L. and Hall, D. (eds) *Rural Tourism and Recreation – Principles to Practice*. Wallingford: CABI, pp. 197–201.

Moore, S. A., Smith, A. J. and Newsome, D. N. (2003). Environmental performance reporting for natural area tourism: contributions by visual impact management frameworks and their indicators. *Journal of Sustainable Tourism* 11(4): 348–375.

Ritchie, J. R. B. and Crouch, G. L. (2003). *The Competitive Destination – A Sustainable Tourism Perspective*. Wallingford: CABI.

Sheldon, C. and Toxon, M. (1999). *Installing Environmental Management Systems – A Step-by-step Guide*. London: Earthscan.

United Nations Environment Programme (2002). *Industry as a Partner for Sustainable Development: Tourism*. Paris: UNEP.

United Nations Environment Programme (2003). *Tourism and Local Agenda 21 – The Role of Local Authorities in Sustainable Tourism*. Paris: UNEP.

Yeoman, I., Robertson, M., Ali-Knight, J., Drummond, S. and McMahon-Beattie, U. (eds) (2004). *Festival and Events Management – An International Arts and Culture Perspective*. Oxford: Butterworth-Heinemann.

Websites

Green Globe: www.Greenglobe21.com

For a good example of a small cultural attraction developed in terms of sustainability visit: www.Envolve.co.uk

Initiatives by tour operators: www.sustainabletravel.org

United Nations Environment Programme: www.uneptie.org/pc/tourism

CHAPTER 7

Cultural tourists in a cultural capital: Helsinki

Arvo Peltonen

Learning outcomes

- Recognize the role and contribution of urban culture in marketing a city's image exemplified through the designation as a City of Culture.
- Appreciate the varied positions of stakeholders in the multi-objective and multi-faceted management of major cultural events.
- Understand the role of cultural hospitality in a city's hospitality culture from the perspective of cultural tourism.
- Understand the importance of distribution patterns of urban cultural events in terms of maximizing encounters between supply and demand within the urban structure.
- Analyse the enduring direct and indirect outcomes arising from the City of Culture status.

Introduction

Since 1985 there has been a continuing annual rivalry between 'culturally profiled' cities seeking the status of City of Culture or Cultural Capital of Europe. Such status certainly carries material and symbolic values that are important from the point of view of administrators and politicians in those cities and countries (Corijn and Van Praet, 1994; Richards, 1996a, pp. 27–31; Cultural Capital of Europe, 2004). The aspirations of administrators and politicians in strengthening a city's cultural characteristics and enhancing its image through such status could be termed the 'cultural hospitability' of the city. The attitudes and the political will, for one reason or another, with regard to making citizens' own cultural services available to visitors can be termed 'hospitality culture' or the hospitality instinct of the Cultural Capital.

However, there are difficulties to overcome not only in seeking such designation as 'City of Culture of Europe' for a year, i.e. the application procedure, but also in the delivery of the designed programme for the year. The course of the cultural year requires a multitude of management activities involving different levels of governance and type and scale of events. In this multi-faceted management process cultural institutions, experts and administrators must collaborate in consistent and integrated ways. Understandably, there are many contradictions between the objectives of the various stakeholders involved in planning for being a City of Culture. The citizens should have an equal role and responsibility as consumers of culture and as active producers of cultural experiences. A further problem is that the needs and expectations of 'others', e.g. tourists, are not always known when the goals for the cultural year are defined. In fact, it sometimes seems to be just the opposite, given that on the ground the tying together of culture and tourism is often fragmented (Richards, 1996a, p. 11, 1996b, p. 92). In sum, management strategies that support the development of culturally motivated citizens and tourists must be developed and implemented in a sustainable manner, including economical, social, cultural, psychological and ecological facets of the city. A conceptual tool for gaining such a holistic, integrated approach is potentially that of destination management (Davidson and Maitland, 1997; Laws et al., 2002).

This case study will consider how Helsinki, one of the nine Millennium Cities of Culture, recognized and dealt with the challenges of the event and raised its profile among the prominent cultural (tourism) destinations of Europe. Specifically, the study aims to address the following questions:

- How did Helsinki strengthen its traditional cultural hospitality and become an even more culturally hospitable capital?
- To what extent did the managers responsible for the cultural year in Helsinki consider tourism a means of attaining the goals set for the status?
- How did Helsinki assist tourists to explore Helsinki's cultural aspirations and creativeness?
- Whose cultural dimensions of Helsinki were sold to whom?
- In the longer term, what are the outcomes of resources expended on the application and operation of the cultural year?

In addressing these questions the study draws on the written material that has been published on the year itself. Such material is limited; besides the official reports (e.g. 2000.hel.fi, sine anno/2001), written evaluations of Helsinki's cultural year are rather scant. There is a review regarding the experiences and impacts of the cultural year published by the Municipal Information Centre of Helsinki (Cantell and Schulman, 2001). In addition, there are the findings of a project to investigate the possible improvement of the economic performance of small and medium-sized enterprises (SMEs) in the cultural sector through networking (Andersén and Vaihekoski, 2001) which did involve a number of SMEs that took part in the year's events. Complementary to these sources, students of the Finnish University Network for Tourism Studies conducted interviews (in total 470) and a 'post-action' survey, based on the ATLAS questionnaire (Richards, 1996a) in 2002 to investigate the attitudes of cultural tourists in Helsinki. At the same time, their recollections and perceptions of both the Helsinki Millennium Year of Culture and the other Cities of Culture of that year were surveyed.

European Millennium City of Culture: Helsinki

In total, nine European Cities presented applications to be designated as the Millennium City of Culture. According to Landry (2001, pp. 30–31), the cities emphasized different objectives:

- the enhancement of international visibility imaging
- the upgrading of urban structure through refinement and/or development of culture resources
- the alleviation of social problems resulting from marginalization. This required major strategic choices with the accent on either civic culture and the cultural industry as a practical tool for mediating urban development, or cultural hospitality as an integral part of urban development, a requisite for upgrading everyday living and advancing the quality of life in the urban environment.

Helsinki City Council decided to apply for designation as the cultural capital for the Millennium in 1994. The bidding procedure of Helsinki for City of Culture status was in many ways significant, following on as it did from a deep economic recession and political changes in Europe. The municipal political atmosphere was cloudy, missing a clear vision and philosophical base. Nonetheless, out of these conditions of creative chaos the building blocks of a new strategy were laid. In the strategy of hope, culture-driven development and internationalization were put together (2000.hel.fi, 2001, p. 7; Cantell and Heikkinen, 2001, p. 20). The year 2000 was also timely, as Helsinki would concurrently celebrate its 450th anniversary.

The Millennium year of the City of Culture competition was anticipated with higher expectations than previous years, and excitement accompanied the designation process. The announcement that for the first time since the inception of the nomination, more than one city would be chosen as the City of Culture of Europe was greeted with a mixture of surprise and some degree of contention. The European Council of Ministers based its Millennium year decision on the belief that a holistic view of the variety of the European city cultures, all with their own special cultural flavours, would be gained by designating all nine applicants from different parts of Europe as a Millennium City of Culture. At first, the majority of the Millennium applicants felt that the Council's decision 'watered down' the whole cultural capital idea. The City Council of Helsinki had discussions about postponing the application. However, after further assessing the situation, the members concluded that the pan-European networking between the cities selected that would arise would contribute to bolstering the city's internationalization objectives and, therefore, such networking aligned well with the City Council's strategic vision.

Setting goals for the Millennium year of Helsinki

The following working hypotheses for the Millennium City of Culture were set:

- Helsinki will be seen as a cultural interface between East and West, with important influences from both cultural spheres.
- The city will be recognized as a pocket-sized, future-orientated metropolis with a human scale.
- Helsinki will be understood as an open and flexible, multiple-value city with a creative spiritual atmosphere.
- The status of Cultural Capital will support the revitalization and development of city's economy through emphasizing the interaction between the scientific, cultural and economic sectors, thus creating a driving force for the prosperity of the city and its region in the future.
- The promotion of culture was interpreted as a means of encouraging more people and industrial interests to move into the city.
- Cultural tourism was considered to be one of the fastest growing sectors in tourism and, thus, was seen as an important contributor in the revitalization of Helsinki (2000.hel.fi, 2001, p. 8).

Four goals were established to inform and guide the programme of events and activities for the Millennium year, namely:

- the scope of the future: culture also means investment in the future through the projects that have permanent impact
- finding new perspectives: the project of the City of Culture is a lasting project along with new ways of enriching and updating the urban culture
- internationalization: the projects will work to spread Finnish cultural testimonies across European cultural forums and will disseminate Finnish cultural events within European audiences

- the City of Culture of the Millennium year will be dedicated first to the citizens of Helsinki; events will be planned for the city's inhabitants, with direct impact on their everyday life anticipated. Helsinki's people will be not just the consumers of culture, but also producers of urban cultural events by their own motivations and inspiration. The empowerment of citizens will mean active participation and shared responsibility in organizing and conducting the cultural events (2000.hel.fi, 2001, p. 16).

These goals clearly demonstrated that the Helsinki City of Culture Millennium year was to be orientated mostly towards the residents of Helsinki and surrounding areas. A culturally hospitable environment was constructed for them and with consideration of their needs. However, the project did not exclude 'others', and implicitly set goals for the promotion of cultural tourism. It was recognized that cultural tourists may have an impact on the city's atmosphere as Helsinki's cultural capital was enmeshed within its hospitality culture.

Managing the cultural events

The Foundation of the Helsinki City of Culture [Helsingin kulttuurikaupunkisäätiö] was founded in 1996 to manage the Millennium year in Helsinki rather than designate one of the existing cultural administrative bodies. Its primary purpose was to formulate the project's final objectives, co-ordinate the events and allocate and control the financial resources. This caused some tensions between established cultural and cultural–political institutions, leading to some degree of reluctance on the part of some of these institutions to participate, at least initially.

A managing director was appointed to take overall leadership of the Foundation and a manager designated to oversee each cultural subsector and be responsible for managing that sector's events. Even so, the success of each project-associated activity and event rested to a large extent on the involvement of entrepreneurs, cultural institutions, interest groups and various associations. Ultimately, however, overall success lay in the hands of ordinary citizens.

Of the 3000 or so proposals and initiatives put forward, 500 were chosen as events for the cultural year and were partly financed under the Millennium year banner (2000.hel.fi, 2001, pp. 8–9). These projects involved 400 different organizations and actors. In total, approximately 100 000 people became involved in the city's cultural innovativeness and creativeness.

Apart from the 500 'official' activities and events, many other sponsors and ministries developed their own projects, with the necessary funding, thereby supporting the year's events and contributing to the overall programme. European Union funding through various social and structural funds and community initiatives was also channelled to appropriate projects.

Performance of the Millennium year of culture in Helsinki

Consumers of culture

According to its loosely formulated tourism-management strategy, the Foundation adopted a 'destination management' approach (Laws et al., 2002). That is, facilities and services for cultural projects that were accepted under the cultural year's banner were chosen mainly by evaluating the feasibility of establishing and expanding creative services, activities and structures that would permanently enrich the city's cultural life. Hence, the model would realize the idea of the 'continuing cultural capital' by versatile service networks within the destination (Michell and Heiskanen, 2003). This approach primarily enhanced the cultural hospitality of Helsinki and only in a secondary manner benefited tourists. The linear model of separate value chains as 'tourist-targeted tourism service-satisfaction' was rejected (Dolivo, 2001). The Foundation defined the role of tourism as a means of enhancing the marketing potential of the cultural events and as indirect image marketing of Helsinki. There were, however, also direct marketing aspirations for special segments, e.g. for specialists interested in innovative solutions in integrating the environmental arts and technology (e.g. architecture of lights). Avant garde exhibitions and performances were advertised for special groups of cultural tourists and media people.

The Millennium year involved approximately 5.2 million participants; in a country of 5.2 million inhabitants, a capital city of 550 000 citizens with a metropolitan area of 900 000 people. There were 2 million visitors to paid events and 3.2 million people participated in free-of-charge events (2000.hel.fi, 2001, pp. 31–34). Thus, the Cultural Capital touched Helsinki in an extensive manner. However, with regard to tourism, the statistics of these event visitors is interesting. According to Cantell (2001, p. 91):

- most of the visitors (60–70 per cent) to the Millennium events were from Helsinki and its metropolitan area
- between 7 and 20 per cent were cultural tourists from other parts of Finland
- approximately 7 per cent were international cultural tourists.

In 2002, a visitor survey (sample of 434 people) undertaken by the Finnish University Network for Tourism Studies found that:

- between 40 and 60 per cent of respondents were from Helsinki and its metropolitan area
- 7.9 per cent were foreigners, e.g. international cultural tourists.

The methodological underpinnings to these two sets of data were different and thus it is not possible to draw robust conclusions. However, it could be argued that the Millennium year did not clearly increase the percentage of cultural tourists in Helsinki. This may lead to speculation that the Millennium year was not very successful in terms of promoting incoming tourism. However, it did succeed in encouraging residents to take part in cultural events. This was the principal goal of the year of Helsinki as a Millennium City of Culture.

Encounters in the city

The sociopsychological benefits of cultural exchange are to be seen in the interaction of people, cultural artefacts and cultural performances. To gain maximum opportunities for such interaction, the prerequisite is to develop the citizens' continuing encounters with creative and inspiring cultural experiences. Three different factors, the versatile mixture of which will influence the fulfilment of the objectives set, or 'cultural fusion', are important in managing these creative encounters:

- *Comprehension of verbal interaction* (not only spoken languages, but also the body languages of theatre and music can act as cultural lingua franca). In the case of Helsinki, the verbal dimension was important in exposing the national minorities to cultural events in their own languages: Swedish as the second official language of bilingual Finland, but also the Sami and Romany languages. In some cases the languages of 'newcomers' (e.g. Russian) were used. Naturally, Finnish was incomprehensible to most of the foreigners.
- *Timing of the events* (seasonality, moments of action). The timing and length of the events along the time-frame of the cultural year influenced the number of visitors that each respective event attracted.
- *Spatial distribution of the pattern of events in the urban structure* (coreness versus peripherality). Not all of the 500 events could be traced in the spatial structure. Coreness and peripherality dimensions were therefore used in interpreting the plausibility of 'others' to be involved in the various events and performances (Table 7.1). By hypothesizing the spatial

Table 7.1 Distribution of events of the Millennium year in Helsinki

Category of events (n)	CBD	Downtown	Neighbourhoods	Helsinki (scattered)	Metropolitan Helsinki	Others (no data)
Urban events (60)	21	13	6	10	3	7
Events for children (29)	6	4	2	8	5	4
Art education (28)	6	2	4	8	7	1
Events for all (25)	1	5	2	10	5	2
History (25)	13	4	–	5	2	1
Scientific debates (21)	13	3	–	2	–	3
Literature, cartoon strips (12)	8	–	–	2	1	1
Media (digital) (23)	6	2	–	–	1	14
Photography (20)	12	3	–	3	2	–
Environmental and urban arts (25)	5	11	2	4	3	–
Architecture (26)	17	5	–	–	2	2
Pop and folk music (33)	22	4	1	2	3	1
Classics (29)	18	4	–	2	4	1
Opera (8)	7	1	–	–	–	–
Total (364)	155	61	17	56	38	23

Source: Helsinki, 2000 (2001).

distribution pattern, it could be predicted that the great majority of encounters for both international and domestic tourists should happen in Helsinki's central business district (CBD) and events for larger, more versatile audiences should be organized in downtown Helsinki. Events and activities that primarily targeted local participants should be located more in urban neighbourhoods than in the city centre. In addition, there were events completely based on networking for digital performances and communications, which were compiled mostly for media purposes.

'Encountering the culture' in Helsinki was thus predomi nantly based in and around the central business district. This is about twenty minutes' walk from the pivotal point of the city, the railway station and the area where the permanent facilities for cultural events are located. Certain activities – major exhibitions and events of 'high culture' – were very centripetal. The high concentration of Millennium events in this lofty, symbolic core of Helsinki meant that most domestic and international tourists probably encountered the productions of the Millennium year there. In contrast, 'events for all' were staged in the major residential areas and thus the general tourists probably did not find these events.

Enduring results and memories

In what ways did Helsinki gain in terms of longer term outcomes from the Millennium year? One of the early decisions made in financing the Millennium year was that funding would not be used for the 'walls', but for the events. No projects involving major construction works were commissioned, although there was expenditure on cosmetic facelifting of the streets, parks and other public places. Some buildings in the downtown area were renovated and their function was changed. Such reused buildings served an important role as forums for the events and all of these have continued most of their new functions since the Millennium year. The free green city bicycles that were introduced in the central business district remained at public disposal. The University of Helsinki gained five professorships in urban studies from Helsinki municipality and the Ministry of Education and Cultural Affairs. Notably, some of the events staged first under the Millennium banner have become annual events, e.g. the annual international happening of urban culture, URB.

What memories do citizens and tourists have of Helsinki's Cultural Capital year and the events of the Millennium year? Of the few studies that have been undertaken, one of the most valuable is a longitudinal survey of the opinions of Helsinki citizens (Cantell, 2001). Nine surveys were undertaken during the period 1998–2001, which aimed to register any changes in the opinions and attitudes of citizens regarding the Millennium year. Insights into the findings of this study are as follows:

- 74–81 per cent of participants thought that the year would increase familiarity with Helsinki as a cultural city; the lower figure was in 2001 just after the Millennium year ended (Cantell, 2001, p. 179)
- 72–78 per cent of participants considered that the year enhanced the quality of life of the urban environment
- 70–78 per cent of participants felt that the year increased the influx of tourists to Helsinki.

As such, it appears that the citizens' opinions regarding the impact of the Millennium year were focused on its impact on domestic and international tourism. Although a robust assessment of the impact of the event on tourism is not available, it seems plausible that the actual impact on tourism demand was lower than expected. In this respect, Helsinki did not improve its touristic profile during or just after the City of Culture year.

What did culturally motivated citizens and tourists remember about the Helsinki Millennium year less than two years later? This aspect was a focus of a survey for the Finnish University Network for Tourism Studies, undertaken in March 2002. Besides noting respondents' consumer behaviour and background information, the survey enquired about their reminiscences of the Millennium year in Helsinki and of the other Millennium Cities of Culture. The survey revealed that the aspects that respondents could recall most readily were the environmental artefacts, which changed the urban landscape or had a visible location in the city structure. Performances, concerts and exhibitions staged in unusual venues or by famous performers also stayed firm in respondents' memories. Collectively, the 470 respondents mentioned 150 different events, of which approximately forty could be categorized as being specific to the Millennium year.

The survey included inviting participants to rank Europe's capitals and its larger cities as the cultural cores of Europe. Helsinki was ranked eighth after, and in rank order, the following: Rome, followed closely by Paris and London, Athens, Florence, Barcelona and Budapest. Interestingly, few participants could neither cite cities that have held City of Culture status nor cite the other Millennium Cities of Culture. This indicates that perhaps the concept of the City of Culture as a vehicle for image marketing needs to be reconsidered.

Conclusion

The status of City of Culture will prevail as an important initiative at the municipality and even national level. Its role in the revitalization of urban culture, everyday urban life and strengthening the self-esteem of the city has and will continue to be interpreted as an important venture. For interior and urban political reasons, new member states of the European Union from 2009 will be applying for City of Culture status. Future Cities of Culture will find the programme a practical way to foster culturally motivated urban development at both municipal and national levels.

For Helsinki, perhaps the biggest problem was that the year 2000 was filled with many events without any clear spearheads that could provide focus to the whole year. However, Helsinki City Council made a clear strategic choice in deliberately designing the Millennium year for Helsinki citizens, while still keeping the occasion open for tourists to learn about Finland's culture, especially its urban culture. Although the status of being a City of Culture (among eight others) did not appear to draw greater numbers of tourists into the city, the citizens of Helsinki enjoyed the events being staged by them in their own 'living room'. Helsinki enhanced its cultural hospitality, but perhaps missed the upgrading of its hospitality culture. This latter aspect is thus something that future Cities of Culture will need to address.

References

Andersén, T. and Vaihekoski, M. (2001). *Verkostoyhteistyön merkitys kulttuurialan yritysystoiminnan kannalta, Case: Helsingin kulttuurikaupunkivuosi 2000* [Importance of networking for the business performance in the cultural sector, Case: Helsinki City of Culture in 2000]. Helsinki: LTT-Tutkimus Oy.

Cantell, T. (2001). Kulttuurikaupunkivuoden kansalaismielipide ja yleisöt [Opinions of the citizens and audiences]. In Cantell, T. and Schulman, H. (eds) *Mitä oli kulttuurivuosi?* [What was the Year of Culture?] *Writings on the Year of Culture in Helsinki.* Helsinki: Helsingin kaupungin tietokeskus, pp. 177–194.

Cantell, T. and Heikkinen, T. (2001). Kulttuurikaupungin synty. Kulttuurikaupunkiprojektin tausta ja esivaiheet. In Cantell, T. and Schulman, H. (eds) *Mitä oli kulttuurivuosi?* [What was the Year of Culture?] *Writings on the Year of Culture in Helsinki.* Helsinki: Helsingin kaupungin tietokeskus, pp. 9–25.

Cantell, T. and Schulman, H. (2001). *Mitä oli kulttuurivuosi?* [What was the Year of Culture?] *Writings on the Year of Culture in Helsinki.* Helsinki: Helsingin kaupungin tietokeskus.

Corijn, E. and Van Praet, S. (1994). Antwerp 93 in the context of European cultural capitals: art policy as politics. Paper presented at the Conference on City Cultures, Lifestyles and Consumption Practices, Coimbra, 15–16 July 1994.

Cultural Capital of Europe (2004). Available at: http://encyclopedia.thefreedictionary.com/Cultural%20Capital%20of%20Europe

Davidson, R. and Maitland, R. (1997). *Tourism Destinations*. London: Hodder & Stoughton.

Dolivo, G. (2001). Kulttuuri ja matkailu – kokemuksia Helsingin kulttuurikaupunkihankeesta [Culture and tourism: experiences from the year of city of culture in Helsinki]. Lecture, Matkamessut, Helsinki (18 January).

Helsinki (2000). (sine anno/2001). *Helsinki Euroopan kulttuuripääkaupunki vuonna 2000*, raportti [Helsinki, A Cultural Capital of Europe in the Year 2000, Report]. Helsinki: Helsingin kulttuurikaupunkisäätiö, 65.

Landry, C. (2001). Politiikka, talous, kulttuuri [Politics, economy, culture]. In Cantell, T. and Schulman, H. (eds) *Mitä oli kulttuurivuosi?* [What was the Year of Culture?] *Writings on the Year of Culture in Helsinki*. Helsinki: Helsingin kaupungin tietokeskus, pp. 26–40.

Laws, E., Scott, N. and Paffit, N. (2002). Synergy in destination image management: a case study and conceptualisation. *International Journal of Tourism Research* 4: 39–55.

Michell, R. and Heiskanen, I. (2003). Finland. In *Cultural Policies in Europe: A Compendium of Basic Facts and Trends*. Council of Europe/ERICarts. Available at: http://www.culturalpolicies.net/project.html

Richards, G. (1996a). Scope and significance of cultural tourism. In Richards, G. (ed.) *Cultural Tourism in Europe*. Wallingford: CABI, pp. 9–45.

Richards, G. (1996b). Policy context of cultural tourism. In Richards, G. (ed.) *Cultural Tourism in Europe*. Wallingford: CABI, pp. 87–105.

Websites

http://encyclopedia.thefreedictionary.com/Cultural%Capital%20of%20%Europe

http://www.culturalpolicies.net/project.htm

http://www.hel.fi/tietokeskus/suunnat/artikkelit/artikkeli100.htm

Cultural tourism in South Africa: a case study of cultural villages from a developing country perspective

Dimitri Tassiopoulos and Nancy Nuntsu

Learning outcomes

- Identify why the government of a developing country supports the development of cultural tourism.
- Outline the key management issues that affect cultural villages.
- Describe the expectations of the cultural tourists.
- Formulate suggestions for cultural tourism management within a developing country context.

Introduction

Culture should be the language that should heal and transform the nation

(Former State President, Nelson Mandela, in Galla, 1998, p. 38)

South Africa has a diverse tourism resource base that apart from its biodiversity has a unique cultural diversity that includes mission settlements, sites of slave occupation, urban space for ritual purposes, rock and sites, rock formations and natural landscapes which have national and international cultural significance (South Africa, 1996, p. 38).

In 1997, South Africa was readmitted as a member of the United Nations Educational, Scientific, and Cultural Organization (UNESCO) and in the same year adopted the Tshwane Declaration which, according to Galla (1998, pp. 39–40), encompasses the following guidelines concerning heritage tourism:

- to provide a unique opportunity to combine South Africa's heritage with the tourism industry to create social, economic and environmental benefits
- to offer South Africans and tourists learning experiences on the personality of South Africa
- to assist in providing equitable access to heritage and financial resources
- to achieve a more equitable distribution of the capacity to engage in economic and cultural systems in South Africa.

The government is committed to managing effectively and conserving the cultural resources of the country by ensuring that:

- tourism takes note of the cultural heritage resources within specific communities and environments
- cultural resources are managed to be the negotiated benefit of all stakeholders within a community

- access to management of cultural resources should be as wide as possible within specific communities and should promote co-operation between all stakeholders
- land-use planning and development projects for tourism should include effective protection and sustainable utilization of cultural resources (South Africa, 1996, p. 38).

Until the end of the apartheid era in 1994, South Africa's cultural tourism offering was dominated by cultural sites connected with its European cultural heritage. However, South Africa is home to diverse local cultures, which have evolved their own unique and distinctive music, art forms and traditional rituals, symbolizing their values and beliefs and in contrast to those of the European or Eastern settlers, whose descendants have evolved variations of their ancestors' roots (Lubbe, 2003, p. 87; Department of Trade and Industry, 2004, p. 6). Before 1994, 30 per cent of international visitors to South Africa came for its scenic beauty, while 26 per cent came for its wildlife; after 1994, 27 per cent of international tourists came to see the 'new' South Africa, while 21 per cent came to experience cultural offerings; in other words, 38 per cent of tourists to this country are motivated by culture as a reason for visiting (Lubbe, 2003, p. 96).

The context of cultural tourism in South Africa

In South Africa traditional villages combine cultural factors such as architecture, dress, cuisine, dancing, music and story-telling (Lubbe, 2003, p. 96). The cultural village offering, of which there are approximately forty in operation around the country, has been developed as a one-stop cultural immersion offering for the tourist to meet the indigenous people (Hughes, 2003, p. 4). While a few cultural offerings have been initiated by small businesses and are yielding modest profits, most have required levels of investment far beyond the reach of the local communities. One challenge that these offerings face is that of too much supply chasing too little demand.

Broadly speaking, there is a three-category typology of cultural villages in South Africa. The first category, 'grass-root' cultural villages, refers to cultural offerings that are found within a rural setting where communities share their daily experiences and practices with visitors. The second category, township tours, refers to cultural offerings of communities that are found within an urban setting, such as townships, and form part of the urban cultural tourism experience. A further category of cultural offerings, which are either rural or urban based, are commercial operations, or cultural 'theme parks', where the cultural offering is staged by 'employees' of the operation. Examples of this category are Shakaland in Kwa Zulu Natal Province and Lesedi Cultural Village in the North West Province.

The development and implementation of cultural tourism in South Africa, although guided by national legislative policies and guidelines, is deemed to be the responsibility of provincial and local authorities. In the Eastern Cape Province, for instance, the Department for Sport, Recreation, Arts and Culture has committed itself to supporting the Cultural Industries Growth Strategy. The Eastern Cape Provincial government recognizes cultural tourism as a rapid growth area and a focal point (owing to its contribution to South Africa's anti-apartheid struggle) in tourism worldwide and hence has embarked on an aggressive strategy to develop the cultural and heritage sites that are tourist attractions (Balindlela, 2001, pp. 1–2). The Eastern Cape Tourism Master Plan [Eastern Cape Tourism Board (ECTB), 2003, pp. 25, 32] recognizes that some of the primary features of the Eastern Cape include its cultural traditions and traditional architecture, and defines cultural tourism as 'the movement of people for essentially cultural motivations such as study tours, performing arts and cultural tours, travel to festivals and other cultural events, visits to sites and monuments, travel to study nature, folklore or art, and, pilgrimages' (ECTB, 2003, p. 25). It also underscores that the cultural legacy of the Eastern Cape needs to be developed with sensitivity by considering the interests of the local people through three critical elements (ECTB, 2003, p. 32):

- the history of the local community
- the understanding of the local community's cultural systems
- the consideration and understanding of gender roles and distinctions.

To this end, the ECTB and the Eastern Cape Development Corporation (ECDC) have been active in developing cultural tourism offerings in the province, mainly in the development and promotion of cultural villages, arts and crafts centres, and sourcing investment funds. Cultural tourism offerings must meet a range of challenges to develop sustainably and remain competitive in the cultural village marketplace. The challenges faced can be clustered, according to KPMG (2002, p. 8), into a set of eight strategic themes:

- Investment facilitation: public and private investment in the cultural villages' facilities and infrastructure is key.

- Linking destination marketing and product development: a cultural village needs to ensure that it meets and exceeds the promises made by its marketing communication.
- Market-driven product development: the effort to develop cultural tourism offerings must be based on an understanding of what the market wants and focus on the unique characteristics of the cultural villages.
- Ongoing and focused research: the future decisions about offering development and marketing activities of the cultural villages should be based on sound and accurate market research.
- Partnership: the most effective partnerships and alignments between the public and private sector, between different spheres of government, industry and the community, must be established.
- People investment: in order for a village to succeed and contribute to the livelihoods of the local community it must be supported by the appropriate strategies for training and skills development.
- Quality service and standards: there must be a close alignment between the promises made to visitors and the offerings delivered. There must be a focus on accessibility, safety, cleanliness, service quality, information provision, and so forth.
- Sustainability: the long-term future of the cultural villages is linked to developing tourism in a way that respects and protects natural, cultural and built heritages and lifestyles and leads to improvements in the livelihoods of the local inhabitants.

The World Travel and Tourism Council (2002, p. 4), however, highlights that although South Africa has the potential to become one of the world's great new (cultural) tourism destinations, as many of the strategic and operational aspects appear to be in place, there is insufficient focus on implementation and this has limited the return on investment and caused targets to be consistently missed.

Thus, the following sections aim to assess some of the above-mentioned challenges by exploring tourists' expectations and perceptions of cultural villages, analysing how such cultural villages are managed, and assessing the enabling environment created by government.

Two cultural villages: case studies

The cultural villages are situated along the south-east coast of South Africa, in the Eastern Cape Province (see Figure 8.1).

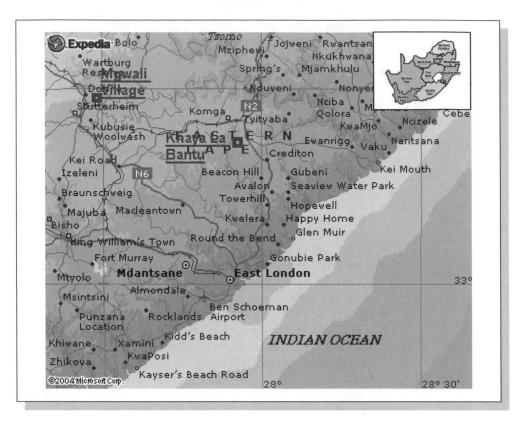

Figure 8.1
Map indicating the location of the two cultural villages in the Eastern Cape (*Source*: adapted from http://www.expedia.com/pub/agent.dll)

The province has a population of approximately 7 million, representing 16 per cent (the third largest) of the South African population, with a non-urban population of nearly 4.1 million (Nuntsu et al., 2004, pp. 519–520). The two Eastern Cape cultural villages illustrate the following: Khaya La Bantu Cultural Village highlights issues related to the understanding of the expectations of cultural tourists, while Mgwali Cultural Village raises issues relating to the management of a cultural attraction.

Khaya La Bantu Cultural Village (KCV) is situated in Mooiplaas, about forty-seven kilometres from East London, alongside the N2 National Road, in the Eastern Cape, and is the homestead of a family who have been living on a working farm for generations. KCV is a Canadian-funded project and has employed a manager to look after its affairs. Furthermore, the management team of KCV has formed a strategic alliance with the local tour operators who in turn provide KCV with access to the occasional cruise tourism business in East London, among others. A pilot study of KCV was carried out in July 2002 to determine tourist expectations and perceptions of this cultural village. Two surveys were conducted concurrently as part of an exploratory study during the period September 2002 to January 2003. These surveys were conducted using two semi-structured questionnaires, whereby visitors to the attraction were intercepted and interviewed.

Mgwali Cultural Village (MCV) is situated about seventy-five kilometres from East London, alongside the N6 National Road in the Eastern Cape, and is a settlement of about 8000 people. The settlement is one of the oldest in the Eastern Cape. The MCV project was initiated on the advice of the Stutterheim Business Centre. During early 2003, in-depth interviews were conducted, using guiding questions, with the various stakeholders of the MCV venture.

Findings

Khaya La Bantu Cultural Village (KCV) (see Case Box 8.1)

Core offerings • • •

Visitors to KCV pay an entrance fee to access this attraction. The attraction has the following core offerings: singing and dancing, the presentation of the red blanket, an interpretation of beadwork and how it is related to the different stages of a woman's life, a visit to the Chief's cattle enclosure (kraal), a beer-tasting ceremony, wood and water bearers, a visit to the women's hut (Intonjane), which is used to check virginity, a visit to the Abakheta hut (circumcisions hut), a visit to the kitchens to see how traditional fare is being prepared, a walka-bout in the village to meet the Sangoma (witchdoctor and healer), an observation of daily village scenes (the stamping of maize and grinding of corn, etc.), partaking in a traditional meal, observing the making of beadwork, and the sale of various crafts made in the village. KCV also organizes a Xhosa Easter Good Friday event for visitors.

Delivering the experience • • •

The village site guides wear casual everyday clothing and conduct all village tours in English only. A substantial percentage (63 per cent) of the visitors, however, feel that the guides

Case Box 8.1   News article about Khaya La Bantu

Xhosa traditions a treat for tourists
EAST LONDON – Most of the 500-odd passengers on the cruise liner *Pacific Princess* which docked here yesterday spent time shopping in the city or experiencing aspects of the Xhosa culture.

About 160 passengers took the excursion to the Khaya La Bantu Xhosa village at Mooiplaas where their visit was given an extra African dimension by the early morning rain.

As the road to the village was too muddy for the luxury buses, the visitors were bundled aboard a fleet of game-viewing Land Rovers from the Inkwenkwezi game park and taken up the track in safari style.

The guests, from all around the world, were welcomed by a bevy of singing and dancing bare-breasted maidens before sampling a traditional meal and being shown around the village.

The tourists and their ubiquitous cameras moved around enthralled, snapping inside and outside the variety of huts that form the village.

Passengers spent almost the entire trip back to the ship discussing the wonders of the village and the scenery despite the low cloud covering many of the distant hills.

All seemed to be impressed with the village's authenticity and at the amount of information imparted on their short visit there.

'The Xhosa experience was just what we came to Africa to see and the way we were brought into the culture was a really pleasant eye-opener for us', Australians Greg and Babs Glass from Adelaide said before boarding.

'We thought the village was very authentic and the experience showed us something very primitive', said Thai doctor Vinai Sawedawan who now lives in Chicago.

For most of the morning the craft stalls on the wharf were visited by people buying curios, from fridge magnets to beaded traditional Xhosa garments and wood carvings.

The *Pacific Princess* sailed at 3 pm yesterday to a rousing send-off from the West Bank High School band.

Source: Elias (2000, Internet).

should be able to speak a language other than English, in order to improve communication with the various backgrounds of the visitors. The majority of the visitors (97 per cent) expected that the content of the cultural village tour be personalized, with small groups for easy information transferral. The majority of the visitors (66 per cent) expected to be allowed to go for walkabouts in the village without guides. Of the various core offerings available to tourists, traditional African dancing (87 per cent) and short African musicals (83 per cent) were indicated as the most popular forms of entertainment experienced during a cultural village tour.

Information provision • • •

> The most commonly used source of information of the visitors is word of mouth (30 per cent), with a large majority of the visitors having been referred by friends and relatives (39 per cent). A substantial percentage of the visitors receive their information about the cultural village from brochures (27 per cent) and tourism bureaux (34.0 per cent). Very few seem to have heard about the attraction via the Internet (3 per cent).
>
> The majority of the visitors expected to receive some form of free printed material, such as a map of the cultural village (81 per cent), information pamphlets/leaflets (72 per cent) or a multi-page brochure (51 per cent) about the attraction. However, no free printed materials were provided by the cultural village for the visitors.

Meeting the expectations of tourists • • •

> The visitors were generally satisfied with the cultural village and as a whole found the experience both interesting and informative. Visitors expressed great willingness to recommend the tour to others because they felt that the visit was enjoyable and fascinating. However, a number of factors were highlighted: unstructured/free time in the village is seen as not adequate for the visitors, smaller groups would be preferred by several visitors, and there was difficulty in getting hold of the facility's contact staff. Access to the facility is seen to be problematic as the facility can only be reached via an untarred road. Most of the visitors (94 per cent) expect to find African crafts, curios and souvenirs for sale at the cultural village and would also like to have proper restaurant facilities and improved toilet facilities.

Mgwali Cultural Village (MCV) (see Case Box 8.2)

Core offerings • • •

> On arrival at the marketplace, a tourist to MCV is offered a brief overview of the village's history and an opportunity to meet the village Sangoma, observe village traditional activities in operation, partake in a traditional lunch cooked in a three-legged pot, visit the oldest Reformed Presbyterian church in South Africa, which has been declared a national monument, meet and observe the craftspeople of the village, visit an exhibition of local crafts and visit a traditional hut, and is given an insight into the everyday life of a typical villager. The village also offers backpacker-type accommodation.

Case Box 8.2   News article about Mgwali Cultural Village

Community museum launched

STUTTERHEIM – Mgwali Community Museum – the first of its kind established in the province, was launched at Mgwali village No 3 near here on Friday to resuscitate the culture of the community, restore and rewrite its history.

More initiatives of this nature are expected to be developed in the province.

Mgwali village, which comprises eight villages, resisted forced removals from the then Republic of South Africa to the Ciskei homeland in Frankfort (Edonqaba), near Bisho. They won the battle in 1985.

Mgwali is one of the oldest missionary stations in the province, and the settlement is rich in religious, social and political history. It was established in the early 1800s under the influence of Reverend Tiyo Soga.

The museum has been built by the community in the form of a number of Xhosa huts which serve as an exhibition centre.

It is situated in an area which is used for market gardening and it poses as a tourism village where market day is held once a month.

Sport, Arts and Culture MEC Nosimo Balindlela said the initiative is in line with the department's policy imperatives to encourage communities to establish their own museums to resuscitate their history and heritage as well as rewriting the history which was distorted by the previous governments.

Her department donated R30000 to the museum for training of the staff.

Balindlela said 'rural areas were rich in history and are the treasury of our heritage' and encouraged the youth to use the museum effectively to get to know their history better.

'We were barred for a long time from learning about our history', she said.

The museum does not benefit from a government subsidy.

Balindlela promised the government was going to grant it a subsidy and build a concrete structure but she could not give time frames. Meanwhile, the museum depends on donations.

The Eastern Cape Tourism Board (ECTB) promised assistance in promoting the museum in both the domestic and international tourism markets.

ECTB development senior manager Ernest Booi urged the Amahlathi Municipality and the Public Works Department to improve the 25 kilometre road infrastructure from the town to the museum as well as the water supply to the museum.

Spoornet's David Mbeki said community development was not solely the job of the government and urged the private sector to form a partnership with the government.

The Eastern Veterans' Association said 'we fought for freedom and now, for a better life for all, will be jealously guarding these projects which intent to uplift the people'.

Mgwali community leader Mzwandile Fanta, former Mgwali Residents' Association chairman who was detained several times by the apartheid government for being at the forefront of the resistance to the forced removal, said the museum had united the community and would shape its economic future as well as fight unemployment.

Fanta said the museum was started by a group of women who were involved in a sewing project early in 1991 with funds from Operation Hunger.

Source: Feni (2002, Internet).

Administration • • •

> The staff of MCV work on a voluntary basis and depend on the goodwill of the visitors for donations (Ntlangani, 2003, p. 38). The Business Advice Centre, a non-governmental organization, in Stutterheim provides MCV with all the information and guidance required to make decisions and administrate the project. The Stutterheim Business Centre also facilitates financial loans through the ECDC to service the machinery (i.e. sewing machines) that are used for the production of goods on sale.

Staffing function • • •

> Appropriate skills training for the staff is provided by the Stutterheim Business Centre. However, the management of MCV believes the capacity building provided by the Stutterheim Business Centre to be inadequate, as they do not have training in budgeting, auditing and general finance (Ntlangani, 2003, p. 38).

Finance function • • •

> The financial management structure, according to Ntlangani (2003, p. 39), is not well organized. The sourcing of financial loans, by ventures in rural areas, from commercial banks in South Africa is seen as difficult, especially if they have no collateral. MCV has no operating capital and in most cases manages this function on a laissez-faire basis.

Production function • • •

> The production of goods that are sold to visitors is labour intensive. The products produced and sold are traditional smoking pipes and dolls made from waste material found in the environment. Cultural dances are staged. Accommodation on a per-night basis is provided for visitors to MCV (Ntlangani, 2003, p. 40). The management of MCV also provides a catering service for visitors. The management team finances the purchasing of raw food and material, for sale to visitors, from their personal resources (Ntlangani, 2003, p. 41). This is due to the lack of operating capital within MCV.

Marketing function • • •

> The marketing function is poorly implemented and consequently there is no market intelligence available that identifies

the target markets of MCV or how best to position and build MCV as a brand. The Stutterheim Business Centre, according to Ntlangani (2003, pp. 42–3), promotes MCV via the local newspapers, radio and Internet. Brochures on MCV are produced by the ECTB, with word of mouth being the main promotional tool for MCV.

Discussion

One aspect of cultural tourism is the way in which different cultural groups communicate. According to Keyser (2002, p. 353), cultural shock and cultural arrogance are often the underlying causes of conflict between tourists and host societies. In the case of cultural visitors to KCV this may be caused, for example, by the confusion around language or symbolism of the cultural village, and may lead to visitors' experiencing frustration. Alternatively, demands by visitors to view practices such as the male initiation rites in the Abakheta hut (circumcisions hut) and the rites in the women's hut (Intonjane), which are used to check virginity, are areas of potential conflict as both practices have been highly secretive. The KCV and MCV communities may permit some rules to be broken and may forgive their visitors, but if there is a continual disregard of their local sensitivities this may be perceived as a display of cultural arrogance by the visitors. If this is left unresolved, the frustration and disappointment may result in destroying local goodwill and lead to community backlash, including hostility, rudeness and poor service. There is need to educate, and consequently sensitize visitors to the norms and values of cultural villages such as KCV and MCV. Other areas for potential conflict, especially where the developed and developing contexts (of guest and host, respectively) converge, are differing interpretations of the specifications for the quality of facilities, products and services, and what constitutes a fair price for a product or service rendered. However, according to Keyser (2002, p. 356), some host communities have managed to combine successfully the conservation of their traditional practices with their utilization of such tourism to their sites as a source of income.

The long-term effect of increasing competition from other cultural village offerings in the area, at this stage, seems unclear in regard to KCV and MCV. Furthermore, the long-term sustainability and value of their alliance with the local cruise tourism industry and tour operator industry require closer inspection. The effective management of cultural villages ultimately is the key to whether they will be sustainable or not. In the case of MCV it is clear that there is a gap between what management is taking place and what should be taking place. There seems to be too great a dependence on the local business advice centre and there appears to be a need for greater capacity building. In the context of a developing country, the aforementioned issues need to be carefully monitored and the relevant stakeholders need to be mentored to ensure that the projects survive on a long-term basis. Culture is increasingly becoming not just a tool for human development, but also a source of economic development in South Africa. In analysing tourism, the emphasis is usually placed on the perceived tourists' right to travel and to have access to cultural sites and manifestations in the places they visit; however, it still needs to be determined at what point cultural tourism begins to detract from the authentic cultural richness and vitality of the places visited by tourists in South Africa.

In the context of South African, a range of strategies needs to be applied to reduce the potential conflict and to boost the potential positive impacts of cultural tourism (Keyser, 2002, pp. 365–368). Potential visitors often need to be prepared for destinations, such as KCV and MCV, where the culture is known to be different to their own, by accessing beforehand information about the culture of the host community. Each culture has particular values, rituals and norms, and tourists need to recognize and respect local cultures; consequently, codes of conduct or guidelines can be very helpful as tools to reduce social and cultural impacts. Providing appealing and informative interpretation can be viewed as another strategy to reduce sociocultural impacts. Interpretation should be seen as a process of explaining to visitors the significance of the destination they have come to visit so that they can better understand and enjoy the heritage of the destination. There is also a need for government and the tourism industry to initiate programmes to inform the public about tourism and to obtain feedback from the local population about their perception of tourism. In South Africa, community involvement is seen as central in the tourism planning and management process. Community-managed projects, such as KCV and MCV, are an attempt to allow communities to decide the type of growth they would like to see and to assist them in implementing their plans.

Conclusion

There is a gap between the government's policy on cultural tourism and its actual activities on the ground. Pivotal is the level and type of assistance, beyond policy formulation, that national and local government can provide in creating an enabling environment for cultural tourism to grow sustainability in South Africa. If, however, community-based and other tourism development processes are not planned, implemented and managed according to market demands, far too many South Africans, especially the poor, will face not merely missed opportunities, but also the hard reality of failed or underperforming offerings to which tourists simply do not go (Department of Environmental Affairs and Tourism, 2002, p. 5).

I believe we should move quicker on the concept of cultural tourism to expose the rich cultural diversity and archaeological heritage ... to a wider audience

(Adv. N. Ramatlhodi, 2000)

Acknowledgements

The authors would like to acknowledge the support of Border Technikon in undertaking this research, and contributions of the postgraduate students, A. Tyali and G. R. Mbolekwa.

References

Balindlela, N. (2001). Conference on women in writing. Eastern Cape Province: transcript of a MEC speech made on 12 January.

Department of Environmental Affairs and Tourism (2002). *Responsible Tourism Development Guidelines*. Pretoria: Government of South Africa.

Department of Trade and Industry (2004). *The Tourism Sector*. Available from: http://thedti.gov.za/publications/tourism.htm (Accessed on 15 March 2004).

Eastern Cape Tourism Board (1999). *Tourism Marketing Plan*. South Africa: Government Printers.

Eastern Cape Tourism Board (2003). *Eastern Cape Tourism Master Plan: 2003–2007*. East London: ECTB.

Elias, L. (2000). Xhosa traditions a treat for tourists. *Daily Dispatch* (2 February). Available from: http://www.dispatch.co.za/2000/02/02/easterncape/CXHOSA.HTM (Accessed on 15 March 2004).

Feni, L. (2002). Community museum launched. *Daily Dispatch* (May 27). Available from: http://www.dispatch.co.za/2002/05/27/easterncape/BCOM.HTM (Accessed on 15 March 2004).

Galla, A. (1998). The Tshwane Declaration: setting standards for heritage tourism in South Africa. *UNESCO* 20(4): 38–42.

Hughes, H. (2003). What is remembered and what is forgotten: a decade of defining culture and heritage for tourism in South Africa. Proceedings of the Second De Haan Tourism Management Conference: developing cultural tourism. Nottingham: Nottingham University, 16 December.

Keyser, H. (2002). *Tourism Development*. Cape Town: Oxford South Africa.

KPMG (2002). Tourism development framework for the city of Cape Town: background information. Unpublished document. Cape Town: KPMG.

Lubbe, B. (ed.) (2003). *Tourism Management in South Africa.* Cape Town: Pearson Education South Africa.

Ntlangani, B. S. (2003). Management of a tourism micro-enterprise: a case-study of a cultural village. Unpublished Masters Dissertation. Durban: Regent Business School.

Nuntsu, N., Tassiopoulos, D. and Haydam, N. (2004). The bed and breakfast market of Buffalo City (BC), South Africa: present status, constraints and success factors. *Tourism Management* 25(4): 515–522.

Ramatlhodi, N. (2000). *Opening of the Provincial Parliament.* Northern Province: transcript of a MEC speech made on 27 July.

South Africa (Republic of) (1996). *White Paper: Development and Promotion of Tourism in South Africa* (Tourism White Paper). Pretoria: Government of South Africa, Department of Environmental Affairs and Tourism.

Tassiopoulos, D. (ed.) (2000). *Event Management: A Professional and Developmental Approach.* Cape Town: Juta.

World Travel and Tourism Council (2002). *South Africa: The Impact of Travel and Tourism on Jobs and Economy.* UK: WTTC.

Websites

Department of Arts and Culture (DAC): http://www.dac.gov.za/reports/reports.htm

Department of Environmental Affairs and Tourism (DEAT): http://www.environment.gov.za/

Eastern Cape Tourism Board (ECTB): http:// www.ectourism.co.za/

Khaya La Bantu: http://www.dispatch.co.za/1999/01/11/features/HOLIDAY.HTM

Lesedi Cultural Village: http://www.lesedi.com/

Mgwali – Experience true Xhosa Culture: http://www.border.co.za/harrison/stutt/mgwali.htm

South African Heritage Resources Agency (SAHRA): http://www.sahra.org.za/

South African Tourism (SA Tourism): http://www.satourism.co.za/

Tourism KwaZulu-Natal: http://www.kzn.org.za/kzn/investors/ 36.xml

Part Three

Environmental Management and Sustainability

CHAPTER 9

Sustainability and environmental management

David Leslie

Introduction

The demand for cultural tourism and corresponding attention to the development and promotion of cultural heritage has witnessed substantial growth over the past decade. This rise in both demand and supply has been influenced by a combination of the ongoing growth in international visitor numbers, and continuing expansion in the range and choice of destinations fuelling a highly competitive marketplace. As the choice of destination for traditional forms of tourism has increased, so too has the diversity. Countries and regions that have witnessed decline in their traditional markets have sought to promote other forms of tourism, thus the attention being paid to the development of cultural tourism. This facet of tourism demand is also recognized as holding potential for tourism development in other hitherto less popular localities as a way of promoting tourism and realizing the associated economic benefits. In some ways such development has contributed to sustaining the cultural heritage of the area and of the community. However, to attract substantial demand, the cultural resource must be substantive in some way; for example, in scale or acclaim, such as the Seven Wonders of the World, or world renowned, as illustrated by the Taj Mahal or, in contemporary terms, distinctive, as in the Guggenheim Museum. On a smaller scale, an alternative approach for destinations is to create a thematic approach based on the related elements of an area's cultural heritage (McKercher and du Cros, 2002). In much the same way, we can identify the promotion of cities as cultural tourism destinations; witness the EC's 'European Capital of Culture' and the UK's recent 'City Culture' promotional campaign. Thus, cultural tourism encompasses the past and the present; a diversity well exemplified by Butcher (2001). However, in order to gain significant economic benefits from tourism there is a need for substantial demand and thus the requisite supporting superstructure and infrastructure. Whilst this is essential to facilitating access and meeting the needs of tourists it also brings additional pressures on the destination's environment and the cultural heritage itself.

Thus, development and promotion are not without their challenges (Richards, 2001) and problems, not least of which is the impact of the visitors. At the international level this has been recognized for some time, as well illustrated through the process, procedures and requirements of the system introduced by UNESCO for designation as a World Heritage Site. This designation attests to the significance of our cultural heritage in that of the 754 World Heritage Sites, 582 are cultural attractions (United Nations Environment Programme, 2003). Also, it exemplifies the problems inherent in both seeking to sustain the cultural heritage and at the same time promote access and thus the need for considered strategic environmental management of such sites. In effect, designation enhances promotion and thus visitor numbers and hence can be a double-edged sword; a situation which is equally applicable, allowing for scale, to the cultural heritage of any community or society considered as holding potential as a tourism attraction. But, although such designation may be seen to contribute to sustaining cultural attractions of international significance there are still challenges to address, as illustrated by the case on Stonehenge (see below); the very same challenge, albeit on a smaller scale but no less important, faced by any society's, or any community's, cultural heritage. The challenge involves a complex range of problems and issues that require more sustainable solutions than what may be seen to be more 'end-of-pipe' remedies. Hence, there is a need for environmental management and the incorporation of the objectives of sustainable development; in effect, an approach that is based on contemporary environmental management theory (Southgate and Sharpley, 2002).

This requires recognition of the value of cultural heritage, which has traditionally been seen as the historic environment: the built heritage, icons to past cultures and so forth. But sustaining this past in general has been and in many cases continues to be problematic as it is rarely recognized for its intrinsic value alone. It has to compete for government resources with often more important areas such as health, education and safety, thus gaining support and resources increasingly requires more than substantiation of any intrinsic value, but articulation in terms of potential economic benefits. Thus, attention is being paid to tourism and the development of cultural tourism. Although tourism development is often berated for its negative impacts, particularly on the physical environment, undoubtedly it has played and continues to play a significant role given its potential to generate economic activity, in drawing attention to the cultural heritage. This is perhaps more apparent when considering sites of comparatively small scale in a particular region. For example, the Aude region in southern France, noted for its medieval history from the Cathar period and the city of Carcassonne, is now being promoted as 'Aude, the Cathar Country' (European Commission, 2003). The varied elements of the cultural heritage involved may each be of limited potential and thus threatened, but when thematically linked and presented collectively they create a promotion of substantial tourism potential, thereby enhancing the potential to gain additional resources to help sustain the region's community and cultural heritage.

Such developments reflect visitor interests, in that culture as represented by historical interest invariably ranks closely behind scenery and climate as major criteria for destination choice. This interest in an area's heritage, in past culture, leads to speculation that visitors will also have a propensity to be interested in contemporary culture and thus complementary areas – customs, produce and products, etc. – to have a sense of discovery, to learn something new and contact with local people. This combination of the past with the present reinforces the substantive point that these cultural 'resources', in effect the social capital of the community, are not present for the consumption of tourists but are part of the community, past and present. This interest by tourists through the development of cultural tourism can play a part in contributing to sustaining both the community and its resources. However, in developing such resources to promote tourism several important factors must be considered and addressed, not least of which is how the relationship between sustaining the cultural heritage and tourism is managed effectively to achieve a balance between conservation and tourism (McKercher and du Cros, 2002). However, the focus here is on those factors relating to the interface between the attraction and the visitor. The social/cultural dimensions require interpretation and presentation to enhance the visitor's experience which, to a large extent, is based on the way that the visitor interacts with the site, the displays, etc., and thus may be considered of paramount importance (Moscardo, 2000). However, and particularly significant in this context, while interpretation and presentation may be seen as fundamental in contributing to sustaining the cultural heritage, the opportunity is presented to advise visitors of their impacts and how these may be reduced, although there is little evidence as yet that tourists are influenced by 'green' credentials through promoting their awareness (Leslie, 2001; Cottrell et al., 2002). Given that the impact of tourism on the environment is a function of consumer demand and underpinning such demand are the attitudes and behaviour of people, including visitors, then any steps taken to promote their awareness of such impacts should be welcomed even if, as yet, they have been found to be of little influence. A third factor is that interpretation has a role in informing and thus facilitating access to a wider audience. Raised awareness should increase a sense of value for these cultural resources and thus contribute towards progress in achieving the objectives of sustainability. It is therefore sustainability to which we first turn our attention in the following discussion, which leads on to introducing Agenda 21 and local Agenda 21 plans. The central role of the community is identified and subsequently discussed, before introducing the case studies that follow.

Sustainability

The quality, and thus attractiveness, of a destination environment, a combination of its many physical and cultural facets, is the result of centuries of development. This development has been shaped by the prevailing socioeconomic forces and physical dimensions of the local and regional environment. To maintain this attractiveness requires recognition and, as appropriate, development of those very dimensions that have helped to shape it and continue to influence the character of the place. The key to the future of this combination of nature and what is appropriately termed 'social capital', in other words cultural heritage, the real raw material of tourism, lies in recognition of these factors. However, nowhere today is an island safe from the influences of wider economic and societal forces or from global issues such as pollution. Places are:

Facing a historical challenge: to maintain an acceptable standard of living for all people, while conserving or restoring the viability of the natural environment and hence, the very basis of human life
(Welford, 1995, p. 25)

Thus, to sustain a destination, planning and development must encompass effective responses to change and the need to maintain investment. This is evident from the expanding profile of environmentalism in the twenty-first century, which bears witness to the rise of green politics since the 1980s and wider societal concerns over matters pertaining to the impact of people and industry on the environment. These concerns expressed at international level are manifest in the Brundtland Report, conceptualized in the phrase 'sustainable development'. This is perhaps most clearly explained through what it aims to achieve which, as noted by Church and McHarry (1999), is:

- to protect and improve the environment
- to ensure economic security for everyone
- to create a more equitable and fairer society.

The route to sustainability lies in recognizing, promoting and developing the linkages between these economic, social and environmental objectives. This approach can contribute substantially to maintaining levels of employment, and can be influential in the creation of new enterprises and therefore new employment opportunities, thereby supporting and potentially adding to diversity in the employment market.

The foregoing aims and objectives reinforce the significance of people and society and in total the importance of the quality of life. The balancing of these aims is fundamental to the development of sustainable communities that are the foundation for achieving sustainable development. Thus, programmes introduced to further the objectives of sustainable development must address all the aims. To achieve any degree of success they must include effective participation by the community or communities involved (Desai, 1993; Church and McHarry, 1999). Desai is particularly of interest for the work on developing sustainable communities through an approach termed 'Bioregionalism', which is when industries are created and revived based on sustainable land use. There is integration between conservation, heritage and community, aspects of which are all illustrated in the following case studies.

Of significance in this context was the launch of Agenda 21, an action plan for the twenty-first century designed to promote and provide guidance towards the achievement of sustainable development.

Agenda 21

Agenda 21 includes substantial attention to encouraging the active involvement of all people in society in planning development. The promotion of community participation is emphasized in Chapter 28 of Agenda 21, which calls for all local governments to prepare local Agenda plans. This chapter also exemplifies the recognition that for progress to be made towards sustainable development by far the majority of actions propounded need to be undertaken at the local level, the very level where the impacts of tourism are most conspicuous. The widespread advocacy of 'responsible' and 'sustainable' tourism also echoes Chapter 28's explicit recommendations for community involvement in the setting up of initiatives.

In other words, Local Agenda 21 plans simply cannot escape being relevant to tourism, especially given that tourism is implicated in most dimensions of global change. However, it is more in the nature of the diversity of tourism, the many domains with which it interacts, and its economic and social importance that brings this about, than in any concerted recognition of the sectoral significance of tourism as a consumer of the environment. Clearly, as the most globally manifest industry, with a rising profile as a factor in world trade, apparent in the General Agreement on Trade and Service, and with increasing importance as a cultural vector, tourism needs to be part of this local policy formulation. Whether tourism, or rather the related activities, is compatible with sustainable development is a matter of debate. It may justifiably be argued that it is not. While this debate should be recognized, it is a debate outside this context. Further reinforcing this perspective is that the planning and development of tourism are also increasingly seen as facets of local government, and thus tourism comes within the remit of local Agenda 21 planning; therefore, community involvement is implicitly being promoted in tourism development at the local level (Leslie and Hughes, 1997). Thus, local Agenda 21 plans can provide both the stimulus and guidance for seeking more sustainable solutions and the requirement for environmental management planning.

Community participation

It is not an easy task to gain effective community participation at any level of governance. However, valuable work has been undertaken to help guide the process in general at local government level (e.g. Young, 1995; Bearhunt, 2001); even so, and as the case study on New Lanark attests, it is fraught with potential problems. Further, and as a note of caution, there is a danger that the trend towards promoting community involvement on the part of national and local government is resulting in as much emphasis on the processes and mechanisms involved (e.g. creation of partnerships and application procedures) as on outcomes. In other words, there is a shift in the way that 'success' is evaluated.

In effect, local people should be at the heart of the process: this means all sectors and groups within a community and must also embrace small businesses to achieve their aims. Indeed, this has been advocated by many organizations and for some time. For example, as cited by Ghazi (1997, p. 4), the Organization for Economic Co-operation and Development (OECD) has advocated comprehensive community involvement in planning for the:

- presentation, protection, enhancement of the quality of the resource base; and
- social, cultural and physical carrying capacity benefits to local residents.

This quote encompasses the factors fundamental to the sustainability of a community and, as such, its cultural heritage.

Furthermore, it succinctly accentuates the significance of the resource base. Thus, in terms of sustainable development it is the community's resources that are being developed and promoted for tourism. This should be the foundation on which tourism is developed; in other words, a resource-based, not a market-led approach. The principles of sustainability therefore become the overriding objectives of the environmental management of cultural tourism; in effect, the community's heritage, both of the past and, in terms of contemporary developments, of the future. A key facet of this heritage lies in the elements of intangibility. Thus, it is not just a matter of recognizing the economic potential of this cultural heritage in terms of cultural tourism, but also realizing how this social capital plays a role in terms of proving a 'sense of place', contributing to quality of life and the influence of change over time. This wider significance of social capital, of cultural heritage, has often been little realized, yet it is a fundamental asset of the community that '... can be used to evoke a sense of continuity of culture, enrichment of people's lives, as a link with the past to allow society to make sense of the present' (Du Cros, 2001, p. 166).

Facets of this are evident throughout the following case studies.

The case studies

The three cases presented in the following pages are evidence of diversity in time, place and significance. This suggests that the visitors' motivations will be diverse, ranging from curiosity and education, to exploration and to see something different, or just an excursion, somewhere to go. While this is so, the different approaches taken by the authors serve well to illustrate and develop many of the main points made above. In particular, they illustrate the value of cultural heritage in terms of 'place', the significance not only to their communities but also to society at large, and the need for considered strategic planning and development if the integrity of these cultural attractions is to be sustained. A key element of this is environmental management, which brings into focus the need for capacity management. Too many visitors at any one time will destroy the overall ambience, whereas too few visitors will place additional pressures on resources and the probable need for additional external funding, which may be difficult to access. Popularity can also bring other problems; negative impacts increase, possibly leading to take-over by a management agency, resulting in a loss of influence of the local community (Moscardo, 2000).

The first case in this section may be seen to represent the modern face of cultural tourism in the UK, an example of the 'heritage industry', namely New Lanark in Scotland. This is not so much contrived, but rather the regeneration of industrial heritage with interpretation and presentation of its cultural significance in terms of industrialization and industrial Britain. It is small in scale, localized and compact as a result of its geographical location and topography, being located in a valley and by the side of the River Clyde. However, its significance is manifest in the designation as a World Heritage Site. Although comparatively small, it reflects the complexities of such developed cultural attractions and notably shows facets of sustainable development through, for example, the attention given to the conservation of the locality, the reuse and renewal of old structures and artefacts, capacity management and maintaining investment. In many ways it exemplifies Franklin's comment on the 'heritage industry' in the UK in that it provides 'A chance to showcase local culture to create social identify and to have some say and control over how others, especially tourists, understand local people' (Franklin, 2003, p. 194). What is important in this context is that New Lanark is home to a diverse community of people. Community involvement is seen as the cornerstone of sustainable development and thus New Lanark provides an unusual opportunity to research community involvement in a situation wherein the community, in effect, is very much a part of the cultural attraction.

The problem of conflicting interests is, arguably, inherent in environmental management whenever there is more than one stakeholder. This is perhaps nowhere more often the case than in developments relating to the cultural heritage. This is well illustrated in the case study on Stonehenge, which evidences many of the general points noted above, such as the implications of designation as a World Heritage Site, the impact of visitors and sustaining the site in something like its current condition for future generations. Perhaps because of the significance accorded to Stonehenge today, and the conflicts between the many and varied stakeholders and interest groups, the management of the site has been taken over by an external agencies, beyond the direct influence of the local community. This approach, given the resources needed, is undoubtedly appropriate and may be considered a simple solution to the problem of protecting the site and its sustainability. However, as the case study illustrates, it is fraught with problems as regards how to manage this environment appropriately, how to develop the site, its interpretation and presentation, and how to facilitate access while managing visitor numbers and addressing the needs of various interest groups. In effect, the solution to sustaining Stonehenge has generated a different set of conflicts and debates.

An early point made above was how the development and promotion of cultural tourism are comparatively recent, in contrast, for example, to 'sunlust' tourism. This is especially evident in the case of Templo Mayor, the ancient heart of the Aztecs, in Mexico. This case serves to remind us that recognition of the significance of cultural heritage occurred during the latter half of the twentieth century. Although the constraints of space prohibit detailed discussion of the latter-day attention to and development of Templo Mayor, the overview presented provides many insights into the complexities of sustaining the cultural heritage of a community, especially in a central urban location comprising substantial structures that bear witness to past cultures and cultural change over the centuries. Within this context, tourism is seen as a positive factor in playing a role in the promotion, presentation and interpretation of this multi-faceted heritage, yet at the same time bringing another set of problems coupled with conflicting interests. The latter especially contributes further to the difficulties in addressing the problems and the need for sensitive and creative management of the environment, which incorporates not only Templo Mayor but also the surrounding culture heritage.

References

Bearhunt (2001). *Pathways to Green Spaces and Sustainable Communities, Ideas for Those Wanting a Share of the £125 Million NOF Fund*. Macclesfield: Bearhunt.

Butcher, J. (2001). *Innovations in Cultural Tourism. ATLAS, 2001*. The Netherlands: Tilburg University.

Church, C. and McHarry, J. (1999). *One Small Step ... A Guide to Action on Sustainable Development in the UK*. London, Community Development Foundation.

Cottrell, S., Van der Duim, R., Ankersmid, P. and Kelder, L. (2002). Measuring sustainability of tourism in Manuel Antonio/Quepos and Texel: a tourist perspective. Paper presented at ATLAS Conference, Estoril, Portugal, November 2002.

Desai, P. (1993). *Bioregional Survey*. Surrey: Bioregional Development Group.

Du Cros, H. (2001). A new model to assist in planning for sustainable cultural heritage tourism. *International Journal of Tourism Research* 3: 165–170.

European Commission (2003). *Using Natural and Cultural Heritage to Develop Sustainable Tourism*. Brussels: European Commission, Directorate-General Enterprise – Tourism Unit.

Franklin, A. (2003). *Tourism: An Introduction*. London: Sage.

Ghazi, P. (1997). Preaching like the converted. *Guardian* (16 July): 4.

Leslie, D. (2001). *An Environmental Audit of the Tourism Industry in the Lake District National Park.* Kendal: Friends of the Lake District.

Leslie, D. and Hughes, G. (1997). Local authorities and tourism in the UK. *International Journal of Managing Leisure* 2(3): 143–154.

McKercher, B. and du Cros, H. (2002). *Cultural Tourism: The Partnership between Tourism and Cultural Heritage Management.* New York. Haworth Hospitality Press.

Moscardo, G. (2000). Cultural and heritage tourism: the great debates. In Faulkner, B., Moscardo, G. and Laws, E. (eds) *Tourism in the 21st Century.* London: Continuum, pp. 3–17.

Richards, G. (2001). European cultural attractions – trends and prospects. In Richards, G. (ed.) *Cultural Attractions and European Tourism.* Wallingford: CABI, pp. 241–254.

Southgate, C. and Sharpley, R. (2002). Tourism, development and the environment. In Sharpley, R. and Telfer, D. J. (eds) *Tourism and Development: Concepts and Issues.* Clevedon: Channel View Publications, pp. 231–262.

United Nations Environment Programme (2003). World heritage and protected areas. *Our Planet* (September): 14.2. www.ourplanet.com

Welford, R. (1995). *Environmental Strategy and Sustainable Development – The Corporate Challenge for the 21st Century.* London: Routledge.

Young, S. (1995). *Promoting Participation and Community Based Partnerships in the context of Local Agenda 21: A Report for Practitioners.* Manchester: Manchester University Press.

Effective community involvement in the development and sustainability of cultural tourism: an exploration in the case of New Lanark

David Leslie

Learning outcomes

- Appreciate the role of the community in cultural tourism.
- Understand the need for community involvement in the sustainable development of the cultural heritage.
- Recognize the heterogeneous nature of communities and identification of factors that impinge on effective community participation.
- Appreciate the importance of informed awareness of the impacts of tourism in influencing the attitudes of community members towards tourism development.

Introduction

The concept of community involvement in tourism planning has long been recognized as a valuable element of tourism development (Murphy, 1983; Allen et al., 1990) and affirmed more recently (Caffyn, 1998; Bramwell and Lane, 2000; Anon, 2002; Singh et al., 2003). Yet the practice is often limited; as Murphy (1991) suggested, the community approach to tourism development planning may be little more than tokenism. Arguably, such an approach is particularly counterproductive to the development and management and sustainability of sociocultural attractions, which inherently are part of the community. However, enabling a community ('the community' being taken '... as the majority of ordinary people resident in an area ...' (Wilson, 1999, p. 38)) to become actively involved in tourism decisions will engender more effective communication and co-operation between the community and tourism planners, thus ensuring co-ordination of effort and requirements in an area of development that is recognized as a dynamic vector of social change and that, in one way or another, will affect the lives of the community. This includes being an element of the tourism package itself (Mann, 2000; Singh et al., 2003). Indeed, 'the community' is as vital to the sustainability of tourism development as the destination's natural and sociocultural resources (Murphy, 1991; Getz, 1994); moreover, they are interdependent (Mann, 2000). Overall, this would undoubtedly contribute towards a more sustainable development approach in the management of cultural tourism.

In effect, this is the objective of Agenda 21, encapsulated in local Agenda 21 plans (Leslie and Hughes, 1997). The community is thus seen to be placed in a position of importance. Indeed,

Mansperger (1995) and Mann (2000) argued that a community approach would provide the local residents with invaluable control measures over their own existence, as tourism decisions would be influenced by their own needs at all times. This would also promote greater recognition of the role tourism plays in promoting and sustaining a community's sociocultural heritage. But, '… for a tourism based economy to sustain itself in local communities, the residents must be willing partners in the process' (Lankford and Howard, 1994, p. 122). If this is not the case then, as Young (1973) argued over 25 years ago, if tourism development continues apace local residents may become antagonistic (Dogan, 1989; Madrigal, 1994; Ryan and Montgomery, 1994). Conversely, better awareness of tourism's impact can promote favourable perceptions of the sector (Caffyn, 1998; Mann, 2000; Singh et al., 2003). Undoubtedly, this is a key requisite for a community contributing fully to the success and long-term prospects of tourism development (Simmons, 1994; Schroeder, 1996; Reid and Sindiga, 1999). Consequently, the additional time and effort required to manage such an approach would be deemed valuable.

However, community involvement in planning has been questioned for a variety of reasons (Murphy, 1991; Prentice, 1993; Ryan and Montgomery, 1994; Pearce et al., 1996). In the context of managing cultural tourism developments, major reservations in summary are:

- The community approach requires considerable additional time and effort to manage, which might not be justified by the proscribed benefits.
- Community involvement could lead to weak management owing to divisions between fractions of the community.
- Homogeneity versus heterogeneity: the approach requires a homogeneous community with a common identity and purpose; a heterogeneous community could create management problems for developers through dissenting views leading to adverse relationships within the community and between developers and the community.

On these specific reservations, does the willingness to enter into dialogue and have a more expansive and decentralized decision-making process necessarily mean 'weak management'? Contemporary management thought would tend to disagree with this view, and it is the management of planning for cultural tourism and development that is of concern here. However, the nature of the arguments has helped to form one of the key research questions that this case attempts to address, namely heterogeneity. Many of the reservations can be seen as symptoms of this overriding factor.

Community participation and heterogeneity

To determine whether the advocated problems associated with heterogeneity are worthy of such attitudes and whether they should prevent adoption of community involvement in tourism planning, those heterogeneous elements of a community, as proposed by Lankford and Howard (1994, pp. 124–5), most germane to the development of cultural tourism are analysed as follows.

Length of residence

It is suggested that native and longer stay residents are more inclined to express negative feelings towards tourism than are newcomers, as their levels of attachment are greater (Broughman and Butler, 1981; Sheldon and Var, 1984). Commentators consequently advocate that the disparity of views suggested above would create dissension when attempting to make decisions in a community involvement manner. However, length of residence has been found to produce less than profound results (Lankford and Howard, 1994), and newcomers may be as adverse to change as their native counterparts, more so in some cases (Wilson, 1999). It could therefore be posited that each category (native, long stay or newcomer) has the capacity to demonstrate negative and positive feelings towards tourism. However, the actual demonstration and scale of such attitudes is very much dependent on the nature of the development. The fact that negative attitudes have been found in every category is thought more pertinent than commentators' fears of dissension, as these feelings may create problems for the development. Thus, to provide the residents with a voice in the form of a community planning programme would enable them to express their views. Consequently, both the developers and the residents would be aware of their own views as well as other perspectives, which is posited to be a firm basis for the development of successful coexistence, thereby contributing to the enhancement of the sustainability of the cultural heritage of the community.

Economic dependency

The level of economic dependency placed on tourism by residents can shape their perceptions of development, e.g. high levels of economic dependency correlate with positive attitudes towards tourism in general (Milman and Pizam, 1988;

Prentice, 1993). Furthermore, a member of the community may hold more favourable perceptions of tourism if a relative, friend or even a neighbour is dependent on tourism (Liu and Var, 1986; Milman and Pizam, 1988). These findings have led researchers to question the possibility of a community comprising resident beneficiaries and non-beneficiaries to reach decisions that are acceptable to both parties. Increasing the community's awareness of tourism's direct and indirect benefits, as noted above, could pre-empt or contribute to resolving possible disagreements between beneficiaries and non-beneficiaries. Therefore, it cannot be stated with assurance that economic dependency will create opposing views. Consequently, the theory that dissension will automatically arise as a result of heterogeneity is again questioned. In addition, it is opined that negative perceptions of tourism may be present before community involvement in planning, and therefore to argue that the management approach should not be introduced for fear of inducing negative consequences for tourism development is not thought to be adequate reasoning.

Age

The age of a resident is also perceived to be an influence on his or her attitudes towards tourism and tourists (Murdock and Schriner, 1979; Broughman and Butler, 1981). It could be suggested that age, although a potentially significant influential factor, is not independent. Other variables, such as contact levels with tourists and varying degrees of development and the type of development, can be seen to influence the attitudes of the young and old. It is for the developers to realize that various age groups could conceivably hold different views. However, there is no basis to suggest that there is a rule. Therefore, the view that contrasting views will be expressed according to age alone is unfounded. Consequently, to suggest that dissension would automatically occur between various age groups if the community approach were to be utilized is again questioned.

Level of contact with tourists

The proposition is that increased levels of contact with tourists will lead to residents expressing less favourable attitudes towards tourism (Allen et al., 1993), or even resentment (Doxey, 1975; Keith, 1998). However, this is more often encountered in small destination areas (Belisle and Hoy, 1980; Faulkner and Tideswell, 1997). In contrast, Sheldon and Var found that

'Residents living in high density areas' who have increased contact opportunities with tourists '... do not appear to be more negative to tourists ...' (1984, p. 47). Therefore, the suggestion that community involvement programmes would be difficult to employ, as dissension would result owing to varying levels of contact with tourists and distance of the tourism zone from the residents' home, is not found to be true in every situation.

The foregoing review of heterogeneous elements serves to encapsulate much of the earlier discussion on community involvement and both reservations and support for its practice. In combination, this represents a substantial review of research studies from which two factors emerge. First, the studies are temporally and spatially diverse, methodologies differ and the communities involved represent destination areas rather than discrete locales. Little attention has been paid to those tourist destination localities that are attractions within which there is a vibrant localized community (Mansperger, 1995; Bramwell and Lane, 2000). Such a situation would provide a valuable opportunity to investigate community involvement in planning and particularly the elements of heterogeneity, at the micro-level. Further, by its very nature the community is an integral part of the attraction by virtue of residency irrespective of its actual involvement in the attraction, i.e. a community-based tourist attraction. The number of such attractions is very limited; however, one such attraction in the UK is New Lanark, Scotland. This case provides the added opportunity to reflect on Murphy's (1983) tenet, supported by Getz (1994), that for suppliers and community mutually to benefit from tourist development there is a need for a symbiotic relationship that takes into account all aspects of the environment.

New Lanark and the community

The primary research objective of this case study was to establish whether the heterogeneous community of New Lanark demonstrates heterogeneous attitudes towards tourism and thus necessarily implies that the community approach cannot be translated into a 'real' situation, namely New Lanark. This involved the following aims:

- to identify New Lanark community's attitude(s) towards tourism development
- to investigate the level of community involvement in tourism planning and development, in order to establish whether the approach is considered valuable

- to determine whether community involvement in planning would further sustain the development of tourism within the village of New Lanark.

New Lanark is located in the central belt of Scotland, situated in a deep valley on the banks of the River Clyde, approximately 40 kilometres east of Glasgow, and has a resident population of around 180 people in sixty-seven households. The village derives its attraction as a tourist destination from its unique industrial, social and cultural history. It was founded in 1785 as a working community by David Dale, and subsequently developed from 1800 under the management of Robert Owen (a key social reformer in the new industrial age). Profits from the cotton-spinning mills were used to finance many social and educational initiatives, aimed at improving the quality of life of workers. A prime example was the creation of the Institute for the Formation of Character, a community and adult education centre that included the first infant school in the world (Beeho and Prentice, 1997). Other practices in the village included free medical care and reduced hours of work.

The village gradually declined in the twentieth century, culminating in the cotton-mills closing in 1968 and turning into 'A rundown slum of a place where families lived only to gain enough sympathy to jump the council house waiting list …. It was an eyesore and an embarrassment, but it was out of the way and could be conveniently ignored' (Anon., 1996, p. 5). However, the majority of buildings had survived from the early nineteenth century (with few additions) and were subsequently revitalized through a mixture of charitable work and public funds. It is managed by an independent charity, New Lanark Conservation Trust, which aimed to 'Restore and revitalise the village as a working community, not to preserve it as a museum piece' (McDonald, 1992, p. 402). In effect, '… New Lanark has been developed to maximize its commercial value, public entertainment, and short-term financial advantage' (Arnold, 1999, p. 16). The charity's success in these areas, and the range of attractions, facilities and services, is well illustrated on its website (www.newlanarktrust.org). It can perhaps best be described now as representing 'A 20th-century living village community within the physical setting of an earlier era' (Beeho and Prentice, 1997, p. 79). Overall, recognition of the Trust's approach to revitalizing New Lanark and sustaining this remarkable industrial cultural heritage is manifest in the extensive awards received, the pinnacle of which was UNESCO designation as a World Heritage Site in 2001.

The 'village community' resides in a mix of owner-occupied and housing association flats in the regenerated tenement houses once occupied by the workers. There is a community spirit among the residents that is most evident through the support given to the Village Group via a community committee which organizes events for the local people, e.g. the annual New Lanark Victorian Fair. The social characteristics of this community, with particular reference to the heterogeneous variables identified earlier, are shown in Table 10.1.

Table 10.1 Social characteristics of New Lanark's community

Social characteristics	Respondents (actual number)
Birthplace	
New Lanark	6
Lanark	15
30 mile (48 km) radius	17
North of Scotland	3
England	6
Length of residence	
2–5 years	9
6–10 years	11
11–15 years	5
16–22 years	10
23 years and over	12
Age band	
16–35 years old	10
36–50 years old	15
51–65 years old	15
66 years old or over	7
Marital status	
Single	9
Married/partner	30
Widowed	5
Divorced	3
Gender	
Female	28
Male	19
Employment status	
Employed, full time	24
Employed, part time	6
Retired	12
Homemaker	2
Unemployed	2
Student, full time	1

Methodology

An attitudinal survey of the sixty-seven households in the village was undertaken using questionnaires, delivered by hand to each residence, designed with the purpose of determining:

- demographic characteristics of respondents as a means of measuring heterogeneity within the community
- residents' attitudes towards tourism development, delineated in terms of the economic, social and physical dimensions of the environment within the context of the village
- the levels of tourism involvement among residents as a measure of its effect on attitudes towards tourism development.

Overall, therefore, the aim of the survey was to establish whether the differences in background of residents produce heterogeneous attitudes towards tourism development and thus the potential implications for the effectiveness of the community approach to planning. The survey also sought to establish social characteristics and level of tourism involvement data to determine whether the very aspects that characterize the community as heterogeneous are the influencing factors when their attitudes towards tourism are formalized.

The response rate to the census was 70 per cent, i.e. forty-seven households, and the social characteristics of the respondents are presented in Table 10.1. Analysis of the data enabled the retrieval of attitudes towards tourism's impacts and future development, and the deduction of causal relationships between attitudes towards tourism, sociodemographic characteristics and levels of tourism involvement. Consequently, it was possible to deduce the community's attitudes towards tourism development, the significance of the identified heterogeneous elements and whether the community approach would further sustain the development of tourism within New Lanark.

Main findings

Community involvement, i.e. the participation of ordinary residents in the locality in planning, has been defined as the enablement of a community to become actively involved in tourism decisions. This is recognized as all the more important when it is the community's cultural heritage that is the basis of the attraction. Secondary research suggested that the community approach was only feasible in theory, as the heterogeneous nature (considered in terms of social characteristics of community members and involvement in tourism) of modern-day communities would induce dissension that could ultimately result in the demise of the tourist attraction. Further, it was identified that the actual demonstration and scale of the community's attitudes towards tourism were not directly dependent on its heterogeneous nature, but rather on the nature of the development. Therefore, heterogeneity within a community does not necessarily imply that this approach cannot be incorporated into a real situation, as the correlation between heterogeneity and dissension was not found to be conclusive.

From the findings it is apparent that there is a significant consensus on many aspects of tourism development within New Lanark, both positively and negatively perceived. However, heterogeneity of response was marked in relation to economic and social impacts, although far less so with regard to the physical environment or the development of the village. Overall, the census was in favour of tourism development. Positive attitudes of respondents were particularly evident in the context of those tourism impacts perceived as being beneficial to their lives, e.g. an improved standard of living and increased recreational facilities. This is not surprising given the attention to the quality of the built environment, i.e. the preservation and regeneration of the old buildings and the physical attraction and visual amenity of the area, which includes the Clyde Falls. Notably, many of the respondents were found to be passive towards tourism's influences within the village. This might be considered paradoxical given that their homes and the locale would hardly be attractive to anyone in the absence of the work of the Trust in regenerating the village, with the support of grants, substantial contributions of which were attributable to the obvious tourism potential of the destination.

Significantly, little evidence of substantial variance in attitudes was found on the basis of social characteristics. This leads to the second key point, namely that of involvement in tourism and development decisions. Variances on the basis of such criteria found that two categories, namely 'New Lanark employees' and 'tourism decision makers', held opinions on tourism development that were significantly different to the other members of the census. The congruence between these two groups demonstrates that the community approach on the basis that heightened involvement and awareness of tourism's impacts does not necessarily infer dissension. Furthermore, involvement in tourism, in a decision-making capacity, induced stalwart support for tourism development, a factor that further endorses the community approach. However, the most positive and least negative attitudes were found in those residents directly involved in decision making, while those residents directly involved in employment in the development showed the highest levels of both positive and negative attitudes. Occupying the middle ground were those residents who were not directly involved. Therefore, in the case of New Lanark increased involvement of community residents in the decision-making process, it is argued, will lead to greater negativity and lead to speculation that the number of residents with negative attitudes will increase, owing to those non-participants deemed ambivalent moving off the fence. To pre-empt such a development a managerial approach to planning as per the diagram presented in Figure 10.1, based on this analysis, should be adopted.

There are certain limitations associated with this case study, which are not a result of the methods used but of the case study approach itself. By definition, this places limitations on the research findings, e.g. generalizations can only be made when referring to identical communities. However, this does not

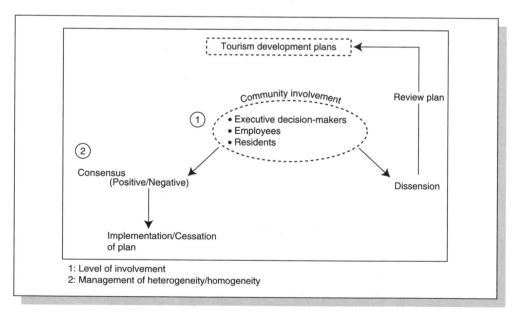

Figure 10.1
Flow diagram of the community involvement process

detract from the conclusions of the case study, as the main purpose was to prove or disprove whether Murphy's community involvement in tourism planning theory would prove viable within the context of New Lanark.

Conclusion

The results generated from this research study suggest that community involvement in tourism planning would further the New Lanark Conservation Trust's aim of 'restoring the village as a living, working community' (Anon., 1996). This is conceivable, as it has been found that 'the community' is an element of the tourism product. Therefore, to adopt a management style (as indicated in Figure 10.1) that would increase the community's potential to work in conjunction with the developers would further induce 'a living, working community'. Recognition of the consensus evident on both the positive and negative impacts of tourism in the village should help both planners and residents to focus on key areas of dispute, i.e. where there is little consensus and/or where there is a negative consensus on any particular area. Further, broadening the number of residents involved in decision making should lead to more residents gaining a fuller understanding of tourism's role in the community and of its potential to create positive outcomes for the village. Personal involvement is argued to cause stronger connections with tourism, which in turn would incur enhanced belief in its future development. Thus, in terms of the promotion and development of cultural tourism, empowering the community through effective participation in the planning processes is seen as essential to sustaining the cultural heritage and is thus a contributory factor in progress towards sustainable development.

Acknowledgements

The author would like to thank Debbie Logan and Tony Harrison for their invaluable contributions to this chapter.

References

Allen, L. R., Long, P. T. and Perdue, R. R. (1990). Resident support for tourism development. *Annals of Tourism Research* 17: 586–599.

Allen, L. R., Hafer, H. R., Long, P. T. and Perdue, R. R. (1993). Rural residents' attitudes toward recreation and tourism development. *Journal of Travel Research* 31(4): 27–33.

Anon. (1996). *Restoring New Lanark – A Description of the Project*. New Lanark Conservation Trust.

Anon. (2002). *Act Local: Community Planning for Sustainable Development. The Duthchas Handbook*. Suthchas Project. Inverness: The Highland Council.

Arnold, J. (1999). Industrial museums in crisis. *Herald* (9 February): 16.

Beeho, A. J. and Prentice, R. C. (1997). Conceptualizing the experiences of heritage tourists: a case study of New Lanark World Heritage Village. *Tourism Management* 18(2): 75–87.

Belisle, F. J. and Hoy, D. R. (1980). The perceived impact of tourism by residents: a case study in Santa Marta, Columbia. *Annals of Tourism Research* 7: 83–101.

Bramwell, B. and Lane, B. (2000). *Tourism, Collaboration and Partnerships: Politics, Practice and Sustainability*. Clevedon: Channel View.

Broughman, J. E. and Butler, R. W. (1981). A segmentation analysis of residents' attitudes to the social impacts of tourism. *Annals of Tourism Research* 8: 569–590.

Caffyn, A. (1998). Tourism, Heritage and urban regeneration – community participation and power relationships in the Stirling initiative. *Environment Papers Journal* 1(3): 25–35.

Dogan, H. Z. (1989). Forms of adjustment: sociocultural impacts of tourism. *Annals of Tourism* 16(2): 216–236.

Doxey, G. V. (1975). A causation theory of visitor–resident irritants; methodology and research inferences. In Conference Proceedings of the Travel Research Association, San Diego, pp. 195–198.

Faulkner, B. and Tideswell, C. (1997). A Framework for monitoring community impacts of tourism. *Journal of Sustainable Tourism* 5(1): 3–28.

Getz, D. (1994). Residents' attitudes towards tourism. *Tourism Management* 15(4): 247–258.

Keith, D. (1998). The darker side to tourism not in brochures. Letters to the Editor. *Dundee Courier* (12 February): 12.

Lankford, S. V. and Howard, D. R. (1994). Developing a tourism impact attitude scale. *Annals of Tourism Research* 21: 121–139.

Leslie, D. and Hughes, G. (1997). Agenda 21, local authorities and tourism in the UK. *International Journal of Managing Leisure* 2: 143–154.

Liu, J. C. and Var, T. (1986). Residents' attitudes towards tourism impacts in Hawaii. *Annals of Tourism Research* 13: 193–214.

Madrigal, R. (1994). Residents' perceptions and the role of government. *Annals of Tourism Research* 22(1): 86–102.

Mann, M. (2000). *The Community Tourism Guide*. London: Earthscan.

Mansperger, M. C. (1995). Tourism and cultural change in small scale societies. *Journal of Human Organisation* 54(1): 87–94.

Milman, A. and Pizam, A. (1988). Social impacts of tourism on central Florida. *Annals of Tourism Research* 15: 191–204.

Murdock, S. and Schriner, E. C. (1979). Community service satisfaction and stages of community development: an examination of evidence from impacted communities. *Journal of the Community Development* 10(1): 109–124.

Murphy, P. E. (1983). Tourism as a community industry – an ecological model of tourism development. *Tourism Management* 4(3): 180–193.

Murphy, P. E. (1991). *Tourism: A Community Approach*. London: Routledge.

Pearce, P. L., Moscardo, G. and Ross, G. F. (1996). *Tourism Community Relationships*. Oxford: Pergamon.

Prentice, R. (1993). Community-driven tourism planning and residents' preferences. *Tourism Management* 14(3): 218–227.

Reid, D. G. and Sindiga, I. (1999). Tourism and community development: an African example. *Leisure and Recreation* 41(2): 18–21.

Ryan, C. and Montgomery, D. (1994). The attitudes of Bakewell residents to tourism and issues in community responsive tourism. *Tourism Management* 15(5): 358–369.

Schroeder, T. (1996). The relationship of residents' image of their state as a tourist destination and their support for tourism. *Journal of Travel Research* XXXIV(4): 71–73.

Sheldon, P. J. and Var, T. (1984). Resident attitudes to tourism in North Wales. *Tourism Management* 5(1): 40–48.

Simmons, D. G. (1994). Community participation in tourism planning. *Tourism Management* 15(2): 98–108.

Singh, S., Dallen, J., Dowlong, T. and Dowling, R. K. (eds) (2003). *Tourism in Destination Communities*. Wallingford: CABI.

Wilson, D. (1999). Consulting the community: a problem in sustainable tourism development. *Environment Papers Series* 2(1): 25–40.

Young, G. (1973). *Tourism: Blessing or Blight*. London: Pelican.

Websites

English Heritage: www.English-Heritage.org.uk
International Union for Conservation of Nature: www.IUCN.org
International Council on Monuments and Sites: www.icomos.org
New Lanark, World Heritage Village: www.newlanark.org
UNESCO: www.UNESCO.org

Managing Stonehenge: the tourism impact and the impact on tourism

Ian Baxter and Christopher Chippindale

Learning outcomes

- Appreciate the wide political, economic and social contexts for cultural sites at different scales (local, national, international).
- Understand the role of certain sites acting as 'cultural icons', and implications of World Heritage Site designation.
- Identify diverse concerns and interests in cultural sites by stakeholder groups.
- Appreciate the potential conflict between conservation and tourism development.

Stonehenge in context

Jaquetta Hawkes, an eminent archaeologist writing in the middle of the twentieth century, succinctly summarized the challenge to managers that has surrounded this prehistoric site for as long as it has been noted on the tourist trail: 'Every age has the Stonehenge it deserves – or desires' (Hawkes, 1967, p. 174). Since the age of the antiquarian undertaking of grand tours of sites and monuments around the country, cultural tourists to Stonehenge have written about their experiences, mused on the site's development and history, and commented on its preservation and presentation.

The site was protected by law as a 'Scheduled Ancient Monument' in 1913, and subsequently gifted to the nation by its owner in 1919. By 1930, 607 hectares around the monument had been bought by public subscription to save it from development, which was vested in the hands of The National Trust (Baxter and Chippindale, 2002). These acts of protection through legislation, ownership by government and public appreciation of the site set Stonehenge on the way to becoming the iconic prehistoric site which we see it as today through promotion of its status, and placing it in the realm of a site to be managed and understood publicly. While the importance of the monument has long been realized by those interested in studying it (mainly archaeologists) and those visiting it (tourists, appreciating the site's cultural importance, partly by virtue of its unique physical form), the site's iconic form and location, sitting at the centre of an extensive prehistoric landscape, have also made it the focus of interest for diverse groups' belief systems and social structures. Thus, the site's link (however tenuous) to Celtic mysticism and Druids makes the site of spiritual importance to modern-day Druids and 'New Age' culture. Stonehenge therefore plays a wide role in modern social structures as well as expression of identity through material culture (Bender, 1998).

A site such as Stonehenge, of international significance, is recognized universally as an important site for a number of reasons. Reflecting the primary significance of the site as a cultural landscape of international importance, the Stonehenge and Avebury World Heritage Area was inscribed by the United Nations Educational, Scientific, and Cultural Organization (UNESCO) in 1986, joining 600 other sites around the globe recognized for their outstanding universal value (UNESCO, 1986; English Heritage, 2000). The iconic status that the site has gained, in carrying multi-layered significance, makes cultural tourism at the site just one of a number of influences and impacts that need to be balanced through careful management (Chippindale et al., 1990). It also raises the issue and influence of cultural tourism at the site to an international field of interest and of material concern at that level.

The pen-portrait of the site found in the 'Discover Stonehenge' leaflet, designed for visitors to navigate around the site (English Heritage, 2002), provides a useful historical summary: 'Today you see the remains of a prehistoric monument that was in use thousands of years ago. It was constructed in three main phases:

- 3050 BC (5050 years ago) – Circular ditch and bank (a henge).
- 2500 BC circa (4500 years ago) – Wooden structure constructed at centre.
- 2500–1500 BC (4500–3500 years ago) – Stone monument constructed, arranged and rearranged over almost 1000 years.'

Quite apart from the site's role on the stage of world cultural significance (in terms of its historical importance), seven issues summarize the current practical challenges faced at Stonehenge on a day-to-day basis (Baxter and Chippindale, 2002):

- The site is of universal value and renown as the most instantly recognizable icon of prehistoric Britain. In 2002, the site received over 750 000 visitors, placing it in the top twenty visitor attractions that charged admission in the UK. Visitor numbers are expected to increase, as the tourism industry develops cultural tourism growth in the UK over the next decade (VisitBritain, 2003).
- Stonehenge is one of 196 protected sites in the wider prehistoric landscape area, but the only one with major visitor interest owing to its upstanding and monumental nature (Figure 11.1). Many of the other sites are earthworks or

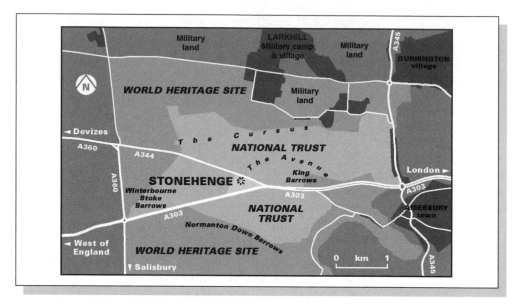

Figure 11.1
Stonehenge within the wider World Heritage Site

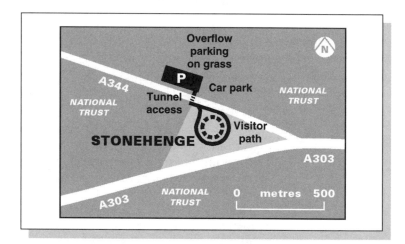

Figure 11.2
The Stonehenge
visitor site

humps and bumps in the ground, which may not convey much meaning to the untrained eye.

- The focus of interest within the World Heritage Site is a fragile upstanding monument/ruin, thirty-two metres in diameter (Figure 11.2): Stonehenge itself.
- The site is closely bounded by two roads: a regional highway (the A344) runs directly to the north of the site and cuts

through part of the monument; a national trunk route (A303) runs 200 metres to the south.

- The present visitor facilities consist of concrete bunkers constructed below ground level in the 1960s which are not now felt to respect either the monument or the surrounding landscape. Temporary structures to aid visitor management have been added on an ad hoc basis (such as Portaloos, and cabins for ticket selling). Visitor capacity for these facilities has been exceeded severely in the past ten years.
- There is no other upstanding building within one kilometre of the site. Stonehenge is set on rolling chalk downland in an wider open arable and pasture setting. Structures and traffic intrude on the visual setting of the monument.
- All land surrounding the monument is owned by conservation organizations; however, it is two different organizations with differing approaches to management (English Heritage owns the site itself; The National Trust owns the surrounding downland).

The Stonehenge problem: conflict

The underlying problem from which Stonehenge suffers is that of conflict. Management of the site must deal with conflicting interests, conflicting physical status on the ground, and conflicting relationships between Stonehenge and its many different public audiences. The site's iconic status also makes it an object of intense public scrutiny and tourism 'desire'. The most pressing problems are the physical impacts on the site itself. Traffic runs hard by the site, and as already noted, the A344 cuts into the monument itself. Pollution, vibration, noise and visual intrusion on the site (quite apart from the health and safety risks of having large numbers of tourists in very close proximity to a busy road) make for unsatisfactory environmental management around the site. The scale of visitor numbers, compared with the car parking available and the facilities available for visitor reception, do not accord with a monument declared a World Heritage Site and are unsatisfactory in tourism management terms. The professionals interested in the understanding, conservation and protection of the site are unhappy with these various impacts on the site, and have an additional desire to return the site to its proper setting and encourage visitors to engage more fully with the wider prehistoric landscape. There are numerous stakeholder/interest groups who either need or want their views to be taken on board, or should be recognized and have their views sought, such as New Age travellers, Druids, local residents, tourists

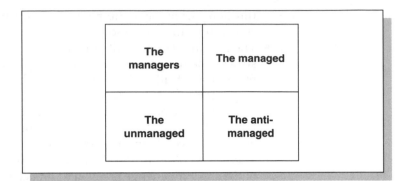

Figure 11.3
Stakeholder charac-
teristics (after
Baxter and
Chippindale, 2002)

and disadvantaged groups. Management of the site as it stands is therefore unsustainable in most senses of the word.

Recognizing that many people are interested in Stonehenge as a place, a stakeholder analysis is usefully undertaken. The characteristics of the stakeholders in Stonehenge can be catego-rized as shown in Figure 11.3.

The managers are those to whom responsibility for legal ownership and day-to-day operation of the site falls. The main players in this category are English Heritage (the English Government's agency responsible for heritage management) and The National Trust (the country's largest conservation charity). The managed are those who interact with Stonehenge, but who are bound by the operational procedures in force for the site. This category is dominated by the cultural tourists vis-iting the site, but also includes the many more passers-by dri-ving along the roads with views to Stonehenge which are constrained by the infrastructure and routing of the highway system. Nevertheless these are still 'viewers' of Stonehenge (Urry, 1990). The unmanaged group are those people who may be aware of Stonehenge but have not visited it and people who have never heard of the site. This is the largest group and equates with the wider 'world' for whom the site is protected and managed as a legacy of past times deemed important enough to be designated as a World Heritage Site. The anti-managed group are those who disagree with the structures in place to manage the site as it is currently. This group may try to subvert established social structures or norms on a wide scale, or may have very specific aspects of site management and pro-tection with which they disagree.

People are not bound by these categorizations and may move from one grouping to another depending on the kind of relationship they have with the site at a particular point in time. For example, the anti-managed category, which might include New Age groups, find themselves ultimately governed by laws and access regulations to the site imposed by the managers. People, before they become tourists, are in the unmanaged category. The categorizations are therefore about the articulation of a person's relationship with the site, rather than the precise actuality.

Once people have chosen to visit the site, they become cultural tourists, and move into the 'managed' category, but as site visitors spend little time associated with the site (other than the duration of the visit). It features in the tourists' itinerary, and they most probably have a picture of it in their mind and maybe their own interpretation of the site. To some extent, it is the visitors who have created and maintain the site as an icon. Yet it is an interesting conundrum that the root of desire for change and improvement at the site is not articulated by this group, which has the greatest physical impact on the site. This is because tourists visiting can be seen as discrete physical presences at the location, perhaps lasting from ten minutes to an hour or so. Collectively they have the capacity to damage the site (and do so, e.g. access to the site is largely restricted to a circumference path some fifty metres distant from the stones), and the turf around the monument has to be replaced regularly (Cathersides, 2001), but they do not hold a collective view on the site. At its most basic level, the visitor journey comprises entering the site's boundary, being charged for admission and organized as a visitor, viewing the site and leaving, or concluding the visitor experience via an opportunity to shop and eat.

The visitors cause the main pressures on the site in terms of volume, wear and tear and explicit need for core tourist facilities. However, those impacts on the site (as well as others, such as environmental and land use), and the calls for change, improvement and restitution of Stonehenge's status, are monitored by those who have longer associations with the site, but may not be located at the site itself, and therefore are not causing the major physical pressures on it. Tourists can therefore fulfil the basic fundamentals of a tourist visitor in getting to see Stonehenge. They can park close by, see the site from the road or pay the admission charge to walk closer to it; they can buy a souvenir, eat a snack or purchase a drink, and obtain some basic interpretation of the monument. Management of the site is secondary to the primary tourism purpose of the visit.

The conflict therefore to a large extent stems from different kinds of pressures from different stakeholders being placed on the site and the feeling (on all parts) that the situation at the site as it stands is not good enough, for all of the implicit reasons already mentioned. The physical pressure on the site is undenied, but the intellectual and managerial pressure is perhaps even greater, but not recognized necessarily as a pressure or an impact. This pressure stems from the desire on the part of the managers to fulfil the wider perceived or hoped-for needs of other stakeholders (especially cultural tourists). As a focus for cultural tourism, a site's facilities need to fulfil basic physical needs; however, it is also thought that a cultural site needs to fulfil the higher level role of contributing to an understanding of the society and location of the site or place. The current limitations on the setting of Stonehenge do not allow for cultural tourists to engage properly with the site, which should (according to the managers) be understood not as a single icon but as representative of a wider prehistoric area. The managers have thus been working over the past twenty years to achieve their goal of improvement, which they see will fulfil all stakeholders' wishes for Stonehenge, and the experience of the site to be improved somehow through provocation of the visitors to engage with the site and surroundings in new ways. When the implications for the site as a World Heritage Site are taken into consideration, Stonehenge is not just characterized for its intrinsic qualities as a site; there is also an expectation in the universal duty of care that the standard of management will conform to the highest standards. Such standards include management of the resource in a sustainable fashion, adhering to World Heritage preservation and tourism principles enshrined in relevant international conventions (UNESCO, 1972).

Solving the problem: vision

The 'problem', such as it is, has been defined that the management of Stonehenge is not currently achieving what it should for its World Heritage and global stakeholders, i.e. everybody, be they people who have had a relationship with the site as visitors or even those who have not yet, but may be seen as potential visitors. There is a professional desire on the part of the identified managers (the conservation profession acting through specific managing organizations) to share and widen knowledge about the site, and return it to its rightful setting. This underlies an effective conservation philosophy for the site. The expectations within World Heritage listing provide the basis for the articulated vision of a 'need to conserve, enhance and interpret the cultural significance of the whole Stonehenge landscape and its outstanding universal values' (English Heritage, 2000, p. 4).

Sustainability is at the heart of proposed solutions to Stonehenge: the impact of visitors on the site should be mitigated against the requirement to preserve the historic features of the landscape setting and the individually identified archaeological sites contained therein. There is a requirement for development of the experience of the site in accord with both the World Heritage Convention, and more particularly the International Cultural Tourism Charter (International Council on Monuments and Sites, 1999). Principles 2 and 3 of the charter are most relevant, stating that 'The relationship between Heritage Places and Tourism is dynamic and may involve conflicting values. It should be managed in a sustainable way for present and future generations', and that 'Conservation and Tourism Planning for Heritage Places should ensure that the Visitor Experience will be worthwhile, satisfying and enjoyable'.

The Stonehenge World Heritage Site Management Plan sets out the vision for the site in this global context (English Heritage, 2000). Aspects of this vision are being taken forward at the practical level in an initiative called 'The Stonehenge Project'. The Management Plan (quoted here at length):

'envisages a landscape which includes an extended core zone of permanent grassland [rather than mixed arable/pasture with associated impacts of ploughing/intensive grazing] surrounded by a wider landscape of sustainable low-intensity mixed farming.

In the long term all farmland in the core zone would be restored to permanent grassland and all inappropriate structures and roads [the current visitor centre and the A344/A303] removed or screened to provide an improved landscape setting for the core of Stonehenge, the protection of the archaeology from ploughing, and an area carefully managed for open access on foot for visitors. The zone would be primarily managed for both archaeological, landscape and nature conservation, and for the access and enjoyment of the very large numbers of visitors ...

With a new high quality visitor centre outside the boundary of the World Heritage Site (WHS) as a starting point, visitors would gain access to the Stones and the heart of the WHS via primary access links, drop-off points and "gateways" ... Pedestrian access beyond the core to the wider, and more tranquil, and more fully presented and interpreted landscape and archaeological sites ... would be possible'
(English Heritage, 2000, p. 5)

The intent therefore is to clear the site of modern clutter, removing the roads (closure and sinking into a tunnel), and creation of a new visitor centre outside the boundary of the WHS. This is represented in Figure 11.4. However, as soon as the vision is turned into a plan, we re-enter the world of practical problems and challenges to address.

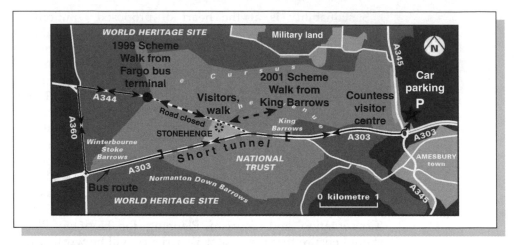

Figure 11.4
Schematic of alternative visitor routes (following project development between 1999 and 2001) and removal of roads from Stonehenge

Solving the problem: actuality

As already noted, there are many stakeholders in Stonehenge and the management of it. Two organizations have the practical problems of management, and working together to turn the vision into reality. The professionals, the government and other stakeholders who have articulated their views on the site have long lambasted the site as a 'national disgrace' (House of Commons Public Accounts Committee, 1993, p. vii). The tourists, however, continue to visit in their hundreds of thousands each year. Their focus is different; it is about the visit and the visual experience rather than appreciation of the site's management. While they may feel that the visitor experience could be improved, they are already at the site when being asked about it. Therefore such improvements are in the future, for another visit, another day some time off. The 'managers' therefore have to act as the beneficial hosts, investing for future cultural tourists, addressing their possible needs and concerns, and aiming to provide an experience that falls in line with law, plans, regulations, conventions, aspirations, desires, needs and so on. This is no small order for the practicalities of managing an entire prehistoric landscape, when in fact it is really just the 'iconic bit' – the monument – that is really worth seeing in the visitors' eyes. The managers want the world to want more of Stonehenge and make the link between environment, space and place: the problem is providing an effective experience for those hoped-for wants.

Current plans provide for a new, yet to be built, 'world class' visitor centre just over two kilometres to the east of the site (identified by the star on Figure 11.4). Situated outside the World Heritage Site, and therefore not subject to the restrictions that the World Heritage label carries (again a dichotomous idea: World Heritage Site labelling intending to make sites more accessible yet potentially restricting the ways in which physical interpretation can be improved). Put out to worldwide architectural competition, the winning designs for the proposed visitor centre are meant to blend with the landscape and yet echo the monumentality of the archaeological remains (English Heritage, 2001). This facility will cater for the more basic mass tourism needs: car parking, catering, shopping, events, corporate hire, road services and toilets. The more intellectual needs for the cultural tourist, the niche tourist who fits most closely with the ideal Stonehenge consumer in the eyes of the conservation profession, will also be fulfilled through interpretive displays introducing the landscape, its history and the processes used to uncover knowledge about the site. Education and stimulation of the visitor to discover the World Heritage Site are at the heart of the interpretation, encouraging the visitor to walk or ride on a transit system out across the landscape.

Yet, in planning and management terms, we seem to be back to vision again: the practicalities of interpretive design for the visitor centre (arguably the most important part) have long been waited for. No details about the internal design and interpretive layout are currently available publicly. The practicalities of encouraging and moving visitors from the visitor centre to the stones (still the recognized focus of any visit) have been advocated, rethought, retold and still not finalized (hence the two routes identified in Figure 11.4). There are so many issues to consider: the fragility of the landscape, the impact of any kind of transit system to transport visitors from the visitor centre to the focus of the site, the perceptions of hoped-for visitors, the different stories that need to be interpreted, the different technologies that could be used, the willingness of people to go and discover the core site from a visitor centre two kilometres distant, and so on. During 2003, debates continued in the press, and among the stakeholder groups, over the removal of the roads, ending in a government choice from three tabled options of a short tunnel for the A303 and closure of the A344 past the stones (Department for Culture, Media and Sport, 2002). The scale of this project led to a Public Inquiry being launched at the start of 2004 (Her Majesty's Inspectorate of Planning, 2003). The visitor centre and wider site visitor provision have yet to be considered at a public level: English

Heritage and The National Trust are reliant on other money to support developments, and the Heritage Lottery Fund (a distributor of UK National Lottery monies) will be expected to support capital infrastructure costs.

There is, therefore, another major stakeholder group in provision for tourism: the financiers for any proposed scheme for visitor facility improvement. This expectation of a 'cultural heritage investment' brings into question the economic value of the kind of tourism venture that is very firmly labelled as a cultural site and therefore subject to the vagaries of market failure (National Economic Research Associates, 2003). Could such a major scheme ever make money; would it be expected to? If not, how big can the costs be to the taxpayers who may be assumed to foot the bill for funding English Heritage? How much are tourists wanting to visit the icon Stonehenge prepared to pay for the wider goals of presenting, preserving and discovering a much bigger landscape? Wider issues of financial sustainability of cultural tourism have yet to be addressed, but the Stonehenge developments begin to raise such questions and an interesting debate in the future may be expected.

Evaluations and conclusions

Stonehenge at the moment is an unsatisfactory case study, as it is very much in a state of flux, with a series of questions and 'don't knows' about how the tourism experience will develop. The intention here has been to show the context for the site and its relevance as a cultural tourism site, the relationship between tourists and the wider stakeholders, and the intentions of the managing stakeholders for site development on behalf of everybody else. It can be seen that decisions made about the site's future have a variety of repercussions, the most far-reaching being that for the site visitor, including the tourist. Numerous visitor surveys have been carried out by a variety of organizations, and visitor opinions on the cleanliness of the site, its catering, desires for improvement, quality of interpretation and so on can be quantified. Views are known about improvements that tourists might like to see, and no doubt that these will be taken into consideration in the planning of the visitor centre. However, the central role that the tourist plays in the past and future of Stonehenge still seems to be little understood. Not much is really known about the complex relationship between the tourist and the site, the tourist as a stakeholder in the site, or the relationships between the managers and the managed. Visions and practicalities have governed Stonehenge as a site to date and are likely to continue to do so. Stonehenge is relatively well understood in historical and environmental terms, but the multi-layered contexts within which the cultural tourist as stakeholder exists, at a World Heritage Site managed in a sustainable fashion, are only at the early stages of study.

References

Baxter, I. and Chippindale, C. (2002). From 'national disgrace' to flagship monument: recent attempts to manage the future of Stonehenge. *Conservation and Management of Archaeological Sites* 5(3): 151–184.

Bender, B. (1998). *Stonehenge: Making Space*. Oxford: Berg.

Cathersides, A. (2001). Stonehenge: restoration of grassland setting. *Conservation Bulletin* 40: 34–36.

Chippindale, C. et al. (1990). *Who owns Stonehenge?* London: Batsford.

Department for Culture, Media and Sport (2002). *'Stonehenge will be Reunited with its Natural Landscape by 2008', Says Arts Minister Tessa Blackstone*. Press Release. London: DCMS.

English Heritage (2000). *Stonehenge World Heritage Site Management Plan*. London: English Heritage.

English Heritage (2001). *World Class Team to Support Design on New Stonehenge Centre*. Press Release. London: English Heritage.

English Heritage (2002). *Discover Stonehenge*. London: English Heritage.

Hawkes, J. (1967). God in the machine. *Antiquity* 41: 174–180.

Her Majesty's Inspectorate of Planning (2003). *A303 Stonehenge Improvement*. Public Notice. London: HMIP.

House of Commons Public Accounts Committee, Session 1992–93 (1993). *Committee of Public Accounts Twenty-ninth Report: Protecting and Managing England's Heritage Property*. London: HMSO.

International Council on Monuments and Sites (1999). *International Cultural Tourism Charter: Managing Tourism at Places of Heritage Significance*. Paris: ICOMOS.

National Economic Research Associates (2003). Economic issues in the heritage sector. Unpublished Report for The Monuments Trust and The National Trust.

United Nations Educational, Scientific, and Cultural Organization (1972). *Convention Concerning the Protection of the World's Cultural and Natural Heritage*. Paris: UNESCO.

United Nations Educational, Scientific, and Cultural Organization (1986). World Heritage Committee Tenth Session (CC-86/CONF. 003/10). Paris: UNESCO.

Urry, J. (1990). *The Tourist Gaze: Leisure and Travel in Contemporary Societies*. London: Sage.

Visit Britain (2003). *Visits to Visitor Attractions 2002*. London: Visit Britain.

Websites

Council for British Archaeology (CBA) (debates and information about Stonehenge and its history): www.britarch.ac.uk/stonehenge

English Heritage (site management, World Heritage Site information, conservation and tourism development): www.englishheritage.org.uk/stonehenge

International Council on Monuments and Sites (ICOMOS) (World Heritage Convention, International Cultural Tourism Charter, and other documentation): www.icomos.org

The National Trust (site management, World Heritage Site information, conservation and tourism development): www.nationaltrust.org.uk

The Stonehenge Project (joint management website with information on site developments): www.stonehengeproject.org

Templo Mayor: evolution and rediscovery. Sustaining Mexico's ancient cultural heritage

Adriana E. Estrada-González

Learning outcomes

- Understand the potential contribution of tourism development to the sustainability of the cultural heritage.
- Recognize the potential of heritage resources as cultural tourism attractions; through their development diversification can occur comparatively easily from traditional forms of tourism to modern tourism products, without considerable investment.
- Appreciate the role of tourism in promoting awareness of and access to cultural heritage, which may otherwise be restricted to scholars and researchers.
- Develop an awareness of the rich cultural heritage of Mexico, and how culture is preserved through generations.

Introduction

Cultural tourism is a relatively modern concept in the tourism vocabulary of Mexico. Although many forms of cultural tourism, ranging widely from history and archaeology to cultural heritage routes, have been used and overused for decades by tourism agents, only recently has it taken real meaning. A mix of these various facets of cultural tourism appears around the magnificent site of Templo Mayor, which is embedded in one of the most populated cities in the world. Some researchers consider it an archaeological site, but for others it has social, historical and even religious connotations; as such it well illustrates different forms of cultural tourism. According to the typology of urban heritage planning, as proposed by Ashworth (1991), Templo Mayor lies in the category of preservation and conservation. A key objective of urban heritage planning that involves archaeological sites is how most effectively to combine and present the potentially diverse ways of using artefacts and specific sites while involving, and seeking a balanced approach between, the many organizations and indeed individuals, and the community, with interest in or involved in some way in the development of any such urban site. Undoubtedly, this is a major task, one that is increasingly central to sustaining urban cultural heritage and overall sustainability.

This case study exemplifies the complexity of such sites through exploring the historic background of Templo Mayor, its transition during the colonization period, its decay and its subsequent rediscovery to be used as a landmark for cultural tourism.

Background

Mexico is a country that gathers history, traditions, mystic sites and people: features readily utilized in the tourism promotional literature for Mexico and the potential destinations therein. For the past sixty years or so, Mexico has promoted three types of destination, namely:

- beaches
- archaeological sites
- colonial cities.

These tourism products were perpetuated by local, state and national councils which were looking for ready-made attractions, natural or built, ready to be sold for tourists' consumption (Torres, 2001). However, this classification relates to the fact that the orientation of tourism policy in those days was demand led. In effect, what is the tourist seeking? As a result, less attention was paid to the destination; a resource-based strategy was not on the agenda. These products required little, if any government (national or local) investment because they already existed as very much a part of Mexico's heritage. That is, beaches are natural resources where tourism was promoted and facilitated by big hotel chains and by local fishermen. Archaeological sites are most often centuries-old pyramids or ruins, while colonial cities are comparatively more recent, dating back some five centuries, many of which exist in one form or another from the early days of the Spanish conquerors.

This approach was fine for much of the twentieth century. However, towards the end of the century it became recognized that a new approach was required to attract tourists (SECTUR, 2001, p. 17). Thus, in the 1990s a different perspective on tourism promotion began to appear and Mexico began exploring a range of potential new destinations and new tourism products. A number of these 'new products' emerged, catalysed by wider trends in tourism demand, through the repackaging of what was already present. For example, trips conducted by biologists to remote untouched areas became 'ecotourism', while guides for exploration tours became guides for 'adventure' or 'extreme risk' tourism. Another activity that had quietly been continuing in the background involved historians and anthropologists who led groups of scholars and students keen to discover Mexico's past through a diverse range of opportunities. Recognition of the extent of this activity and its significance to tourism substantially raised awareness of the heritage and subsequently this awareness contributed to the rise in profile of cultural tourism in Mexico.

Cultural tourism in Mexico

A broad definition considers cultural tourism as the visit to and knowledge of cultural monuments and historic–artistic sites. It encompasses perceptions of a value-added experience for the tourist, which thus is associated with 'quality tourism'. The potential tourist seeks for a place where he or she may receive more than expected. This is why cultural tourism fits so well with a modern profile of tourists, seeking satisfaction through new products and experiences. As such, cultural tourism serves well to differentiate products and destinations, enhancing market segmentation and opening new perspectives and diversification to destinations, which hitherto might have been seen as little other than 'sea, sun, sand'. Closely linked with cultural tourism is the concept of 'heritage', which refers to tangible and intangible values of a society's inherited past that continue on through generations. Heritage is usually something that it is widely recognized and valued by society in general, worthy of preserving; this includes history, gastronomy, architecture, festival and events, archaeology, religion, music and art. Templo Mayor illustrates and encompasses three of these areas, which are outlined as follows.

Historical tourism

Historical tourism encompasses the design, planning and application of historic elements used by tourism as a source of cultural attraction, such as monuments, tangible and intangible resources, and architecture. However, creating a historical place goes far beyond 'simple facts'; for example, the age of the village and its history. Elements such as aesthetic beauty, architecture and events need to be incorporated in diatribes of monuments and places if their history is to be presented and interpreted in a meaningful way. This helps to establish a site in terms of the development of the region, the village or a place with specific functional features, such as infrastructure development and local community participation; in other words, to develop historical tourism in a manner complementary to the sustainability of small, remote communities. One substantive example of this is Chapultepec, which means 'grasshopper hill' in Nahuatl (the language of the Aztecs), which has a diverse and rich sociocultural heritage. This forested area was used as a summer residence for Emperor Montezuma. Over the centuries it has been both a place of residence (e.g. the Viceroy in 1785 built a home there which later became a Military Academy and subsequently a Museum, now known as Chapultepec Castle) and, throughout, a popular park. Today, Chapultepec Park encompasses the Chapultepec Castle, the Museum of Modern Art, the National Museum of Anthropology, the Rufino Tamayo Museum (Twentieth Century Art in Mexico), the Snail Museum (named according to its shape, and containing a history gallery) and a Zoological Park.

Archaeological tourism

Archaeology, an important field of anthropology, relates to 'lost' or 'disappeared' societies and cultures. This discipline considers the study of tangible artefacts of past communities which help to explain not only the society of the time but also lifestyles of people living in that environment at the time.

Mexico is a vast country full of archaeological wealth, as the result of flourishing cultures, whose presence is still very much in evidence as part of Mexico's cultural heritage, manifest in myriad architectural, artistic and cultural features. For example, the first Prehispanic culture in Mexican territory was the Olmec, who lived in 1200 BC near the Gulf of Mexico. They were followed by the Mayan, who flourished between 1000 BC and AD 300, mainly on the Yucatan Peninsula. To the northeast of Mexico City lies Teotihuacan, which flourished between AD 100 and 750 and is considered to be the exemplar of urbanized civilization in Mesoamerica. Since the sixteenth and seventeenth centuries, Mexico's explorers have sought to learn more about their ancestors and their lifestyles and to preserve this invaluable cultural heritage. They began to dig and explore in a more systematic manner the magnificent pyramids around the country. However, it was not until the beginning of the twentieth century, when the development of anthropological sciences turned the exploration, excavation and analysis of information into a discipline, that knowledge of past specific ethnic groups and cultures in the country began to emerge.

Because of this unique diversity, archaeology is capturing the tourists' attention, and at the same time, they are captivated by the impressive vista of the pyramids and monoliths. This attention combines well with the perceived desire of tourists to explore and stay in places belonging to ethnic groups, with strong cultural heritage links founded on their history, tradition and culture in what some commentators might describe as a 'mystic–magical environment'.

Religious tourism

Religious tourism may be considered as the oldest manifestation of tourism, for as Sagaón wrote: 'When Man starts to worship his Gods and shows gratitude to them, he has to travel to holy places to pray' (Sagaón, 2001, p. 6). This union of movement and travel, coupled with the provision of services for tourists, creates the field of religious tourism. The main representations of religious tourism are pilgrimage, fairs and carnivals. The pilgrimage, also considered as procession, is the act of moving from one place to another, often travelling through foreign lands. It is also an ordered march of a group of people, usually with religious connotation.

However, Templo Mayor did not gather devotees in the modern concept of churches, shrines or temples, but certainly it was a place with religious charm, attracting local people and tourists.

The Aztec civilization

The Aztecs, a tribe of nomadic origin, was the last ethnic group to appear in Mexico's historic heritage. Although in comparison with other ethnic groups, the Aztec civilization in Mexico developed quickly and lasted for a relatively very short period, they left an indelible and lasting mark on Mexican history.

The Aztecs, also known as Mexicas, departed from a mythical place called Aztlan (meaning 'lost origin'), on a historical pilgrimage. However, it would be truer to say that the population of this mythical place migrated from their land more as an exodus than a pilgrimage, arguably to escape from rival tribes (Carballo and Martínez, 1988, p. 15). This nomadic migration is considered to have lasted for around two centuries. However, as myth would have it, they travelled on until they found the sign, predicted by their prophets, of 'the promised land' for their new settlement: 'an eagle standing on a cactus, in the middle of a lake, and devouring a snake' (Adair, 1996, p. 73) at a place called Texcoco. This image became incorporated in tradition and is now the civic emblem of Mexico. The new city, named Tenochtitlan, a piece of land surrounded by a lake, served their purpose well in that any enemies would be readily visible on the shoreline and could be repelled well in advance; thus a new era of sedentary life began (see Figure 12.1).

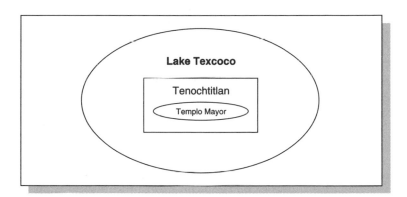

Figure 12.1
A new era of
sedentary life

The actual date of the founding of Tenochtitlan is disputed, varying from the exact (1325) to the beginning of the fourteenth century. This uncertain conception of dates emerges from the fact that Aztecs recorded time in cycles of fifty-two years, a quite different standard from the linear record of the Western calendar. More recent discoveries, found on the outskirts of Mexico City, suggest that the Aztec settlement could be older, by some 300 years, suggesting that it was in its splendour by the year 1000. The relics found include ceramic urns and tools, showing evidence of the development in the region.

Templo Mayor

Templo Mayor is the most important religious structure in the Aztec region. It comprises a group of pyramidal foundations located at the very heart of Mexico City; adjacent to which is the Cathedral and the City Hall (Palacio Nacional). Undoubtedly, it is an 'obligatory stop' for local people and tourists. To place Templo Mayor in a contemporary perspective, it is necessary to refer to Mexico City. This megalopolis of millions of inhabitants is the consequence of a historical evolution of four cities in one: the prehispanic period, the colonial period, new development during the nineteenth century, and post-1910 (or the revolution period). Each of these cities opened the door to the next period, but to do this, it was necessary to destroy and plunder the previous city (Carballo and Martínez, 1988, p. 15). However, traces and monuments from the original city remain today. Templo Mayor is one of those monuments that stand as a living memory of Mexico City's past, and arguably more importantly of Mexico itself.

Origins

Templo Mayor, with its double pyramid building, was dedicated to the Gods of Rain (Tlaloc) and War (Huitzilopochtli). Not only was it the ceremonial centre of Tenochtitlan, it also represented the main settlement of public and ecclesiastic power. It has been estimated that in the fourteenth century the population was approximately 300 000 inhabitants. Even though this population was huge for that time, the overall design – the infrastructure with its network of channels connecting the four points of the city – allowed for ease of access to the temples and ceremonial sites. As the city developed, so Templo Mayor grew; according to some estimates to as much as twelve times its original size. It is possible through the way the site is displayed and presented today to review the six phases of construction that have been identified.

- Phase 1: dated to 1325. This phase relates to a building that is not visible from the outside of archaeological site. This building was the first temple built in the area and was constructed of mud and wood. It was discovered in 1989 when further excavation works took place.
- Phase 2: dated to 1390. During this period the two temples were built, considered to be the most important structures and seen today at the archaeological site. In the interior of the temples are found mural paintings depicting civil, religious and war events. At present, two-thirds of the temples are below ground level.
- Phase 3: dated to 1431. It has been argued that the take-over of the nearby village, Azcapotzalco, facilitated the extension of the temple as a consequence of the extra labour brought in from the village. During this stage, the treasures located inside the temple were of considerable value.
- Phase 4: dated to between 1454 and 1469. During this period it is evident that fine-quality products, such as arrowheads of jade, and clay pots with designs in traditional Aztec colours, were produced in Templo Mayor. The resources used include raw materials from both the Pacific and Atlantic coasts.
- Phase 5: dated to around 1480. Unfortunately, the archaeological rests (remains of pyramids, platforms and artefacts) have been lost. The main visible feature is a platform, all that remains of the old plaza.
- Phase 6: dated to between 1486 and 1502. Another set of minor temples was built during this period. This essentially completed the major expansion of Templo Mayor, a time

generally perceived as the heyday of the city. However, it expanded spatially as the power of the Aztecs grew and they conquered outlying villages, which contributed enforced labour, further adding to their power.

On their arrival at the city the Spanish conquerors saw the temples and called them mosques. To convey an idea of the magnitude of the place at that time, the ceremonial area contained twenty towers and the capacity of the largest temple has been calculated as being up to 1000 people. The Spanish conqueror Hernán Cortés reputedly described the city as marvellous and referred to its splendour and refinement, and the beauty of the landscape created by the Aztecs.

When the Spanish conquerors arrived, Templo Mayor comprised seventy-eight buildings. The ceremonial centre was formed by sixty buildings within a 500 metre square, out of which radiated the major avenues of the city. Templo Mayor was the symbolic centre of a large tribute network for the Aztecs, a place of worship, funerary rests and sacred offerings. The centre was dominated by the sixty-metre high temple, which was the temple seen by the Spanish conquerors on their arrival at Tenochtitlan in 1519. Shortly afterwards, in 1521, the destruction of the Tenochtitlan area began, and as a consequence, Templo Mayor declined.

On the arrival of Spanish conqueror Hernán Cortés, King Montezuma was the Aztec ruler. Their historical meeting took place in Templo Mayor. Subsequently, there was a period of war-like situations during which time buildings, bridges and the whole city, including the temples, were devastated. The worst part of this historical period is the fact that the local people had the task, in effect, of destroying their city to build a new one. The ancient temples remained but, and this was not an uncommon practice, the new Spanish temples, churches and religious sanctuaries were built on top of them, using the materials from the temples. Templo Mayor became the home of the conquerors and their public and religious buildings.

Rediscovery

The earliest recorded discoveries of Templo Mayor were of stone sculptures found towards the end of the eighteenth century; however, and as noted above, little in the way of excavation took place until around the beginning of the twentieth century. Although archaeologists discovered a corner of Templo Mayor in 1913 it was not until the 1940s that sustained excavation began to rescue the valued objects and monuments that constituted the ceremonial place. The initial finding and later activity at the site is largely explained by the development of the city's infrastructure, notably the sewerage system. Even so, formal restoration works did not start until 1978, which led up to the official inaugural function on 12 October 1987, and further archaeological excavations and the construction of a museum on the site, designed discreetly to avoid any visual intrusion with the adjacent colonial architecture. The museum has eight halls re-creating, in a symbolic manner, the original constitution of Templo Mayor, and houses displays of the sculptures, urns and artefacts excavated on the site.

The renewed interest in the site and its significance has led to a number of substantive developments. In 1991, the Program on Urban Archaeology was established; this has promoted scientific surveys to study the seven blocks of the historical centre, which confirmed the sacred place of Templo Mayor. These surveys have been diverse in their aims, involving not just archaeology, but also research into the anthropology, biology and history of the period, and approaches to and techniques of restoration.

A particularly contentious area of debate, which has been ongoing for decades, arises from the location of the Metropolitan Cathedral, which is just in front of Templo Mayor. A conflict of interests has developed over further excavations of Templo Mayor and the effects that this will have on the Cathedral, because below its construction lies part of the historic city of Tenochtitlan. What we can be sure of is that the Cathedral lies on the original site. The significance of this and comprehension of the conflicting interests become all the more apparent when it is realized that construction of the Metropolitan Cathedral began in 1563, sixty years after Templo Mayor was finished.

Templo Mayor as an attraction for cultural tourism

Today Templo Mayor lies as an archaeological site right in the centre of Mexico City. It stands as a museum, and an open-air area displaying the main pyramids left by the course of time – markers to Mexico's cultural heritage. It is of wider significance in terms of world history, but also an outstanding and unique element of cultural tourism in global terms.

Certainly, it is a 'must visit', always on the itinerary of guided tours, and stands on a par with the Cathedral and the National Government Palace (Palacio Nacional). Thus, the challenge for the tourism planners and destination management is to reach a stage of development at which the main actor, the visitor, gains a level of awareness of its cultural significance and thereby is enabled to realize the value of Templo Mayor. Secondly, and equally important, is the need to consider the sustainability of this place. Located, as it is, at the very heart of the city, the site is exposed to erosion, pollution and over-crowding. Although it is permanently restored and managed by the National Institute for History and Anthropology, it requires almost daily attention to keep it from deteriorating further. Herein lies the nexus of the problem: the balance between development and the environment. That Templo Mayor is a monument to cultural tourism is inescapable and that tourism has played a significant role in debate in support of its excavation, presentation and interpretation is evident. However, visitors also have negative impacts on this and indeed the adjacent heritage sites. The question is thus how to achieve a balance.

At this stage, the main goal is to gain as many visitors as possible, in order to inform, transmit and re-create the origins of Mexico's native civilization, as well as of the transition period to Templo Mayor.

For national tourists, it is a place for worship, a legend, the history of the origins of the Mexican nation and a sightseeing place. Whatever the perception may be, cultural tourism is related to Templo Mayor, and every single effort is worthwhile to maintain the cradle of Aztec civilization for future generations.

Site evaluation and future visions

Since its inauguration in 1987, Templo Mayor has evolved from being predominantly a site of special interest for scholars and researchers to a tourist attraction of substantial cultural significance.

Paradoxically perhaps, the presence of Templo Mayor at the heart of Mexico City has contributed to both the modernization and preservation of the historical centre of the city. Templo Mayor, with its museums and cultural events relating to the life and legacy of the first inhabitants of this city, receives approximately 700 000 visitors per annum. A considerable number of these visitors are schoolchildren on guided tours, for whom developing their awareness and understanding of their cultural heritage is remarkably important. Other visitors are domestic or foreign tourists searching for their roots and seeking knowledge and understanding of past cultures.

The challenge today is to maintain and promote its value as a tourist attraction while seeking not to destroy its allure as a mystical place. This is increasingly recognized, not solely in the context of Templo Mayor but more widely. Terms such as urban revitalization, heritage planning, conservation and preservation are present more frequently in working agendas to develop the image of a place, whether it is an archaeological site or a beach.

Conclusion

The tourism sector in Mexico offers a wide variety of tourism products for almost every preference. However, cultural tourism is still an incipient field in Mexico. For decades, tourists have been visiting and touring places that contain a meaning: it may be a pyramid, a church, a village, or a remote lake or river. These particular places need to promote awareness and convey the importance of their preservation and revitalization. Today, many communities, not only in remote areas but in urban areas as well, are dependent on the activities and associated revenues of foreign tourists, many of whom visit out of the interest and desire to travel in areas with a strong cultural heritage.

Mexico's richness of archaeological sites is enormous. This captivates the attention of local people and tourists. As a result of this interest, national institutes and national policies are adapting and developing plans to unveil, restore, preserve and conserve monuments, architecture, ruins and pyramids, historical landmarks and even complete cities. At the same time, Mexico has recognized the need for change, has identified new trends, and is shifting away from the traditional market-led approach to more resource-based strategies. This approach shows signs of greater awareness of the issues of sustainability, of sustainable development, the need for a balance between economic development and the environment. This shifting emphasis and the concomitant recognition of the societal significance of the country's cultural heritage – today's and tomorrow's cultural tourism attractions – is to be welcomed.

Significantly, cultural tourism for Mexico is a recent phenomenon that can be developed without considerable investment, but that holds substantial economic potential. This is the main reason to develop the field of cultural tourism. However, to be sustainable such development must be in balance with the environment and, indeed, the needs of the community. In such an effectively managed way, cultural tourism holds the potential to play a major role in contributing to the sustainability of this uniquely diverse cultural heritage.

References

Adair, M. (1996). *Frommer's 96. Mexico*. New York: Simon & Schuster.

Ashworth, G. J. (1991). *Heritage Planning*. Groningen: Geo Pers.

Carballo, E. and Martínez, J. L. (1988). *Páginas sobre la Ciudad de México 1469–1987*. México: Consejo de la Crónica de la Ciudad de México.

Sagaón, M. T. (2001). *Turismo Religioso en México*. Monterrey: Tesina UMNE.

SECTUR (2001). *1° Informe de Labores*. México: Secretaría de Turismo.

Torres, J. C. (2001). *Revista Semestral 'Unidad y Diversidad'. Revista Digital de Planificación, Empresas y Desarrollo Regional*. Available: http://www.itox.mx/Posgrado/Revista4/art2.html (accessed on 10 March 2004), http://archaeology.la.asu.edu/tm/, http://www.ovpm.org/ville.asp?v=1

Websites

Consejo Nacional para la Cultura y las Artes: http://www.conaculta.gob.mx/pa.htm

Instituto Nacional de Antropología e Historia: http://www.inah.gob.mx

Templo Mayor Website: http://azteca.conaculta.gob.mx/templomayor/

UNESCO World Heritage Cities Website: http://whc.unesco.org/nwhc/pages/sites/main.htm

Part Four

New Media and Technologies

CHAPTER 13

New media and technologies: trends and management issues for cultural tourism

Marianna Sigala

Introduction

Advances in information and communication technology (ICT) and recently the evolution of the Internet have been instrumental in transforming the production, interpretation, exchange, marketing and consumption of cultural services as well as in managing visitors' experiences and behaviour (Sigala, 2003a). ICT affects all functions of cultural organizations including conservation, exhibition, marketing and administration (Stam, 1992; Solima, 1998) by permeating all stages of visitor cycle, i.e. pre-sale services, on-site services and post-sale services. Internet tools have enabled the electronic management and publishing of content, the development of virtual cultural-heritage exhibitions and/or the 'webification' of existing, 'bricks and mortar' cultural-heritage attractions, as well as the emergence of several virtual communities of curators, visitors, educators and others with similar interests in culture and heritage. Moreover, the introduction of multimedia information systems enables the heritage-cultural industry to redefine its role and models by allowing it to redesign traditional products and promote new cultural experiences by involving a worldwide network of potential visitors, who may also be able to participate in the production of the cultural service.

However, most studies so far have merely focused on technical issues and learning tools such as the digitization and electronic storage of collections for educational and dissemination purposes (Khoon et al., 2003). Consequently, limited research has been devoted to the interaction between culture-heritage, tourism, ICT, the Internet and visitor experiences, and therefore little knowledge exists with respect to how best to use ICT tools in cultural attractions (either virtual or physical) for enhancing visitor services and satisfaction and supporting sustainable destination management. In this vein, the major objective of this section is to explore and analyse these latter issues in depth. To achieve that, first this introductory section will discuss the Internet and ICT features and capabilities substantially transforming the operational and marketing practices of heritage-cultural organizations, and then synthesize them into a theoretical model that can effectively consolidate and identify any potential ICT impacts on heritage-cultural tourism. First-hand practical and in-depth knowledge regarding specific issues is provided by three additional case studies, the importance and key elements of which are also introduced in this section. The case studies are: online visitors' learning experiences and construction of online authenticity, virtual community information systems and destination community tourism development; and destination management systems and sustainable heritage tourism development.

ICT and Internet features and capabilities: implications for managing visitors' experiences and behaviour

Attempts to understand and thus manage visitors' behaviour within heritage-cultural organizations and destinations have been numerous and from multiple perspectives, e.g. the social approach, the cognitive approach (i.e. visitors' intrinsic and extrinsic motivations), social cognition (e.g. interpretation, visitors' involvement and participation) and environmental psychology (e.g. routing, mapping) (Sigala, 2003a). By consolidating all approaches, Goulding's (2000) research provided a holistic framework indicating that the following factors influence visitors' behaviour: (1) social factors: cultural identification; continuity of theme and story; conversation and story building from evaluation of stimulus; social interaction; (2) cognitive factors: the creation of mindful activity; involvement and engagement; inner reflection and imagination; variation of stimulus to create a meaningful 'whole'; perceived authenticity; and (3) environmental aspects: scene setting; routing and mapping; crowding density levels (in the case of technology-based or enhanced heritage environments, this factor reflects website-device information design, functionality, navigation and searchability). The features and characteristics of recent ICT and Internet advances and their exploitation can substantially impact on and enhance the social (community), cognitive (learning, authentic experience making) and environmental space of heritage-cultural visitors. The impact of ICT advances and features on these three factors influencing visitors' behaviour and experiences are analysed below, as well as in the subsequent case studies.

Recent ICT advances and Internet technologies share three major, unique but also interconnected capabilities that in turn have a substantial impact on the management of cultural-heritage visitors' behaviour, services and experiences (Sigala, 2003b). Ultimately, as discussed in detail below, these three unique features of new ICT advances consist of vital innovation drivers, business model and role transformers of the heritage-cultural industry, as they enable operators to unlock and embed the value and intellectual capital of their visitors, and other communities of interests within their experience, making capabilities and supply chains. Overall, as explained below, the three ICT features enable the extension of the cultural ecology of museums by making the online museum experiences more spiritual, engaging, moving and social.

Interactivity

New media enable interactive and/or real-time communication. Consequently, relationships between heritage-cultural organizations, curators, historians, educators, visitors and any other type of stakeholder can become more interactive, two-way and rich in information, creating new paradigms of product design, heritage interpretation and visitor service. For example, the website of the Science Museum of Milan (www.museoscienza.org) features a chat box that serves as an online guide, while its services are enhanced through its integration with the following data sources: collections database, library database, guided visits booking system, website, internal bookshop and online web international bookshops. Another well-developed online chat application is WebTalk-I (Bertoletti et al., 2001). For example, in the Museum of Science and Technology of Milan, the application named 'Virtual Leonardo' allows users to co-operate while accessing a site with a number of pages describing different machines invented (designed but never built) by Leonardo da Vinci. Virtual Leonardo allows users to visit the museum together, exchange opinions, and interact with the world and with each other in a number of ways. Net2Gether (http://www.net2gether.com) is another interesting tool for two-dimensional collaboration over the web. It provides a chat window under the usual browser window. Chat is organized in groups, and each group has a leader. The leader is able to push the webpage being visited into the browsers of the other participants. Other interactive applications that also benefit from the second feature of the new media, i.e. connectivity, include the virtual communities technologies that are discussed later.

Finally, interactive services are being further advanced not only by efforts to enhance the multimedia information richness of the communications, but also by efforts to complement communication, services and heritage interpretation with personalization features. In other words, the interactivity of new ICT is being advanced by adaptive personal learning systems and capabilities. So, although real exhibitions are limited to linear presentations, in multimedia-based exhibitions multiple hyperlinks allow visitors to recognize the meaning and significance of an object in various contexts of culture and to understand the complexity of interconnections of cultural appearances. In this way, user-interactive hypermedia enable a multifaceted interpretation, while a new learning-adaptive generation hypermedia and multimedia application is being developed (Zimmermann et al., 2003) for developing personalized virtual environments and personalized visitor experiences. Speech, music and sound effects are dynamically arranged to form an individualized and situated soundscape offering online exhibit-related information as well as creating context-specific atmospheres. This idea relates to the concept of situation-aware content, where information is most effective if presented in a cohesive way, building on previously delivered information. The latter may be accomplished by using comparisons and references to space and time, which in turn may aid the visitor in becoming orientated within the museum, as well as around the various exhibited objects. This dynamic composition of the soundscape can be personalized through each visitor's online behaviour, the history of the visit (by log files and cookies), and interests or preferences either expressed explicitly by the visitor or inferred from the visitor's behaviour (Hayes-Roth, 2001). Doyle and Isbister (1999) presented a more sophisticated application whereby the agent guide tracks users' words in a chat environment and provides more or less detailed tour information accordingly. By doing this, the interactive conversational character will be able to establish a customized person-to-person dialogue while also guiding the user through the virtual exhibition.

In other words, if the information is provided in a manner that flows and relates pieces to each other, this process can create mindful behaviour by stimulating visitors' interest and, hence, their desire to enquire, analyse and learn. It is essential also to consider the importance of creating an overall experience that truly addresses the needs of online visitors. This requires not only providing visitors with a vast amount of information, even if wonderfully presented, but also allowing them to have a pleasurable and entertaining time on the website.

The optimal online multimedia website should support strong personalization of all presented information in an effort to ensure that each visitor is allowed to accommodate, develop and interpret the visit according to his or her own pace and interests (Dyson and Moran, 2000). Simultaneously, website features should provide the appropriate amount of impetus to foster learning and self-development so as to create a richer and more meaningful experience. For example, visitors registering on the website and obtaining a password will be provided with additional services, such as better navigation support. For these visitors, profiles will be stored to gain insight into their interests and the perception of the exhibition in general. The ideal website should not only guess what the visitors are interested in, but also consider what they have to learn: orientating visitors, providing opportunities for reflection and allowing them to explore related ideas, thereby greatly enhancing the educational value of the visit. In essence, the website should stimulate new interests and suggest new paths for exploring the online exhibition, while a system supporting visitors' browsing should consider their agenda, expectations and interests. The impact of the new ICT/Internet tools and features on interpretation and visitor management are summarized in Table 13.1, in which the benefits of such tools are categorized according to the five principles of interpretation provided by Tilden (1950).

The interconnections and implications between cultural-heritage websites' design, functionality and features, visitors' meaning-making experiences, learning experiences and interpretation are discussed in detailed in the case study on eternalegypt.org (Chapter 14). By adopting a post-modern approach and after reviewing both the technology and heritage literature, this case study clearly illustrates the implications of the functionality and features of website design on interpretation and on the construction of online personalized, constructivism authentic meaning-making experiences. Technology implications for interpretation practices are also discussed in the case study on Venice (Chapter 16), but from a destination management perspective.

Connectivity

The open and global nature of the Internet as well as of new technological devices (e.g. mobile devices, mobile phones and interactive television) are fostering the creation of a shared global heritagespace. The radical increase in connectivity is giving rise to new communication and co-ordination mechanisms both across heritage organizations and visitors, and within groups of visitors and other interested parties. This technological connectivity facilitates the creation and fostering of heritage-cultural networks and communities as well as their inclusion into the heritage-cultural operators' value chain.

In contrast to e-mail communications, which are one-to-one, not very interactive and may lead to spam mail, virtual communities (using electronic mailing lists, newsgroups, web-based forums, chat rooms, etc.) are becoming increasingly popular with the general public. Such tools provide one-to-many and many-to-many communication practices, enhance collaboration among visitors, curators and other interested parties, and increase websites' 'stickiness', and visitors' interest

Table 13.1 Principles of interpretation: impact and examples of ICT/Internet tools

Principle	ICT impact	ICT application/ example
Information on its own is not interpretation	ICT contextualizes and personalizes information, thus enhancing meaning	Hypertext technologies that link information with other relevant facts and data Thinking maps and navigational tools
Any interpretation that does not somehow relate what is being displayed or described to something within the personality or experience of the visitor will be sterile	ICT personalizes information according to people's interests and goals and situations ICT links information sources	Web forums and discussions Mobile devices that localize information based on visitors' location Intelligent software that personalizes experiences by learning the users by either collecting and analysing users' information and/or comparing the latter with other users' profiles
Interpretation is an art, whether the materials being presented are scientific, historical, architectural or environmental	ICT applications not only involve techies but also require much expertise in marketing, psychology, IS, interpretivism theories, etc.	Multimedia and interactive/engaging presentations
The chief aim of interpretation is not instruction, but provocation	ICT increases edutainment ICT fosters visitors' fun ICT instils interest among communities of visitors, local communities, curators, etc.	Web forums and discussions Online newsletters and newsgroups Online chat and discussion tools
Interpretation should aim to present a whole rather than a part	ICT contextualizes and localizes information	Hypermedia applications Web chatting and forum tools Website maps and navigational tools Virtual tours

and loyalty (Sigala, 2003a). Through discussion lists, guest books and member programmes, the heritage-cultural technology spaces become a meeting space where actual and potential visitors share opinions, suggest new themes for exhibitions and events, and build up their cultural experience. Interactive games and forums encourage individuals to partake in mindful, exploratory behaviour, while presentations accompanied by hypertexted information allow for 'inner' (intrinsic) directed contemplation. The interactions between the heritage-cultural operator and the visitors, and among the visitors, produce a huge amount of information that can be stored and searched within the technology heritagespace. The benefits of mailing lists, newsgroups and web forums for cultural and heritage websites are widely discussed by Bernier and Bowen (2002a,b, 2003). Several heritage operators currently offer a discussion forum on their website (e.g. the Tate, the Kew Bridge Steam Museum, West London, UK, the Spellman Museum of Stamps and Postal History at Regis College, Weston, Massachusetts, USA, and the online Museum of Fine Art). Overall, virtual community tools can be used to achieve the following (Sigala, 2003a):

- Attract new visitors through appealing content and personalization of online experiences.
- Promote the participation of visitors and other actors through the production of the cultural experience.
- Building visitors' loyalty through the organization of forums and members' programmes in which the exchange of information becomes a crucial tool for developing personalized and long-lasting relationships with visitors.
- Reach potential visitors:
  ○ identify relevant audience
  ○ reach a large number of potential visitors with a single message.
- Communicate with existing visitors.
- Conduct market research:
  ○ find out latest trends
  ○ visitors' needs and interests
  ○ what visitors talk about and look for.
- Create customer databases and profiles for customer relationship management strategies: this will allow institutions to develop an in-depth understanding of visitors' evolving needs, expectations and requirements, and then to customize cultural supply.
- Build a reputation by helping visitors.

- Increase traffic by directing people to a website.
- Support community and sustainable tourism development by enhancing or integrating with destination management systems.

The advantages and functionalities of a virtual community-based information system that enables communication exchanges among tourists and local people, and so supports community-based tourism development, are analysed and illustrated in depth in the case study about Chania, Greece (Chapter 15). This virtual community information system can be developed either independently or as part of a destination management system. The development and exploitation of a new generation destination management system that can be applied for supporting sustainable destination management and enhancing interpretation practices are also investigated in detail in the case study about Venice, Italy (Chapter 16).

Convergence

Digital technologies are converging, making the Internet and new media ubiquitous. In other words, visitors are able to access and transfer the same information at any time, with any device, anywhere. The emerging wireless application protocol (WAP) technology, for example, permits mobile Internet access. Convergence allows heritage-cultural operators to integrate their PC-based online, mobile and offline management practices. A recent ICT application that aims to increase visitor participation with online users is the Telebuddy project described by Hoffmann and Goebel (2003), which aims to connect a live audience in a museum environment with an online community on the Internet. Telebuddy is a physical avatar equipped with camera, microphone and speakers and connected to the Internet. As a puppet or physical avatar, the Telebuddy provides a visible body for the eyes and the ears of the Internet: The avatar resembles a real person who has the capability to see (through a camera), hear (with a microphone) and talk (through a speaker). The puppet also contains an infrared sensor to specify its position in a building. Like a 'buddy', it can accompany a pedestrian visit to exhibitions or interesting locations, and can talk about the shared experience. Online users access the Telebuddy system via an Internet platform and communicate with people in remote places. With Telebuddy a novel user experience of feeling present at distant locations – feeling 'tele-present' – can be achieved.

In general, handheld mobile devices have several functionalities that can be integrated with other technological applications and traditional practices for enhancing heritage-cultural visitors' experiences and services. Major functionalities of mobile services include (Proctor and Tellis, 2003):

- Interactive survey and response: the system asks for and records visitors' opinions about exhibits, which can be incorporated into a knowledge database for later access, search and analysis by other visitors, curators and/or managers.
- Creative play: visitors can mix their own soundtracks to accompany their viewing of exhibits.
- Location-specific content delivery: content is delivered to visitors according to their location.
- Visitor tracking: a system can track the locations of visitors and relay them to a digital map at the distribution desk. This system also alerts staff if a device fails or if the visitor appears to be in need of technical assistance.
- Visitor paging: staff can page visitors ad hoc through the mobile devices, as well as send out pre-programmed, timed alerts, e.g. regarding the start of a video programme in the institutions.
- Visitor profiling: the wireless system tracks visitors' use of the content with a record of which exhibits they visit, how long visitors spent on the exhibits, what type of enquiries visitors posed, their demographic profile, etc. The visitors' profile can then be used for personalizing other visitors' tours (through collaborative filtering applications), market research purposes, rearranging collections, managing real-time visitors, tec.
- Visitors' e-mail facility: visitors can e-mail themselves or others with further information on objects and artists on the tour, to follow up later.

The case study on eternalegypt.org (Chapter 14) also describes some of the enhanced services that operators can provide by integrating online and mobile applications. For example, an online visitor to eternalegupt.org can create his or her own personalized tour on the website, download this tour into their mobile phone, follow this tour while at the cultural site, print the tour for a souvenir, or e-mail or text it to a friend. The enhanced mobility and benefits that mobile heritage applications can provide for tourists, local people and destination planners are also discussed in depth in the case study on Chania, Greece (Chapter 15).

ICT-driven experience innovation in the heritage-cultural sector

The three ICT features should not be considered separately. As will become apparent from the three case studies, interactivity, adaptive learning, connectivity and convergence are interconnected, and their combined functionality drives innovation within the heritage-cultural sector. This ICT-driven innovation facilitates an experience-centric rather than a product-centric view of innovation within the sector that redefines the operators' role, business model and supply-chain network. Each case study illustrates that ICT advances are transforming the basis of value within the heritage sector, from heritage-cultural products to co-created experiences. In all three case studies, there is an enhanced base of competence comprising three co-creators of heritage-cultural value: the operator and its network, the visitor, and the communities of visitors and other interested parties. In this vein, the innovation mandate for heritage-cultural operators is to leverage that competence base to expand and enhance the environment, enabling an ever wider range of potentially desirable experiences for individual visitors. This is a fundamentally different approach to innovation than the current preoccupation with new product development, product-heritage destination differentiation, process improvements and visitor management.

The transformation to an experience-innovation perspective is a quantum leap that requires the redefinition of everyone's role and perspective. Although heritage products and services are all embedded in an experience-based approach, the attention of managers and operators must shift dramatically to focus on the experience space (not products and services) as the locus of innovation and on the experience network (not just the company and its partners) as the locus of competence. The experience space is different to the product space. In the experience space, the visitor is central and an event triggers a co-creation experience. The events have a context in space and time, and the involvement of the visitor influences that experience. The personal meaning and understanding (the socially constructed authentic experience as explained in the case study on eternalegypt.org) are what determine the value for the visitor. Ultimately, the innovation driver in not the heritage product, the ICT system network that supports it, or the social and skills network that includes operators, curators, visitors and the broader community. Instead, the innovation value is the co-creation experience that stems from the visitor's interaction with all four elements (Figure 13.1). Thus, heritage experience is

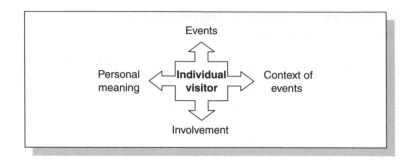

Figure 13.1
Heritage experience
space

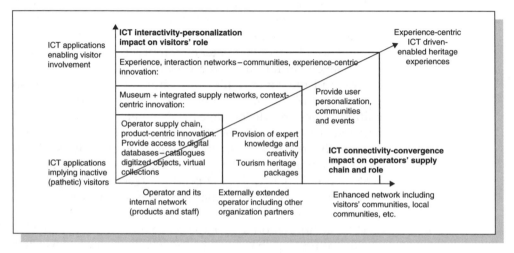

Figure 13.2
Role of ICT applications in enabling heritage experience-centric innovation

defined by the experience of a specific visitor, at a specific point in time and location, in the context of a specific event.

Each of these technological capabilities (interactivity, convergence and connectivity) has already played a role in product-centric innovations and in, so doing, has favourably affected visitors' experiences. But the difference between that role and the role they could play in experience-centric innovation is a matter of intent and perspective. The intention of experience innovation is not to improve a product or service per se, but to enable the co-creation of an environment populated by operators and visitors and their networks, in which personalized, evolvable experiences are the goal, and products and services evolve as a means to that end (Figure 13.2). From that perspective, a new technological capability is meaningful only when it is focused on improving the experiences desired by the visitor.

Conclusions and implications for future research

ICT and current Internet technologies are empowering and re-engineering the role of cultural and heritage institutions as well as transforming their visitors' management and interpretation practices. Despite the increasing number of cultural and heritage technology applications, little is known on how best to exploit Internet and ICT tools to create meaningful visitor experiences, support sustainable heritage tourism development at the destination level, and instil and drive innovation. This section aims to fill in the gaps. To achieve that, after introducing, analysing and consolidating the major ways in which ICT advances can enhance visitors' experiences and satisfaction, and heritage destination management, three case studies explore in more depth the way in which ICT drives experience-centric innovation practices within the sector. The first case study focuses on the development of authentic online heritage-cultural experiences by illustrating practices from eternalegypt.org, the second case study analyses the development and use of destination systems for engaging and enhancing community participation in tourists' heritage experiences in the city of Chania, and the third case study demonstrates how destination systems can be used for developing sustainable heritage tourism by referring to the case study of Venice. However, since the success of any technological application depends heavily on its ultimate adoption, future research should investigate socioeconomic and cultural barriers, and factors significantly affecting the take-up of such applications by visitors, heritage-cultural institutions and other interested parties.

References

Bernier, R. and Bowen, J. P. (2002a). Online: museum forums. *New Heritage* 4(2): 62–63.

Bernier, R. and Bowen, J. P. (2002b). On-line museum forums: whence and whither? *MCN Annual Conference*, Toronto, Canada, 4–7 September.

Bernier, R. and Bowen, J. P. (2003). A tour of web-based discussion forums: is there a museum community out there? *Spectra, Museum Computer Network.*

Bertoletti, A., Moraes, C. and Costa, A. (2001). Providing personal assistance in the SAGRES virtual museum. In *Museums and the Web, 2001.* Seattle, WA.

Doyle, P. and Isbister, K. (1999). Touring machines: guide agents for sharing stories about digital places. *AAAI Fall Symposium on Narrative Intelligence.*

Dyson, M. C. and Moran, K. (2000). Informing the design of web interfaces to museum collections. *Museum Management and Curatorship* 18(4): 391–406.

Goulding, C. (2000). The museum environment and the visitor experience. *European Journal of Marketing* 34(3/4): 261–278.

Hayes-Roth, B. (2001). Adaptive learning guides. In *Proceedings of IASTED Conference on Computers and Advanced Technology in Education*, Banff, Canada, June.

Hoffmann, A. and Goebel, S. (2003). Designing collaborative group experience for museums with Telebuddy. Available at: http://www.archimuse.com/mw2003/papers/hoffmann/hoffmann.html

Khoon, L., Ramaiah, C. and Foo, S. (2003). The design and development of an online exhibition for heritage information awareness in Singapore. *Program: Electronic Library and Information Systems* 37(2): 85–93.

Proctor, N. and Tellis, C. (2003). The state of the art in museum handhelds in 2003. Available at: http://www.archimuse.com/mw2003/papers/proctor/proctor.html.

Sigala, M. (2003a). Internet heritage and cultural tourism under virtual construction: implications for online visitors' experiences and interpretation management. *Tourism Today* (3): 51–67.

Sigala, M. (2003b). Developing and benchmarking internet marketing strategies in the hotel sector in Greece. *Journal of Hospitality and Tourism Research* 27(4): 375–401.

Solima (1998). *La gestione impredioriale dei musei*. Padova: CEDAM.

Stam, D. C. (1992). Taming the beast. *Museum Management and Curatorship* 2: 45–60.

Tilden, F. (1950). *Interpreting our Heritage*. Chapel Hill, NC: University of North Carolina Press.

Zimmermann, A., Lorenz, A. and Specht, M. (2003). The use of an information brokering tool in an electronic museum environment. Available at: http://www.archimuse.com/mw2003/papers/zimmermann/zimmermann.html

Websites

Kew Bridge Steam Museum: http://www.kbsm.org/forums

Museum of Fine Art, http://www.museum-of-fine-art.com/cgi-bin/ikonboard/ikonboard.cgi

Spellman Museum of Stamps and Postal History: http://www.spellman.org/forum.php3

The Tate: http://www.tate.org.uk/judgeforyourself

In search of post-modern online authenticity: assessing the quality of learning experiences at eternalegypt.org

Marianna Sigala

Learning outcomes

- Analyse and explain the concept of authenticity from a post-modern sociocultural as well as a technological perspective.
- Explain the concept and the meaning of online authenticity in a post-modern approach and analyse its relation to constructivism learning theories.
- Develop a model for creating constructivism and post-modern visitors' experiences at heritage websites.
- Identify the website tools and functionalities that can contribute to the construction of online post-modern authenticity.
- Illustrate the practical implications of the post-modern authenticity concept by analysing the case study of eternalegypt.org
- Discuss the theoretical and practical implications of this study.

Introduction

With the advent of the Internet, increasing numbers of heritage tourism operators are exploiting its features and tools for 'webifying' their operations and providing more enhanced visitor experiences and services (Sigala, 2003). The mushrooming of heritage-cultural websites raises several questions about whether this digitization of cultural products destroys their meaning or whether it leads to an electronic heritage commodification and commercialization. Traditionally, the concept of authenticity has been one of the most fundamental and widely adopted issues for evaluating the quality of heritage experiences (e.g. Chhabra et al., 2003; Xie and Wall, 2003). However, although in the offline world of heritage the concept of authenticity has attracted much academic debate (see literature review by Burnett, 2001), in the online heritage field, authenticity has received limited interest from both the tourism and the generic literature. Specifically, no in-depth discussion exists regarding how the concept and dimensions of authenticity are constructed online. Consequently, there is a lack of knowledge regarding the website features and functionalities that heritage operators' websites can use for building and enhancing their authenticity.

In this vein, this study fills in this gap by proposing and analysing a framework that can be used for building and evaluating online authenticity. The framework is based on a visitor-centred learning experience philosophy, which in turn is adopted from a constructivist-collaborative educational perspective. Although this philosophy has already been applied for both theorizing and creating examples of participatory and collaborative museum websites (Friedlander, 1998; Teather, 1998), as well as for evaluating the online learning and meaning-making experiences of visitors to museum websites (Teather and Wilhelm, 1999), the value of these emerging ideas for building authentic online heritage experiences has not been explored. However, the importance of creating meaning-making visitor experiences for enhancing online authenticity is nowadays highlighted not only in the heritage but also in the technological literature. Therefore, this study first analyses the concept of authenticity and the role of meaning-making visitor experiences in building authenticity (from both a heritage and a technological perspective), then explores the implications of these premises on the creation of authentic online heritage experiences. A framework for identifying and evaluating website features and functionalities that enhance and create authentic heritage experiences is presented, while its practical implications are illustrated by several examples and the case study of eternalegypt.com. Finally, the practical and theoretical implications of the study are presented.

In search of authenticity: the role of meaning-making experiences

Authenticity, or at least the perception of it, is an important attribute (Cohen, 1988; Boniface and Fowler, 1993; Waitt, 2000) as well as a determining factor in the quality of heritage tourism (see literature review by Chhabra et al., 2003). The concept of authenticity has gone through a long tourism and heritage academic debate that started in the early eighteenth century (Burnett, 2001). However, although much debate still centres on the claims of authenticity associated with historical objects, the move towards heritage as an opportunity to view the past through narratives and thematic portrayals of experiences has been predicated on the trend towards 'witnessing' the past through engagement and experience at the heritage attraction (Burnett, 2001). So, perspectives have varied from those of Boorstein (1964), who saw tourists as being duped and seduced to visit contrived attractions, through MacCannell (1976), who viewed tourists as modern pilgrims in search of the authentic, and Wang (1999), who argued the existence of different authenticity types, to Cohen (1988), who suggested that authenticity is socially constructed and so has different importance to different market segments.

Analytically, MacCannell (1976) assessed the authenticity of cultural and heritage tourism products depending on whether they are made or enacted by local people according to tradition. Taylor (2001, p. 33) also equated authenticity with originality, claiming that tourism sites, objects, images and even people are not viewed simply as contemporaneous productions, but rather as signifiers of past events, epochs or ways of life. In this vein, authenticity is constructed on a reproduced act of something genuine (Zerubavel, 1995) and it connotes traditional origin and culture. However, nowadays (Chhabra et al., 2003) authenticity pays homage to the 'original' concept.

Cohen (1988) has questioned MacCannell's and Boorstein's views of authenticity by arguing that authenticity is not a 'known entity' but rather a 'negotiated concept' that is open to change, and an outcome of the relationship between tourists and their consumption of cultures and environments. In other words, what one views as authentic or what one would like to be authentic depends on social and cultural norms, the role of history, experts and tastes (Tunbridge and Ashworth, 1996, pp. 10–11). Thus, authenticity is viewed as a social process that is created and is open to change through time and space. The fact that authenticity is open to various interpretations and that visitors' experience is crucial for it, is crucial to this study as it shows that: (1) the different types of heritage website visitors (e.g. curators, cultural experts and tourists) as well as the website developers may hold different expectations regarding authenticity; and (2) authenticity is a socially, collaboratively negotiated and constructed concept. Both facts are consistent with and support the constructivism model of online visitors' learning experiences that will be later proposed as a tool for building online authenticity.

By re-highlighting the centrality of nostalgia as a motivation for experiencing heritage tourism (e.g. MacCannell, 1979; Ashworth, 1992), Chhabra et al. (2003) revealed the importance of the process of sharing feelings, surviving memories, artefacts and sites of the past for creating perceived authenticity and enhancing tourists' satisfaction from heritage tourism products. It was indeed this perceived authenticity, defined as 'consistency with nostalgia for some real or imaged past', and not authenticity in the literal sense of whether or not it is an accurate re-creation of some past condition, that actually enhanced tourists' perceptions about the authenticity and quality of heritage products (Chhabra et al., 2003).

The importance of the visitors' learning experience for creating authenticity is also advocated by Ang (1985), who argued that key to a visitor authentic experience is an 'emotional realism' referring to the way in which the heritage site may engage visitors on an emotional and imaginary level, and engender feelings that are meaningful and 'real'. In his studies,

Bagnall (2003) found that this notion of authenticity is related as much to the context of everyday life as to notions of high culture. Specifically, visitors require that the heritage sites generate emotional authentic responses that foster them to share personal and cultural biographies and life histories, as well as relate the latter to the narratives and interpretation of the site. This was because these learning and exchange processes made visitors feel that they were really consuming the past, or obtaining a good idea of what life was like in the past.

Overall, it becomes evident that the authenticity debate has moved its focus from the heritage-cultural products and their creators, and it is now centred on the perceived experiences of their visitors and audiences. This may not be surprising when considering that the definition of heritage tourism itself has changed from a perspective of sociocultural assets and products to an approach centred on visitors' motivation and perceptions. (For a discussion on the definition of heritage tourism see Chhabra et al., 2003.)

In the technological domain, the debate on the authenticity of digital objects is also centred on the concept of the visitors' learning experiences and their internalization of the meaning of the past. A group of experts (CLIR, 2000) has concluded that a digital object can be authenticated in at least two senses:

First, a user should be able to determine the object's origins, structure, and development history. Second, a user should be able to determine that the object is what it purports to be.

In other words, the authenticity of online objects can be perceived as a continuum with two extremes. At one end lie the nature and origin of the digital object and the quality of the digital reconstruction, and at the other end the visitors' perceived learning dimension regarding the use and meaning of the original heritage-cultural object. Overall, computer scientists have widely identified a hierarchy of digital objects to which online authenticity should be applied: data, documents, sensory presentations and (interactive) experiential works. As one moves up the hierarchy, from data to experiential works, the questions about the authenticity of the digital objects become more complex and subjective, as it addresses experience rather than documentary content (Lynch, 2000). This is because of the following arguments.

As digital objects are defined by a set of sequences of bits, a computational notion of authenticity would aim to establish whether the digital object in one's possession is the same as that which some entity published under a specific identifier at a specific point in time. At this level, digital authenticity is related to the integrity of digital objects (i.e. that digital objects have not been corrupted over time or transit), which in turn can be guaranteed and built by the use of digital tools such as Public Key Infrastructure and digital signatures, as well as digital features that indicate the quality of the digitization process of the original object (i.e. number of pixels, colours of the original reflected in the digital object, etc.). However, bits are not directly appreciated by human sensory apparatus, but rather they are rendered, executed, performed and presented to people through hardware and software systems that interpret them. For example, differences in monitors can significantly alter the way things appear, even though monitors display the same bit stream. The quest for authenticity is so transformed to a question of the sophistication of hardware and software systems to understand the bits. Documentary objects are primarily characterized by their bits, but the craft of Internet publishing begins to make a sensory presentation of this collection of bits to turn content into experience. Text displayed through a web browser takes on a sensory dimension, as the words that make up the text being rendered no longer tell the whole story. Digital objects that are performed, e.g. music, video and images that are rendered on screen, incorporate a stronger component. Issues of interaction with the human sensory system, e.g. psychoacoustics, quality of reproduction and visual artefacts, become more important. The bits may be the same across space and time, but because of these differences the experience of viewing may be different. In the most extreme case, experientially rendered digital objects such as virtual reality and simulations, the focus shifts to the behaviour of and interaction among the rendering system, the digital object and the user. Therefore, authenticity of digital objects is not only a simple question of the fixed set of properties of the digital file, but rather a sociotechnically and experientially blended concept constructed by the interaction of human and technology tools in a given space and time (Lynch, 2000).

Meaning-making heritage-cultural websites: a tool for building online authenticity

Given the importance of the socially constructed, meaning-making process of the past to the concept of authenticity, Morrissey and Worts (1998) advocated that on the Internet the importance is to place technology in the service of understanding and enhancing the human experience. Thus, they warn against museums that provide more online information and instead advocate uses of technology that facilitate meaning making. The challenge then is to understand how technology can illuminate and enhance the complex relationships between people and objects. At its best technology can facilitate experiences in which visitors can both transcend and live more fully their daily lives, thoughts and activities. Technology should also be used for challenging people to consider or create new meanings, to see their experiences in a context that connects them to other people, places and times. Thus, heritage operators should exploit Internet tools and create webpages that stimulate emotional responses and foster the sharing of experiences, which in turn can construct an 'emotional realism' and a socially constructed personal authenticity.

In this vein, Hein (1999) has reviewed several educational theories (Kolb, Gardner, Myers and Briggs), each with its own epistemology and learning theory, and synthesized them in such a way that assists the development of museum websites that facilitate and encourage multiple voices and the exchange process of stories, both outside and inside the institution and between staff and visitors. Moreover, his model advocates that on the Internet the aim of museums is to present their meaning in a manner that focuses on visitors, their knowledge and meaning-making processes, which in turn are built on experiences and understanding. Consequently, his model was adapted for developing and identifying the website features and functionalities that enable the construction and enhancement of a socially constructed personal authenticity. Although Hein's model was not developed for assessing online authenticity, its value in evaluating visitors' experiences and satisfaction of museum websites, as well as in supporting online free-choice learning and museum meaning-making experiences, is already advocated in the literature (Dierking and Falk, 1998; Teather and Wilhelm, 1999).

Hein's model of museum website visitor experience is presented in Figure 14.1. The model identifies four types of learning that are parallel to the museum education online experience. The model consists of two axes that move from objective information to subjective knowledge, and from knowledge to meaning that is negotiated between the museum and the visitor. At the heart of this model is the presentation of museum information from a self-reflective perspective that attempts to situate information in the context of the institution's nature, strengths and weaknesses. The message is then formed not as a declaration but as an argument, and contains complexity and layers that invite visitors to weigh their own view against that of the museum. In other words, museum webpages should not promote and reflect an objective authenticity,

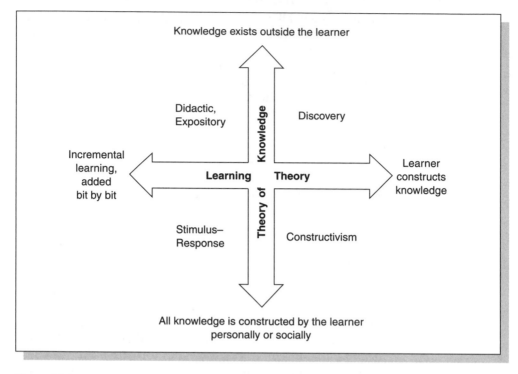

Figure 14.1
Hein's summary of approaches to learning in the educational literature

but rather provide the technological tools that can facilitate the construction of a socially negotiated and collaborative learning-based authenticity.

Practical implications of Hein's model: the case of eternalegypt.org

The top-left quadrant reflects the didactic, expository education of the traditional authoritarian 'school' environment and of the 'teacher' mode of communication. Museum webpages that emerge from the didactic approach are sequential and based on an integrated order with a single correct navigation path, beginning and end. Didactic webpages describe what is to be learnt from the web presentation, as the content of the webpages implies that what the webpages are providing represents a single authoritarian 'truth'. The stimulus–response mode, rooted in early behaviourist work, is similar to the didactic, expository approach, except that it makes no claim for the scientific or objective truth of teaching. Hein (1999) argued that few museums would admit that they follow such an educational approach, even if this was the underlying message. Discovery learning shifts the focus from the teacher to the learner, or the visitor. Active learning involves the learner in hands-on, interactive experiences, and has been adopted as an approach by children's museums, discovery galleries and science museums (Hein, 1999). However, in the top-right quadrant, Hein (1999) presented a particular type of discovery learning, one that arrives at a single 'truth' through 'learning by doing'.

In constructivism, the learner is actively involved both in the way their mind is engaged and in determining the nature of knowledge. Social constructivists look to the setting outside the individual that impacts on their reading of meaning: politics, economics and social phenomena. Radical constructivists also posit that knowledge exists only in the mind of the learner, so that the validity of the ideas (or authenticity) is evaluated not by an objective truth (i.e. an authenticity centred on the heritage product or technological features), but by their position within the constructed reality of the learner. In either case, the situation of the learner, whether defined within their singular mental functions or as affected by broader social phenomenon, drives a visitor-centred model of learning and so of the socially and visitor constructed/negotiated authentic experience. These arguments are also consistent and surround the arguments of post-modernism regarding visitors' heritage authentic experiences that link 'active' modes of consumption with 'thoughtfulness' and 'learning', and 'passive' modes with 'fun' and whatever may be implied to be in binary opposition to 'learned' (Voase, 2003). However, the concepts of passive and active have received much criticism, and they also have several operationalization limitations (Voase, 2003). In contrast, the dimensions of the learning and knowledge theories seem to reflect better the arguments of post-modernism that require the cognitive rather than the physical engagement of the heritage-cultural visitor, as well as the subjective, socially constructed and visitor-centred, rather than the objective product-centred authentic experience.

The constructive museum website would invite visitors to construct their own knowledge and meaning. It would use a wide range of active learning approaches, present a wide range of points of view by different 'experts' and provide many entry points, with no specific path and no identified beginning and end. Such a website would enable visitors to connect with objects and ideas through a range of activities and experiences that involve their life experiences. Some websites have entered or even extended this quadrant by fostering visitor participation in the construction not only of the narratives about what they see, but in what they see, in the very nature of the museum, not just of their experience. They invite the participant into the selection of object or event and in layering their meaning with that provided by the site and by other visitors' records of their views.

The website http://himelacn.org/LACN is an important example as its emphasis is on 'people's understanding and participation in their community through culture' through the Internet. The mode of relating to the content is participatory and collaborative among the cultural and educational organizations and individuals. Castle Toller in Upper Austria (http://fgidec1.tuwien.acat/1002situations/) provides an idea of visitor meaning-making within the frame of ecomuseology on the Internet. Two artists, Michele Kolnicker and Michael Kiselinger, created the Heimat Museum, a virtual museum, to gather ideas and images of 'heimat', 'home' or 'homeland' in German, through the topics of childhood, community, food, language, living-spaces, surrounding, things and school. Although the origins of the project lay in the idea of preparing a display of web-originated stories in the castle for a regional festival in 1994, the website continues as visitors to the site add stories, memories and images to reflect their idea of 'heimat'.

Overall, Teather and Wilhelm (1999) argue that museum websites that embody constructivism principles provide opportunities for their visitors to engage with museum or content in three layers:

1. The nature of the museum object or collection, and its relationship to ideas, experience and personal meaning
2. The institutional and societal context in which the museum operates
3. The personal meaning brought to the museum by the visitor, and its role in the museum experience.

Overall, although the first generation of online heritage websites was typified by a stories/thematic solution to narrative formation as well as searching interfaces, the next generation heritage website should be transformed to a knowledge website that would move towards tailored but also more adaptive responses to different usage situations and visitors. Thus, to enhance the authenticity of the online experiences, heritage websites should rethink the collections, structure, classification, presentation and navigation of their heritage objects as well as their online interpretive, i.e. meaning-making, processes. Table 14.1 summarizes different website features and functionalities that heritage websites can exploit for enabling the construction of constructivism-collaborative online authenticity. These features relate to the information, navigation, interaction and presentation design of websites.

Based on Table 14.1, Table 14.2 presents and analyses the website features of eternalegypt.org. Online visitors can follow tours established by the museum or browse among the museum artefacts in a less structured way: by individual artefact, by time, by sites and museums, by collections, by map, by topic or by taking individual recommendations from the museum (Figure 14.2). However, all search features are interconnected through a type of a mind map (the connections) that allows online visitors to navigate the website in multiple and interrelated ways. At the heart of the Eternal Egypt project is a Content Management System that is a story-making machine, a tool for weaving images, multimedia and information about people, places and objects into narratives. This is accomplished by treating individual content 'elements' such as artefacts or biographical information as the building blocks of larger narrative 'modules', which can be grouped into stories. Reusable and recombinant, these modules enable extreme flexibility in the on-demand creation of meaningful content for Eternal Egypt. Overall, eternalegypt.org tends to create constructivism online experiences, since it provides several tools with which visitors can develop and follow their own online experience and create their own heritage meaning. Consequently, the website allows the development of personalized tours and navigations; however, eternalegypt.org can further use several other features, as discussed in Table 14.1, to enhance its online authenticity according to a post-modern perspective.

Conclusion

Although the concept of authenticity has undergone much debate in the offline heritage field, in the online world authenticity is still an unexplored issue. Thus, this study aimed to investigate the concept and the dimensions of online authenticity. To achieve this, a review of authenticity within both the technological and the heritage literature was conducted, and revealed the importance of meaning-making visitor learning experiences. Consequently, by adapting and using learning theories the study developed a framework for identifying and assessing website features and functionalities that can be used

Table 14.1 Website features and functionalities supporting and fostering constructivism, post-modern online authenticity

Website feature and functionality	Meaning/significance and further applications	Examples
Providing to online visitors the possibility to create alternative pathways through collections of information while posing greater contextual possibilities around objects through the inclusion of additional multimedia and text-based information	• Empowers the user to create pathways through new organizations of information, thereby contributing to the development of the knowledge environment • Predetermined thematic tours or collection descriptions showing highlights of the collections should be followed up by an advanced search using keywords and a browser to further mine data • Provision of information in various forms to suit the conceptual maps of a range of users, such as timeline/chronologies and information hierarchies by theme and subtheme, as well as more innovative mindmaps for visually connecting objects, ideas, metaphors and related themes, and for offering an engaging, interactive experience	EMP Digital Collections (Experience Music Project, http://www.emplive.com), HyperMuseum (http://www. HyperMuseum.com), History Wired (Smithsonian National Museum of American History, http://historywired.si.edu/index.html)
Exploiting the associative and hyperlinking abilities of the technology in the creation of object-centred histories that allow for the layering and exploration of the multiple meanings and contexts of selected objects	• This method can present and deconstruct the documentation/interpretation process as a post-structuralist, post-modernist text. It invites the user to explore collections in more depth while allowing self-guided interpretations • Provision of links to webpages outside the website of the organization	Revealing Things (http://www.si.edu/revealingthings/)
Enriching information content and multimedia capabilities as well as enabling the online exchange of different voices and views	• Juxtaposition of subject, provision of disciplinary/cultural multiple perspectives and contexts, and information on the use and manufacture of objects and visualizations showing their creation histories	

Improved research capabilities through more intelligent searching, browsing mechanisms and possibilities to devise combinations and to mine data

- Use of first person voices and quotes, significance statements, curatorial/expert opinions, artists' comments and primary source material with supporting documents, images, audiovisual information, sound bytes and bibliographic information
- Allows users to put up their own interpretations of this material; supports a constructivist approach to learning, but can also be a threat to curatorial authority
- By exposing the nature of museums' significance and disciplinary/museum assessment procedures through links to policies and curatorial essays, it contributes to the users' understanding of how meaning and value is formulated within the museum context
- Use of multiples and multimedia versions of information presentation and prompts to highlight significant points offers a greater understanding of an object's form through multiple views and its function: zoomable thumbnail images, 3D objects, object movies
- Multiple keyword searches with the use of thesauri (by subject, function and classification) and with mechanisms that suggest search terms, give phonetic spellings and make typological corrections
- Development of a range of logical search schemata, e.g. structured searching, intuitive browsing mechanisms and navigational tools, e.g. well-indexed subject searches and personalization/theming search engines connected to a theme generator function

Hypermuseum model (http://www.HyperMuseum.com)

Table 14.1 *(Continued)*

Website feature and functionality	Meaning/significance and further applications	Examples
	• Advanced searching across databases and comparison of related search results using the indexing of metadata or an existing metadata index • Collection of statements connected to a hyperbolic tree or site map	
Personalization options and other collaborative e-commerce options	• Collaborative filtering and information search. Enables a visitor to find information based on other visitors' suggestions, visitors' previous website browsing history or collaborative filtering Internet technologies and cookies • Mechanisms to elicit responses to search results and collect information from users • Personalization could potentially be achieved through user/task profiles and the future use of searching agents to define profile, mood and required experience	Amazon.com visitors are advised and informed on relative books based on other visitors' comments as well as automatically based on collaborative filtering technologies that compare visitors' online behaviour to previous users' online behaviour and information search

Table 14.2 Website features and functionalities of eternalegypt.org

Tool/functionality	Current features
Providing to visitors the possibility to create alternative pathways	A selection of different website navigation tools such as: ● Connections navigator is a visual tool that was developed to help visitors gain a greater understanding of the relationships among artefacts, characters and places ● *Timeline Highlights* lists artefacts, characters and places of particular interest in the development of Egyptian civilization ● The Topics section offers a structured, hierarchical view of the concepts that make up Egyptian culture ● The Library contains a variety of articles, some of which have been grouped into collections of articles. Library articles and collections of articles describe how individual artefacts, characters and places are interrelated within a theme ● The Sites and Museums page lists museums throughout Egypt that house notable collections of artefacts, many of which are featured on Eternal Egypt. Important archaeological locations are also described here. You can click any link to learn more about a specific site or museum ● The Collection of Articles displays short introductions to each of the articles contained within ● The *Contents* section enables visitors to see an outline of all the articles, artefacts, characters and places that are part of this Collection of Articles. The *Contents* section displays a plus sign next to each article, which expands when you click on it to reveal several related items
Exploiting the associative and hyperlinking abilities	● Connections navigator ● Each cultural-heritage item is linked with the following list of its related characteristics: 　○ *Attributes*: lists physical characteristics 　○ *Type*: lists the category 　○ *Map*: displays key locations 　○ *Timeline*: gives important dates 　○ *Topics*: links to subject overviews 　○ *Sites and Museums*: provides a link to relevant sites or museums 　○ *Connections*: displays related artefacts, characters and places ● Previous, next and home buttons

Table 14.2 *(Continued)*

Tool/functionality	Current features
Enriching information content; multimedia capabilities; enabling the online exchange of different voices and views	• *Contact Us* lets visitors contact the Eternal Egypt team • *Send e-mail online items to friends* • *Text Version* removes the site's graphics for a text-only format that is more accessible for screen readers and slower connections • *About Eternal Egypt* explains how Eternal Egypt was created through a partnership between IBM and the Egyptian Government. It also includes information about the innovative technologies featured on this site, e.g. the digital guide for mobile access • *Image acquisition* and *Content creation* webpages explain the process of object digitization • Multimedia information of objects, including virtual environments, 3D pictures, 360-degree views, animations, webcams and zoomable pictures • Animations of complex topics supplement the textual descriptions and images • *Virtual environments* have been created to show places as they once were or to illustrate the evolution of locations over time in elaborate 3D. These environments, e.g. for the Giza Plateau, Luxor Temple, ancient Alexandria and the tomb of King Tutankhamun, are composed of dozens of panoramic views from virtual vantage points, views no longer available in contemporary Egypt • *Digital 3D models* are offered through the website, but more importantly, the virtual model can be manipulated to generate representations that cannot be created by other means. For example, the model can be virtually restored, replacing missing parts or bringing faded colours back to life. It can be immersed in a reconstructed environment or included in an animation to show its use. Examples of virtual restoration and animations based on 3D models are present in the Eternal Egypt website
Improved search capabilities	• *Search* lets visitors search the entire site using keywords and characteristics • *Glossary* provides an alphabetical listing of unfamiliar terms • *Help* will assist visitors with a particular task or to learn about the site in greater detail • Search by Map of Egypt based on location, by artefacts, character or place, by the Timeline Navigator, by highlights, articles, library and other themes/categories

Table 14.2 *(Continued)*

Tool/functionality	Current features
Personalization options and other collaborative e-commerce options	• *My Visit* creates a record of each page a user has visited for the entire browser session. By Clicking on *My Visit* visitors can review their tour of Eternal Egypt or return more easily to a page that they found interesting • As visitors explore the Eternal Egypt site, they can create their own virtual collection by saving their popular artefacts, characters, places and articles in My Collection, which can also be accessed using a mobile device, e.g. an Internet-enabled phone • *My Collection* can be retrieved from the website on the mobile device, effectively pre-creating a customized tour for access at the historical site. • The Digital Guide keeps a log of the artefacts, characters and places that the museum visitor has selected or encountered with the Digital Guide. So, a visitor can print a personalized record of his or her tour of artefacts. This custom catalogue can act as an ultimate personalized souvenir of a user's visit

for building different types of online authenticity. Overall, a post-modern, constructivism approach to authenticity requires the exploitation of the search, navigation, multimedia presentations and personalization features of Internet technologies for allowing online visitors to create their own personalized authentic experiences. However, the application of such features implies a reconceptualization of traditional museum models and website practices that are challenging the conventional role of curators, visitors and museums. Rethinking the nature and the ways of developing online meaning-making heritage experiences also provides new insights into key areas for change in museum policy, practice, knowledge creation and management. Finally, future research may further investigate how different factors such as culture, socioeconomic profile of a country, and type and ownership structure of heritage institution, may impact on heritage actors' decisions to apply Internet tools and change their models and roles.

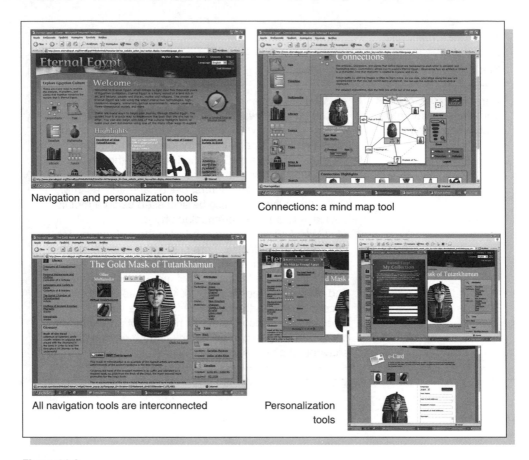

Figure 14.2
Websites features and functionalities of eternalegypt.org

References

Ang, I. (1985). *Watching Dallas: Soap Opera and the Metropolitan Imagination*. London: Methuen.

Ashworth, G. (1992). Heritage tourism: an argument, two problems, and three solutions. In Fleischer van (ed.) *Spatial Implications of Tourism*. Groningen: Gep Pars.

Bagnall, G. (2003). Performance and perfomativity at heritage sites. *Museum and Society* 1(2): 87–103.

Boniface, P. and Fowler, P. (1993). *Heritage Tourism in Global Village*. Sage: London.

Boorstein, O. J. (1964). *The Image: A Guide to Pseudo-events in America*. New York: Harper and Row.

Burnett, K. (2001). Heritage, authenticity and history. In Drummond, S. and Yeoman, I. (eds) *Quality Issues in Heritage*

Visitor Attractions. Oxford: Butterworth Heinemann, pp. 39–53.

Chhabra, D., Healy, R. and Sills, E. (2003). Staged authenticity and heritage tourism. *Annals of Tourism Research* 30: 702–719.

CLIR (2000). Authenticity in a digital environment. Report of a group of experts convened by CLIR to address the question: what is authentic digital object? Available at http://clir.org/pubs/reports/pub92/contents.html (Accessed 18 February 2004).

Cohen, E. (1988). Traditions on the qualitative sociology of tourism. *Annals of Tourism Research* 15: 29–46.

Dierking, L. and Falk, J. (1998). Understanding free-choice learning. A review of the research and its application to museum websites. *Museums and the Web98 Papers. Archives and Museum Informatics*. Available at: http://www.archimuse.com/

Friedlander, L. (1998). Models for a new visitor-centered museum: using the web to create community and continuity for the museum visitor. *Museums and the Web98 Papers. Archives and Museum Informatics*. Available at: http://www.archimuse.com/mw98/papers/

Hein, G. (1999). Learning approaches for evaluating museum websites. In Teather, L. and Wilhelm, K. (eds) *Web Musing: Evaluating Museums on the Web from Learning Theory to Methodology. Museums and the Web99 Papers. Archives and Museum Informatics*. Available at: http://www.archimuse.com/

Lynch, C. (2000). Experiential documents and the technologies of remembrance. In Scammell, A. (ed.) *I in the Sky: Visions of the Information Future*. London: Library Association Publishing.

MacCannell, D. (1976). *The Tourist: A New Theory of the Leisure Class*. Shocken.

Morrisey, K. and Worts, D. (1998). A place for the muses? Negotiating the role of media in museums. In Thomas, S. and Mintz, A. (eds) *The Virtual and the Real: Media in Museums*. Washington, DC: AAM, pp. 147–172.

Sigala, M. (2003). Internet heritage and cultural tourism under virtual construction: implications for online visitors' experiences and interpretation management. *Tourism Today* (3): 51–67.

Taylor, J. (2001). Authenticity and sincerity in tourism. *Annals of Tourism Research* 28: 7–26.

Teather, L. (1998). A museum is a museum is a museum … or is it?: Exploring museology and the web. *Museums and the Web98 Papers. Archives and Museum Informatics*. Available at: http://www.archimuse.com/mw98/papers

Teather, L. and Wilhelm, K. (1999). Web musing: evaluating museums on the Web from learning theory to methodology. *Museums and the Web99 Papers. Archives and Museum Informatics*. Available at: http://www.archimuse.com/

Turnbridge, J. E. and Ashworth, G. E. (1996). *Dissonant Heritage: The Management of the Past as a Resource of Conflict*. New York: Wiley.

Voase, R. (2003). Rediscovering the imagination: meeting the needs of the new visitor. In Fyall, A., Garrod, B. and Leask, A. (eds) *Managing Visitor Attractions: New Directions*. Oxford: Butterworth Heinemann, pp. 254–269.

Waitt, G. (2000). Consuming heritage. Perceived historical authenticity. *Annals of Tourism Research* 27: 835–849.

Wang, N. (1999). Rethinking authenticity in tourism experience. *Annals of Tourism Research* 26: 349–370.

Xie, P. and Wall, G. (2003). Authenticating visitor attractions based upon ethnicity. In Fyall, A., Garrod, B. and Leask, A. (eds) *Managing Visitor Attractions: New Directions*. Oxford: Butterworth Heinemann, pp. 107–123.

Zerubavel, Y. (1995). Recovered Roots. Chicago, IL: University of Chicago Press.

Websites

Archives and Museums Informatics: www.archimuse.com
DigiCULT website: www.cordis.lu/digicult
www.heritagesfutures.net
http://www.icom.museum/
http://www.museophile.com/
www.virtualshowcases.com
http://minervaisrael.org.il/

CHAPTER 15

Intelligent information interactions for cultural tourism destinations

Stavros Christodoulakis,
Fotis Kazasis, George Anestis
and Nektarios Moumoutzis

Learning outcomes

- Discuss the functionalities of a virtual community-based information system.
- Analyse how a virtual community-based information system can support the communication between tourists and local people at cultural tourism destinations.
- Explore the benefits and advantages of a community-based information system for tourists, local people and community-based tourism development planning.
- Illustrate the practical implications of such a system through the case study of Campiello system in Chania, Greece.

Introduction

The proliferation of the worldwide web over the past few years led companies and organizations to try to exploit the web for e-commerce activities. Tourism is one of the most important applications of e-commerce. Several major tourism actors, but also newcomers (mainly information technology companies), have an established web presence. Their websites, visited by many thousands of visitors every day, offer e-commerce opportunities for business-to-business transactions or business-to-customer (tourist) transactions. One particular class of tourism applications in the web is destination information systems (DIS) or destination management systems (DMS) (Christodoulakis et al., 1996, 1997; Werthner and Klein, 1999). These systems typically provide, on the web, information about the tourism offerings of a given destination and may promote e-commerce activities to the potential visitor. The existing DMS, however, do not support advanced models of interaction between tourists (or prospective tourists) of a destination, or interaction between tourists and local people. This is an essential functionality, especially for cultural tourism destinations, to improve online interpretation services and ensure website 'stickiness', e-service quality and online visitor satisfaction (Sigala, 2003).

This chapter describes a system with a robust set of functionalities based on the virtual community concept that provide intelligent information interactions for cultural tourism destinations. These functionalities aim to support the communication between tourists and local people at cultural tourism destinations and can be implemented either as an independent system or as expansions to existing DMS. In this way, information technology can be effectively used to enhance the promotion, engagement and interpretation of cultural sites, and create the baseline for a community tourism planning where local stake-holders will recognize the high degree of interdependencies in planning and managing the tourism domain and promote their common interests.

Background and problem identification

Information systems that support interactions of a virtual community over the web are usually called community-based information systems (CIS). Existing Internet CIS focus on fostering social objectives such as building community cohesion, enhancing community awareness in local decision making, developing economic opportunities in disadvantaged communities, and enhanced training (Schuler, 1994, 1996). Some of them have thousands of users, who also repeatedly visit the community site. However, as existing support for CIS is of general purpose, CIS cannot be easily adopted for advanced functionality for tourism-related communities.

It is argued that it is very important for both tourists and destinations to support advanced information models enabling and enhancing the interaction between tourists and local people at a particular destination, thus reducing the 'community gap'. Major advantages of these systems to both tourists and destinations are detailed below.

First, visitors should be offered tourism destination information with unbiased evaluation. In a CIS, community members such as visitors may provide evaluation information about a site of interest or a service organization (hotel, etc.). Such information may be more trustworthy to other visitors than recommendations given by a destination organization or a travel agent. Sometimes this community-based evaluation information is convenient even for DMS organizations, which may not want to offer their own evaluation (or recommendations) to avoid potential conflicts with partner organizations at destinations. It may also be convenient for the regional administrations, which may be interested in having objective quality of service information delivered to visitors to increase competitiveness of the tourism offerings at the destination, but do not want to be directly involved in such an evaluation.

For prospective visitors with a desire for greater flexibility in their trip planning, contact with a tourism community at the destination offers the advantages of increased security in their planning, as they can not only access evaluations provided by other tourists, but also seek information directly from community members at the destination by asking them specific questions.

Indeed, two-way real interactions should be supported, since it is a great misconception of today's system builders that any information system, no matter how large its databases, can satisfy all potential visitors' questions about the destination offerings.

Another advantage of CIS is the great potential that they create for repeat visits. This is due not only to their better information quality and reliability, but also to the increased opportunities that they offer for human connections between tourists and local people, and the emotional attachment that they carry. Established contacts during the visit may also become trustworthy sources of information and evaluation, creating further security for future visits.

From a region management perspective, virtual communities can promote regional policies such as branding. This can be done, for example, by promoting the creation of specific types of tourism subcommunity with specific interests. From the perspective of prospective tourists, virtual communities can enable the development of collective agreements between potential visitors and local or international companies. By initiating a discussion forum regarding a visit at a specific time and with specific interests, a group of potential visitors may be found which in turn may be in a better position to negotiate collectively better services and rates with destination organizations. Thus, the proposed approach can enhance co-ordination and cohesion within the highly fragmented tourism industry by supporting community-based tourism planning (Jamal and Getz, 1995). A destination community's assets and resources, such as infrastructure, recreational facilities and cultural heritage, can thus be effectively shared by its inhabitants, tourists, public and private sector interests. Tourism development can be managed as a public good whose benefit may be shared by the numerous stakeholders in the local destination. The views of different stakeholders may be shared, and a common understanding and consensus can be reached, thus facilitating the formation and implementation of tourism policies.

A new approach to promote cultural tourism destinations

The major goal of the proposed system is to develop an alternative, quality-based tourism support system through the environmental and cultural characteristics of an area, the anthropocentric perspective and the various local communities, and to promote the concept of 'tourism equals hospitality'.

The approach (Kazasis et al., 2003) may be viewed as a system diffused in the territory to facilitate and support the exchange of information between different communities in a local, physical environment (such as a destination, an area of interest or a visitor attraction) with the aim of building a dynamic shared knowledge base accessed by tourists and local people.

The system presented makes a very practical and illustrative contribution to how information and communication technologies can enhance interpretation, navigational and curator services for a cultural destination (e.g. Chania, Crete, and Venice, Italy). This is achieved mainly be creating collaborative environments and increasing the contextuality of the cultural sites to stimulate mindful experiences for tourists (Sigala, 2003). Specifically, the system supports multimedia presentations enabling personalized experiences and interpretation, navigation and search tools including detailed maps of the territory, virtual community services and tools, as well as online and offline interaction tools. The overall functionality is based on a sophisticated knowledge base that provides the means to handle all kinds of information flow.

Information management strategies

The approach followed is based on an interaction model that maps digital information over physical spaces. The users can access the system through a variety of interfaces, both innovative and conventional (personal computer, web access, public kiosks, etc.). Examples of some of the most innovative interfaces are the outcomes of the research and development in the Campiello project: paper-based interfaces (giving interactive access to the system through conventional paper, in various graphic and narrative formats), large public screens (allowing interactive access to the system by a group of persons) and mobile communication devices.

The system's maintenance model is based on the concept of reward: the more the users upload 'valuable' information, the more the system gives access to 'valuable' information. This model also supports a distinction between 'public' information, which circulates freely within the system and becomes a public resource, and 'private' information, which is circulated in the system but is only made available as a 'travel diary' to some users. Both types of information contribute to the creation of a shared knowledge (information plus personal experiences) that is based on a combination of 'cold' data (the basic functional information) and 'warm' data (the description of the experience of the community of users and information about local cultural events).

205

The information model is mostly based on the concept of 'push information': information is mostly circulated with the model of push media (edited information is proposed to users according to their profile and to their physical location), but the system stimulates users' reaction in the form of annotation (comments, ratings and further contributions attached to the core piece of information). This annotated information is recirculated within the system, giving origin to an exponential growth (with over-annotated information also progressively moving from cold data to warm data).

The social model of the approach allows different roles for users and professional editors: anybody can assume roles ranging from passive use (simply retrieving information), through active contributors (information given and retrieved), to cultural managers and moderators (available for the editing of information, facilitators and managers of the shared knowledge).

The spatial model of the approach is strongly related to the notion of mapping digital information over material physical spaces (Churchill et al., 2004) and builds various interaction models on this model. However, the system also takes full advantage of the potential of remote communication and participation: access to shared knowledge is given also to remote users. Information is connected to the physical space via distributed interfaces to access content: Space is the main structure to navigate and interact, while mobile and ubiquitous computing is augmented with personalization.

The Campiello system

During the i3 LTR Esprit Project Campiello (http://www.campiello.org) the above model and its implementation were followed by the partners of the project, to develop applications and intelligent interfaces for a variety of devices promoting the tourism product of the cities of Venice and Chania, Crete, to facilitate the creation of connected communities and to connect the members of the communities (local inhabitants, past, present and future tourists, and cultural managers) with local people or tourists.

Special care was taken so that the system's knowledge base would support in a uniform manner diverse community interaction means with completely different characteristics regarding both their computational and presentation capabilities. The partners of the project investigated three new methods of communication between social teams and information repositories (Revised Campiello System, 2000): intelligent paper, community walls and mobile device interfaces. The knowledge base of the system may be accessed by users using their regular home computers, their mobile devices or a community wall. The user interaction models are different for each of the above cases. Nevertheless, Internet remains the linchpin allowing access to the information model from anywhere using various user interfaces.

Intelligent paper technology allows the programming of common paper with a specific behaviour by encoding non-visible information related to the actual content of the paper. Based on this, a user may leave a trace on a paper and the system will recognize it and respond by presenting information that matches the user's personal interests. Two types of application have been implemented: personalized newspapers and travel guides. The former allows personalized news presentation according to the user preferences already known to the system. The user may then comment on or rate a topic and receives the comments and ratings for this topic made by other people of a community with the same interests. The latter creates personal-ized maps according to the user's interests and geographical location, allowing a user to see how other visitors and local people evaluate the sites or the tourist services provided in the area, and to leave his or her own comments or ratings for these.

Community wall technology is based on the use of large interactive screens located in public places where people are gathered and communicate. The information presented is mainly related to warm data (news, comments, ratings, suggestions) provided by various communities, and is dynami-cally refreshed according to various rules such as the information inserted in the system by other sources, the interest shown or the rating of a specific topic.

Mobile devices, combined with Global Positioning System (GPS) technology for identifying location, support the finding of paths of maximum interest to the user and the presentation of multimedia information to a visitor while wandering in a city. Such information includes the history of a building, events relevant to the user's profile, or even a nearby person who shares the same interests.

The environment provided is complemented by the web–user interface, which integrates all of the above function-ality as well as the traditional structuring of tourist 'cold' infor-mation for the destination.

Intelligent interactions scenarios

In ancient Greek cities the *agora* was the place where citizens gathered to meet each other, discuss various topics (e.g. politics and philosophical issues), exchange goods and generally communicate with each other. Nowadays, the concept of the agora is less concrete. Social and economic activities are distributed in various physical and virtual places.

In the Campiello project the paradigm of the agora has been used to conduct a large-scale real-life experiment where the Campiello system is used to facilitate the creation of connected communities in the city of Chania and to connect the members of the communities (local inhabitants, past, present and future tourists, and cultural managers) with local people or tourists. The experiment has ensured the active participation of local inhabitants in the construction of the cultural information, and has supported new and improved connections between the inhabitants and the cultural managers and tourists. The approach followed was to integrate Campiello interfaces with the usual activities of users. From this perspective, Campiello has acted like a parasite that collects information and generates seeds that grow as time passes. This information is then fed back to the users in the form of recommendations, general information, description of places, and so on.

In summary, the experiment included the following three scenarios:

- *'Students describe their own city'*: this scenario addressed the need to create links between local people (students in local schools) in cultural tourism cities (Chania and Venice) and their own city, and to allow them to become active managers of their cultural heritage.
- *'People create and participate in communities'*: this scenario addressed the need to create links between groups of people and to advertise cultural events organized by local communities so that potential tourists, actual tourists or other local people could participate. Students from local schools were invited to share experiences from their everyday life or school activities (e.g. exhibitions of artefacts or school festivals) or to seek advice for school projects.
- *'The Old City of Chania reveals itself'*: this scenario modelled the physical territory as an interface with the information space of Campiello. The nature of the agora was fully supported in this scenario in the following way: a user navigating through the city using a mobile device can obtain information about the buildings and streets that he or she sees, plan a route, see comments or recommendations from other users, and leave his or her own personal comments and recommendations.

User classes and profiles

Three major classes of users were involved in the Chania experiment: local people, tourists (future, current or former tourists) and cultural managers. Emphasis was placed on the establishment of channels for communication between these users. This communication used various devices and was supported by the knowledge base in terms of necessary data describing the preferences of people, user communities and comments on places made by various people.

The Chania experiment handled communication channels that were established between users and the flow of information. Communication channels refer to the services provided to support conversations between users with similar interests present in the same position in space and time in a virtual and/or real space. Information is inserted by experts who use special services. This information is integrated in the Campiello knowledge base, provided that it meets specific requirements. Mediators who make decisions of a social, political or qualitative nature provide these requirements. At the other end of the flow, the users of Campiello receive the information that resides in the system through the most appropriate medium.

The knowledge base

The cornerstone of the approach is its knowledge base, which efficiently supports a rich set of services and diverse interaction means. The information stored in the knowledge base is described by a schema that captures the semantics of objects handled by the system. The schema is divided into five major parts, as presented in Table 15.1, and the services that exploit the knowledge base are described in Table 15.2, grouped into four categories.

Evaluation

The Campiello system was thoroughly tested at a public open event to evaluate the capability of the system to reach its own concept and objectives, as well as to verify the usability of the various technologies of the system and interfaces developed during the project (Figure 15.1). The aims of the feedback collection and the evaluation were:

- *Acceptance of the concept of Campiello*: the evaluation parameters set for the specific objective were: demographic, to analyse the population participating in the event; profiling

Table 15.1   The knowledge base scheme

Items, contexts and persons	Describe the basic modelling abstractions for the description of information items, users (people) and semantic frameworks (contexts). Destination/region/subregion, tourism attractions/sites of interest, service organizations and events are examples of tourism-related concepts modelled by Items. Contexts are used to group items with common semantics or typology. For example, cultural site (e.g. Ancient Kydonia in Chania, Crete) can be associated with the context of Minoan Palace/City, Venetian Construction and Venetian Church. The virtual community of the Archaeologists of Crete is also represented by a context. Visitors, local people and experts (e.g. archaeologists) are described by the concept of persons
Traces	Describe the interaction of users with the system and the mechanisms for recording these actions. Evaluation information (e.g. ratings, comments left by visitors to a tourism attraction) is a specific type of trace
Filters	Describe the mechanisms for expressing user interests. For example, a filter expresses the fact that a visitor is interested in archaeology and specifically Minoan sites and nearby restaurants with traditional dishes
Descriptions	Used to model the content of information items. A historical event (e.g. the Battle of Crete) may have several descriptions in various templates, associated with the living memories of local people, the official reports of organizations or the discussions of the virtual community of historians
Map	Refers to the associations between the information items and their spatial representation. The information for a tourism attraction (e.g. the Archaeological Museum of Heraklion) is indexed on top of map (or maps) and accessed through it. The community of Archaeologists of Crete also has a representation on the map

interests, to analyse the acceptance of the various types of information provided by the system; touristic, to investigate the possibility of Campiello providing tourism services in the future; popular items (e.g. events, places), to locate the most interesting (to the visitors) activities of the local communities; and 'campiellized' parameters (i.e. contact with the local people, acceptance of Campiello, keeping relations with local people), to analyse directly the main ideas of Campiello.

- *Usability of the technology*: the evaluation parameters set for the specific objective were: usability, learnability, aesthetics,

Table 15.2   Knowledge base services

Content creation	These services correspond to functions that manage travel diaries (traces of user actions) and topics of discussion (abstract places where people 'meet' each other with the objective of exchanging information related to the discussion)
Content access	Services related to the management of user profiles (containing demographic data, user interests, filters and traces), information searching and recommendations, and personalization of information. Content access uses and extends traditional collaborative filtering (Shardanand and Maes, 1995; Resnick and Varian, 1997). Personalization is supported via a combination of content-based and collaborative filtering (Anestis, 2001). User profiles are compared to find groups of users with similar interests, called friends. Friends may also be explicitly indicated by the user, or may be found by matching only a part of the profile indicated by the user. To personalize a service for a specific user, the traces of his or her friends are examined and items with high ranks are suggested to him or her. The particular methodology gives a solution to the well-known 'cold start' and 'over-specialization' problems found in traditional collaborative and content-based filtering literature (Babalanovic and Shoham, 1997; Pazzani, 1999)
Communities of people	Services related to virtual communities management. Examples of communities are members of a family, a group of friends, archaeologists in Crete and hotel owners. Communities are used to establish and maintain links between people. Specific roles may be assigned to certain members of each community
Map support	The map services were designed to provide users with online maps, adaptive to user-defined criteria. These criteria apply to the information (Items) to be projected on the maps and may refer to the content itself (contexts, time, etc.) or to spatial attributes. The interface also allows spatial queries to be performed and movement directions to be acquired

how prone the technology is to error, handling, reliability, stability, map usability and content creation.

The main evaluation methods that were adopted were the questionnaires and the logging of user actions when interacting with the Campiello system:

● *Questionnaires*: two types of questionnaire were produced. The first one was about the usability of the technology and

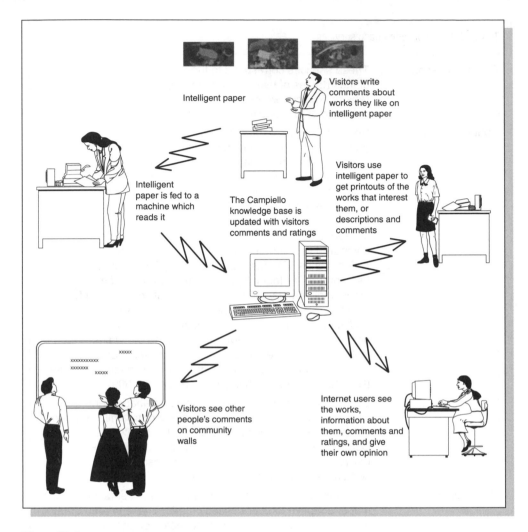

Figure 15.1
The Campiello system during the public open event in Chania, Crete

the second about acceptance of the concept of Campiello. Out of the 1000 questionnaires of the first type that were distributed, 300 were completed. More than 70 per cent of the users evaluated the system for more than ten minutes. Twenty-eight per cent only registered onto the system and visited the introductory pages, 33 per cent spent more time browsing, and 39 per cent tested many of the services offered. More than 4000 questionnaires of the second type were distributed and about 600 completed (15 per cent). More than 50 per cent of the visitors contacted local people and almost 30 per cent expressed their wish to keep in contact with the local people they met. The most interesting result was the wide acceptance of the Campiello concept and the willingness of visitors to use a system like Campiello in the future.

- *Logging user actions*: the system automatically collected statistics and measurements about its use. The basic purpose of this mechanism was to record the users' actions in the system, which were classified into various types. Each user action was recorded in a transparent way through the creation of a trace. The trace types were Rate, Comment, Visualize, Registration, Print and Read e-mail. In addition, the type of interaction device (web, intelligent paper, community wall or mobile device) was recorded for each trace. In this way useful conclusions were extracted regarding the use of each interaction device. During the evaluation process about 5000 traces were recorded in the knowledge base. The number of registered users approached 500.

Conclusions, recommendations and future visions

A new approach to the promotion of tourism attractions has been presented. The approach, starting from DMS functionality, attempts to bridge the community gap (i.e. the lack of any interaction between the content providers and the content consumers) and to provide support for the promotion of a visitor attraction. The approach handles both typical tourism information about an attraction and warm knowledge, related to the experiences of other visitors and local people associated with the attraction.

The major concept of the Campiello system, creating rich social links between people living in or visiting a cultural tourism destination, will play a critical role in marketing and sustainability of cultural tourism attractions in the near future. The successful evaluation of the Campiello concepts ensures that new business models are viable by exploiting existing cultural assets and enriching them with social knowledge that is created by interactions among people.

Recent advances in digital television technologies provide another interesting direction of development of end-user interfaces and services, which is well suited for hotels and the homes of local people and tourists before, during or after the visit to the destination (http://www.up-tv.de/). Taking into account that digital television is a more user friendly medium than traditional computer and web interfaces, and that it represents a wider audience who could receive personalized target advertising, it is a great opportunity for tourism destinations to provide intelligent information interactions and a challenge for existing DMS to reach a broader public through personalized services.

Usage scenarios resembling the scenario 'Students describe their own city' may evolve in an open e-learning environment interconnected with the Campiello system through appropriate interoperability interfaces. In this way, the involvement of organized local groups, e.g. schools, could be ensured in the long run and new types of tourism could be supported, e.g. agrotourism and ecotourism.

The integration of the aforementioned technologies is a big technical challenge. Viable approaches may use service-orientated architectures that allow for the modular design and implementation of independent services, which may then be used to compose more complex services using diverse end-user devices including ubiquitous access to personalized information services (http://www.digital-ecosystem.net/).

Acknowledgement

The Campiello project consortium was comprised of Consorzio Milano Ricerche, Dip. Di Scienze dell' Informazione, Domus Academy, Xerox Research Centre, Grenoble Laboratory, FORTHnet, Municipality of Chania, Technical University of Crete (TUC/MUSIC).

References

Anestis, G. (2001). Designing an information system to support virtual communities of users. Masters Thesis, Department of Electronics and Computer Engineering, Technical University of Crete, Chania.

Babalanovic, M. and Shoham, Y. (1997). Fab: content-based, collaborative recommendation. *Communications of the ACM* 40(3): 66–73.

Christodoulakis, S., Kazasis, F., Moumoutzis, N., Servetas, A. and Petridis, P. (1996). A Software bench for the production of multimedia tourism applications. *Conference Proceedings on Information and Communication Technologies in Tourism.* New York: Springer, pp. 18–28.

Christodoulakis, S., Kontogiannis, P., Petridis, P., Moumoutzis, N., Anastasiadis, M. and Margazas, T. (1997). MINOTAURUS: a distributed multimedia tourism information system. *Conference Proceedings on Information and Communication Technologies in Tourism.* New York: Springer, pp. 295–306.

Christodoulakis, S., Anastasiadis, M., Margazas, T., Moumoutzis, N., Kontogiannis, P., Terezakis, G. and

Tsinaraki, C. (1998). A modular approach to support GIS functionality in tourism applications. *Conference Proceedings on Information and Communication Technologies in Tourism.* New York: Springer, pp. 63–72.

Churchill, E., Girgensohn, A., Nelson, L. and Lee, A. (2004). Blending digital and physical spaces for ubiquitous community participation. *Communications of the ACM* 47(2): 39–44.

Jamal, T. and Getz, D. (1995). Collaboration theory and community tourism planning. *Annals of Tourism Research* 22(1): 186–204.

Kazasis, F. K., Anestis, G., Moumoutzis, N. and Christodoulakis, S. (2003). Intelligent information interactions for tourism destinations. *Conference Proceedings on Information and Communication Technologies in Tourism.* New York: Springer, pp. 1–9.

Pazzani, M. A. (1999). Framework for collaborative, content-based and demographic filtering. *Artificial Intelligence Review* 13: 393–408.

Resnick, P. and Varian, H. R. (1997). Recommender system. *Communications of the ACM* 40(3): 56–58.

Revised Campiello System (2000). Deliverable D3–4.3: EP 25572.

Schuler, D. (1994). Community networks: building a new participatory medium. *Communications of the ACM* 37(1): 39–51.

Schuler, D. (1996). *New Community Networks: Wild for Change.* Reading, MA: ACM Press and Addison-Wesley.

Shardanand, U. and Maes, P. (1995). Social information filtering: algorithms for automating the 'word of mouth'. *Conference Proceedings on Human Factors in Computing Systems*, Denver, CO, pp. 210–217.

Sigala, M. (2003). Internet heritage and cultural tourism under virtual construction: implications for online visitors' experiences and interpretation management. *Tourism Today* (3): 51–67.

Werthner, H. and Klein, S. (1999). *Information Technology and Tourism – A Challenging Relationship.* New York: Springer.

Websites

http://www.campiello.org/
http://www.digital-ecosystem.net/
http://www.up-tv.de/

Destination information, marketing and management systems and sustainable heritage tourism development

Dorothea Papathanasiou-Zuhrt and Odysseas Sakellaridis

> **Learning outcomes**
>
> - Illustrate how destination information, marketing and management systems (DIMMS) can be used for supporting sustainable heritage tourism development by balancing demand and supply needs and trends.
> - Identify and analyse the benefits of DIMMS for tourists and destinations.
> - Debate the benefits of DIMMS for heritage interpretation and discuss the role of interpretation in sustainable heritage tourism development.
> - Demonstrate the applicability of the previous arguments by analysing the usefulness of a DIMMS in the case of Venice.

Introduction

The message character of post-modern society, and awareness of the interpretive nature of human knowledge and instruction, render information technology (IT) as a powerful mechanism to produce, store, interpret, distribute and control messages and messengers, regulating the manifold hierarchies of communications. Tourist destinations need such effective mechanisms to attract their clientele by communicating visitation benefits to them. Tourism planning is hence shifting from sectorial policies and from central to local level, considering all stakeholders. Since unsustainable tourism uses are usually due to information deficiencies between visitors and providers, heavily visited cultural destinations in Europe need to develop smart systems to transform heritage assets into indispensable components of a new tourism product, to provide travel incentives and catalysts for destination attachment, and to connect products, providers and consumers through appropriate information management.

The aims of this study are to demonstrate the problems caused by mass cultural tourism to heritage cities such as Venice, to clarify the reasons and to illustrate how industry-related, enhanced destination information, marketing and management systems (DIMMS) may re-engineer the heritage tourism sector enabling supply and demand to interact within the framework of sustainable development. Statistical evaluations in this study reflect tendencies and are based on data obtained during fieldwork by students who participated at the Socrates Intensive Program (SIP) 'International Experiences in Tourism Planning and Management, Venice 2003', under the co-ordination of Professor Gerda Kearny-Priestley.

217

Tourism uses of heritage assets

Perception and valorization of heritage assets

There is a significant difference between heritage tourists and tourists at heritage places (Poria at al., 2003, p. 238), mainly because heritage places are at the same time multiple attraction poles for cultural and non-cultural activities (Jansen-Verbeke, 1998, pp. 739–742). Undeniably, artefacts per se cannot stimulate travelling, unless potential visitors attribute to them certain values, or signify them with certain meanings. Apart from economic values, heritage assets also possess non-use values, which allow them to enter the tourism market. People value the existence of heritage items even if they do not consume their services directly (existence value), they wish to preserve the option of possible future consumption (option value) and they strive to bequeath the assets to future generations (bequest value) (Serageldin, 1999, pp. 25–28; Throsby, 2001, p. 11). What may render heritage as an asset to successful tourism products is a mix of factors deriving from both demand and supply: the visitors' perception of a place, personal interests and beliefs, globally acknowledged values, a well-marketed destination image, market and social trends, and appropriate heritage management. In this vein, heritage tourism may be defined as a social phenomenon interacting with supply and demand, where visitation incentives are based on the place's distinctive cultural features as well as the visitor's perception and evaluation of them.

Successful heritage attractions are visitor friendly, physically, intellectually and economically accessible. They meet visitors' needs and market requirements, create the tourist experience and give value for money, while maintaining the authenticity and integrity of the site (Garrod and Fyall, 2000, p. 686). In many cases these prerequisites are not met. Heritage managers consider themselves guardians of regional and national assets, but are external to the tourism business. Their function as providers of public access to heritage attractions is limited. They do not follow policies that render the assets conveyors of meanings, thus creating a place's identity and visitor attachment to destinations. Economic matters do not come before their consideration, although the future of the attractions as public goods depends greatly on financial solvency (Garrod and Fyall, 2000, p. 684), while notions such as carrying and service capacity (Masters and Barrow, 2002, p. 8 ff.) are likely to be unfamiliar. Should invaluable travel determinants, the heritage resources, be offered to the tourism market below cost (Serageldin, 1999, pp. 23–36), then local and national taxpayers must carry the burden of sustaining quality (Mourato and Mazzanti, 2002, p. 51 ff.). If heritage assets, the main heritage tourism incentives, remain external to markets, they cannot be conserved (Mourato and Mazzanti, 2002, pp. 51–54; Throsby, 2001, pp. 10–16, 2002, p. 102 ff.; van der Borg, 2003, p. 1), while tourism pressures contribute further to their decay.

Tourism in historic centres

Historic cities have not been artificially developed as tourist resorts, but have established their reputations as centres of historic, economic and cultural activities much earlier. Their tangible attractions are therefore irreproducible, immovable, remarkably concentrated in small spatial cores and heavily visited because their reputation renders demand inelastic. When visitor flows exceed tourism carrying capacity (TCC), major attractions are severely congested, followed by the downgrading of the quality of all services offered. Russo and Caserta (2002, pp. 245–260) note that the Butler destination life-cycle model does not really apply to cultural heritage destinations. Decline there means augmentation of the visitor–resident ratio, 'banalization' of tourism products (Russo, 1999, p. 42; Russo and Caserta, 2002, p. 46), excessive use of heritage assets and infra structure services and deep discouragement of sophisticated high-spending visitors, whose incentive to choose a destination lies within their cultural perception of that destination.

The demand pattern

A sample tourist profile is provided in Table 16.1. In general, the jewel of the Adriatic, Venice, attracts approximately seven million excursionists and three million tourists a year (van der Borg, 2003, p. 7). It has lost two-thirds of its local residents since 1951 (Russo, 1999, p. 42). Russo and Caserta (2002, p. 247) note that the reduction in time budgets generates informational gaps, resulting in overuse of centrally located cultural assets and non-use of less famous attractions. Excursionists in particular contribute to the tourismification of historic cities (van der Borg et al., 1996, pp. 311, 314; Jansen-Verbeke, 1998, p. 731). They concentrate at major fame attractions, which are logically the only ones to be reached with a minimum of information, whereas low quality invades markets when the percentage of visitors rises. The problem is accentuated by the policy of the periphery, which uses its vicinity to the heritage assets to attract clients. Without contributing to their conservation,

Table 16.1 Tourist profile of the Socrates Intensive Program (SIP) sample

Profile of the SIP sample (about 200 valid questionnaires)

Gender	Male 50% Female 50%
Tourism generators	Domestic tourism 10% Incoming tourism 90% (European 70%, other 30%)
Mode of transport to Venice	Flight carriers and train: 70% Other: 30%
Accommodation type	Hotel 70% Hostel, bed & breakfast 25%
Average duration of stay	Five days
Travel character	Self-organized: 80%
Group size	Not exceeding five people

it delegates daily visitor flows to the small spatial core of historic centres, causing further pressures on transportation, queues and heritage resources. The periphery becomes the area of benefits because it earns the major part of the tourist expenditure, through accommodation, catering and shopping. The heritage city becomes the area of costs because tourists spend a high share of their budget outside the central area; it also has to sustain the overused central attractions and infrastructure using resources other than tourist revenue, such as taxation and subventions.

Although perceptions build the motivation to travel and regulate behaviour at the destination, informational asymmetries between supply and demand, as well as poor heritage management, seem to be the main reasons for mass cultural tourism 'occurring now for the first time in history' (Russo, 2001, p. 172). The profile of the SIP sample is perfectly concordant with the rules of mass cultural tourism: their visit was self-organized in small groups, but with respect to cultural consumption they lost their autonomy and behaved like mass tourists. Although 60–65 per cent believed that there are many environmental problems in Venice and that tourism is partly to blame, they were not willing to contribute up to three Euros to ameliorate the quality of the heritage assets.

Visitation pattern: time pressures, informational asymmetries and congestion

Spatial features, transport modes, available time and information influence tourist flow patterns. Table 16.2 and Figures 16.2 and 16.4 provide information regarding the visitation patterns and the information availability of the sample. Figures 16.1 and 16.3 give some idea of the special location of Venice's attractions, which might also explain visitation patterns. Small time

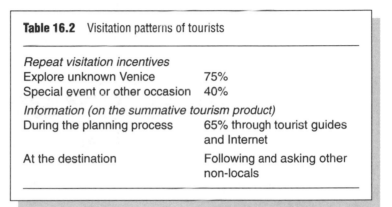

Table 16.2   Visitation patterns of tourists

Repeat visitation incentives
Explore unknown Venice   75%
Special event or other occasion   40%

Information (on the summative tourism product)
During the planning process   65% through tourist guides
                                                              and Internet

At the destination   Following and asking other
                                                              non-locals

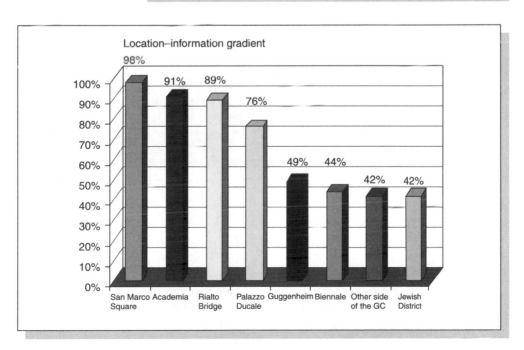

Figure 16.1
Pattern of visitation to Venice's heritage core

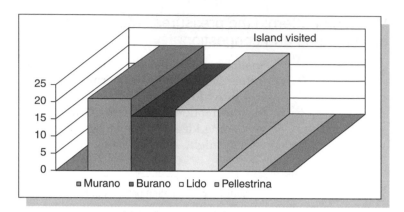

Figure 16.2
Pattern of visitation to Venice's proximate islands

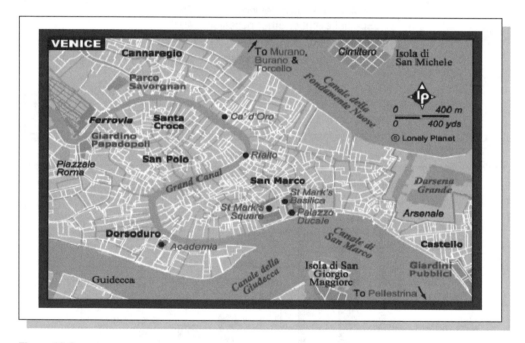

Figure 16.3
Centrally located heritage attractions in Venice

budgets (the average duration of a daily trip is eight hours; Russo, 2001, p. 174) and asymmetric information between visitors and producers define the visitation pattern, rendering traditional information tools ineffective.

Equipped with poor information, visitors put great pressure on the small historic centre; for example, San Marco's Square has exceeded its TCC and local people no longer frequent it.

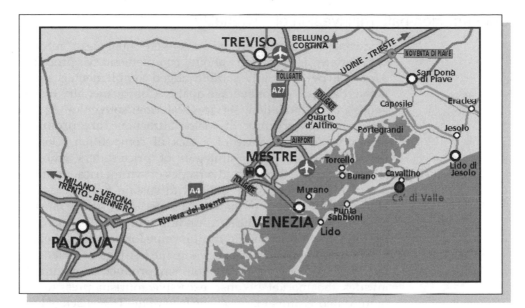

Figure 16.4
Venice: periphery and islands

Only one in forty-four visitors enters a museum in Venice, and only one in fifty-five a church. Cultural expenditure is less than 3 per cent of visitors' total budget, at US $179.40 per capita per day for tourists and US $68.40 for excursionists (van der Borg, 2003, p. 7).

Seventy per cent of the SIP sample considered the performance of centrally located cultural institutions good; 80 per cent ignored the significant advantages of the Venice Card (van der Borg, 2003, p. 22–23), which is local government's main tool by which to re-engineer the cultural sector. The fact that cardholders do not queue does not influence purchasing decision at all. Visitors assume that the card will not benefit them: only 20 per cent of the sample would have bought it if they had known about it.

Visitors in the SIP sample moved around the city using mainly vaporetti or going on foot, finding their way around using a map or a tourist guide (70 per cent) or signposts (30 per cent). Signage in Venice City is remarkable poor, recycling information to and from major attractions. The distance of less famous attractions from the central primary ones determines the visitation pattern, and distance decay drastically affects visitation incentives. Lack of information gives birth to the congestion effect: 'I don't go to places I don't know of'.

Consumption pattern: invasion of low quality

Unaware of quality, SIP visitors were unable to retrieve appropriate information about complementary products. Almost 40 per cent of the sample judged complementary products as being of low or average quality. Complementary tourist goods (accommodation, services, catering, souvenirs, etc.) in the immediate vicinity of major attractions are produced monopolistically because of a lack of competition. Quality depends on the profit strategies of price-setters who, as monopolists, are the main adversaries of symmetrical information, while taxpayers are obliged to sustain heritage assets. However, the quality of the tourist experience is built on supply and the quality of the surrounding context: all elements of the tourism product should recoup value for money, especially in a heritage tourism context, where the heritage experience is the basic component of the tourism product. Low quality invades the market because excessive tourism pressure by uninformed visitors increases the load of the TCC. Lack of time does not allow inspection before purchase. Flows join other flows, causing the bandwagon effect (Towse, 1991, in Russo and Caserta, 2002, p. 250): 'I go where others go'.

Destination information management and marketing systems: towards sustainable heritage tourism development

Tourism uses and DIMMS

New tourism, including re-emerging urban tourism, is the innovative framework concerning all players: undifferentiated conservative and economizing mass customers have given way to sophisticated seekers of qualitative travel experiences. Besides demand for classic services, new tourists exert pressure on the tourism industry for the development of new products, services and experiences. Experienced travellers with a strong environmental conscience and respect for local cultures enter *en masse* the phase of self-designing the travel process. Since travelling is no longer the mere bridge of time between arrival and departure, tourism organizations are exploiting features and capabilities of information and communication technology to meet the sophisticated requirements of the new tourists (Rachman and Buchanan, 1999, pp. 12–15).

Destination information management and marketing systems (DIMMS) are computerized systems specifically designed to facilitate information about a destination's tourism product (Chen and Sheldon, 1997, pp. 151–176) through integrated databases. Spatially equally distributed DIMMS represent rich data and process models, bridge temporal and spatial distance, store data independently of the program's runtime, facilitate communication through qualitative and quantitative execution guarantees, and combine enhanced data processing to satisfy a growing visitor potential in each destination (Aberer, 2000). Permanent quality control concerning information is especially vital to DIMMS, because it guarantees its credibility (Ebner, 1992, p. 1), whereas its distribution depends on the successful representation of a destination's assets.

Demand and supply dictate the structure of DIMMS as a national, regional or local operating system. National DIMMS usually consist of a database management system (DBMS), which covers the tourism product nationwide. This structure allows local tourism offices to access information through telecommunication connections. In this way, national tourism offices control all the subdivisions, providing access to CRS–GDS. All regions access nationwide information about the tourism product. This is essential to trips with multiple destinations, where at each destination information is crucial to plan the next step. National DIMMS facilitate the channelling of customer flows to regional and local ones; otherwise, suppliers depend on foreign travel agencies and tour operators, who do not have the same interests as local producers.

Local DIMMS provide online information distribution within the borders of every region. Lacking standardization is a strong disadvantage, and the complexity required to connect to other systems outside the country is difficult to overcome. Interconnections within other regions require synergies and consensus, but players with a competitive mentality will not be eager to share information sources (Haimeyer, 1995, p. 105).

Resources for the development and functioning of DIMMS come from central, federal or local government or the private sector. If CRS–GDS are included, fees are required to enter the participants' list, or a percentage is set up, as a provision corresponding to the reservations made. Interconnections with CRS–GDS enable market widening through proper channelling. DIMMS create communication environments with CRS–GDS and connect suppliers globally with travel agencies and autonomous travellers. Should suppliers share costs, then DIMMS could create strong similarities to CRS–GDS. In this case the tourism product cannot be diversified on a market segmentation basis. If no fees are required, suppliers enter the participants' list and DIMMS build an integrated system covering niche markets, alternative tourism activities, accessibility networks, accommodation and transport, political, cultural and environmental affairs, event marketing, weather forecast, online shopping, etc.

Tourism benefits and smart DIMMS

Information is crucial to primary and secondary tourist goods. Industry-related DIMMS (Ritchie, 2002, pp. 439–454), interconnected with various information sources at the destination, at entry points or distant locations guarantee appropriate information distribution. Since the worldwide web solves partially the problem of the intangible nature of the tourism product, DIMMS fill informational gaps concerning a place's summative tourism product, while exporting the place's brand image.

Still evolving, DIMMS constantly take into account the latest developments in technology and market demands, acting as tourism counsellors, who reduce the time and money budget needed to acquire information, enabling a vast customer pool to detect the desirable choices. Smart DIMMS offer a complex source of information concerning a holistic tourism product and the expected real benefits (Rachman and Buchanan, 1999, pp. 14–21), while serving visitors and producers through the exchange and processing of information about tailor-made and ready-made products at local, regional and national levels. They guide existing and potential markets to discover the unique features and attractions of a destination, rather than presenting exchangeable commodities, as these usually appear in the catalogues of tour operators. Accessible twenty-four hours, DIMMS prepare visitors upon arrival, mitigate language difficulties, generate bookings and sales, offer edutainment, give an overview of accessibility networks, including public transport schedules, traffic and weather forecasts, regulate tourist flows through multicriteria networks of tourism resources within a region, and decongest major attractions through appropriate information and visitor flow management.

The use of multimedia technology in the web signals new ways of communication and promotion. Smart DIMMS (Aberer, 2000, p. 11) should be able to handle semantics in information systems (data mining, information retrieval and intelligent information agents), co-operative information systems (pragmatics, autonomy and self-interested agents; Steiner, 2000, p. 33 ff.) and the use of other media in information systems (multimedia data management and multimedia retrieval), and realize new forms of distribution (connectivity, processing caps) and software agents. Future DIMMS will include mobile computing, intelligent agents and self-organizing information systems (Aberer, 2000, p. 13).

Smart DIMMS benefit visitors through:

- immediate connection of products and providers
- monitoring quality and validity of the information
- simplifications of the procedures that save time and money, e.g. integration of:
  - multimedia info points, kiosks and touch screens, maxi-screens, web phones, line @ and other terminals
  - informative signboards
  - newsletter management via mail and/or SMS
  - management of submitted demand via telephone, fax and e-mail services
  - integration of intelligent geographical maps with functionality of routing; interactive maps
  - accessibility and communication networks; intraregional connections
- interfaces with:
  - CRS–GDS and other systems of online booking
  - software for hotel management
- twenty-four-hour, real-time management of accommodation types (modalities, availability, rates, special offers, immediate confirmation of reservations, etc.)
- reservation of additional services (guided excursions, heritage trails, car rentals, fitness and spa reservations, restaurants, beach and ski passes, theatre, cinema, etc.)
- weather and traffic forecast
- users' guidance in the region's assets: social, aesthetic, historic, scientific, special values, ecosystems, biodiversity and geodiversity, along with a thematic glossary of local culture, aiming to forge customers' loyalty
- thematic browsing
- multicriteria tourist nets: highly interactive networked tailor-made packages
- information structuring based on the principles of human–computer interaction
- online edutainment and prizewinning games.

Smart DIMMS also benefit destinations, by:

- local economies through strategic alliances of the public and private sector
- regional platforms: offer to the public and private sector the know-how required to spread and commercialize their products
- inclusion of small and medium-sized enterprises: initiates their independence from the tour operators

- online shopping of strictly locally produced traditional items creates brands in many ways
- monitoring the quality and validity of the information
- destination branding based on the icon value of the tourism product
- management of tourist demand and tourist flows through information policies:
  - decongestion of tourist pressure at major fame locations, coastal zones, mature locations by the creation of a holistic destination product
  - spatial diffusion of the tourist flows based on diversified products (promotion of complementary, additional and alternative emerging locations and destinations offering a wide range of activities)
  - enhancement of seasonality through product differentiation (cultural roads, special events)
  - raising expenditure per capita and redistribution of the tourist revenue through virtual destination guidance
- destination representation based on heritage interpretation.

DIMMS as a tool for heritage interpretation

Heritage interpretation is a multidisciplinary process of message communication, aiming to reveal effectively to visitors a place's natural and cultural wealth. Meaning and relationships of a given culture, approached through guidance and personal participation, whether at the destination or in virtual environments, are the goal of any interpretation.

Information is definitely not interpretation, although it constitutes the backbone of interpretation. Interpretation translates an expert's technical account into a message in the language of the visitor, relating the context to his or her everyday life and experiences. An interactive framework among resources, interpreters and visitors makes learning a pleasure-generating process: through first-hand experiences interpretation involves visitors in the explorative learning and entertainment process (Papathanassiou-Zuhrt and Sakellaridis, 2003, p. 6).

To adapt the natural and cultural phenomena of given heritage tourism contexts to the needs of specific target groups, interpretation interlinks various disciplines from natural, cognitive and human sciences (Moscardo, 1996, pp. 376–397). Key issues in the interpretive process are the planner's ability to master human cognitive mechanisms of acquiring and retaining information, and to adapt through hermeneutic information, adapting scientific context and terminology to a recreational learning environment in favour of the visitor in given heritage tourism contexts, such as sites, collections and trails.

Interpretation enables visitors to receive, understand and remember messages, encouraging them to use and evaluate the information in certain ways. It bonds sustainable development policies, raising public awareness, environmental education and communication. Visitors learn to understand, appreciate, value and care for the cultural and natural heritage resources interpreted to them. The benefits of interpretation are multiple for the economy, ecology and society. Interpretation:

- meets the increasing demand for educational visitor experiences
- creates visitor satisfaction, positive word-of-mouth reports, high revenue, longer visits and repeat visitation
- enhances civic pride, environmental conscience and respect for local communities
- reduces environmental and cultural damage by explaining the impacts of various behaviours and suggesting appropriate alternatives
- substitutes experience for places that are very fragile and/or difficult to visit (e.g. caves, sacred temples) or topics that are impossible to experience directly (e.g. disease, prehistoric or cosmic conditions)
- web interpretation exports a resource's image globally, bridging the spatial and temporal distance between web navigators and cultural operators
- provides visitors with relevance and makes them part of the experience.

Information technology enables the (re)presentation, exploration, celebration and dissemination of heritage assets. Whereas the linearity of printed texts constrains the reader's imagination, hypermedia environments mark the web as a medium. Disruption of linear sequences, autonomy of reading and learning processes are distinctive features of the hypertext compared with the written word. In hypermedia environments decisions are unavoidable: readers establish a heuristic, non-sequential autonomy. The hypertextual environment links formerly separate entities in a meaningful way to one another, and by presenting facts and reasons in one format they become the new narrative medium. This medium enhances visitors' participation, the ability to explore and move back and forth in given settings, so that learning becomes a pleasure-generating process.

With the significance of linking given, the new task for DIMMS should be to extract the semantics from the knowledge implicit to the media, and associate between media representations and semantics without a heavy manual input (Lewis et al., 1999, p. 4). DIMMS can and should develop narrative tools to support the conceptual framework of heritage interpretation, so that heritage assets can be made attractive through provocative, coherent collocations and accessible to a wider public. To design effective web-narrative structures, interpreters exploit the semantic and episodic memory potential (Mullholland and Collins, 2002, p. 2). DIMMS interpretation should consider the following three keystones:

- *Interactive interpretation framework*: smart digital narratives, giving up chronological arrays and terminology, incorporate typical exhibits. They construct a plot, an array that allows any cultural and natural setting to be viewed from different perspectives. Heritage objects are autonomous narrative elements belonging to larger narrative structures. As visualized culture narratives they become storytellers who validate other elements and structures as long as they are (re)presented in the prevailing historical and socioeconomic context that created them (Pletinxc et al., 2003, pp. 225–231).
- *Interpretive representation through processual information management*: computational ontologies arrange, present and classify heritage representations according to various taxonomy principles. They demonstrate how a work of art is the inspiration source of a series of cultural products (Throsby, 2002, p. 10) and secure the contextualized learning process. Conceptual models reveal temporal and causal relationships between the tangible heritage resources and may present the steps taken to their completion, so that visitors become familiarized with several procedures. Web-based tools such as resource annotation tools (Mullholland and Collins, 2002) enable visitors to create their own collection, their own living heritage spaces.
- *Edutainment*: computational techniques may turn unfamiliar notions, themes, areas and topics into pleasurable experiences. Interpretation as a communication process is based on exploratory learning techniques. The dual character of edutainment consists of entertainment and exploratory learning, a combination that generates the pleasure of being (self) instructed. The prerequisite for edutainment to be effective is that structure and management of information result in meaningful messages for the recipients. Communicating a message effectively means that visitors receive, understand, react, remember and use its content. Edutainment is a powerful tool that benefits visitors through virtual or first-hand

experiences or spiritual enrichment; it benefits places by educating and sensitizing a broad public to their needs and problems.

Conclusion

Heritage attractions in qualitative environmental settings create a destination's distinct profile and generate tourism. To prevent tourism becoming a monoculture, and protect the heritage assets and local people's quality of life, tourism planning has to restructure the cultural sector and manage tourist flows effectively. Valorization, interpretive management and constant monitoring of heritage assets should be major tasks for heritage managers. DIMMS represent a valuable tool to implement sustainable tourism uses. Through visitor care and orientation they help tourists to behave responsibly, create a heritage asset's market value mix by globally exporting its image as a tourism component, achieve satisfaction of tourism professionals through immediate connection of demand and supply, and impact positively on the local economy and the environment.

References

Aberer, K. (2000). *Information Systems Architecture*. EPFL-DSC, Laboratoire de systèmes d'informations repartis, Part I. Available at: http://lsirwww.epfl.ch/courses/fds/20002001ws/Overview_handout.pdf

van der Borg, J. (2003). *The Heritage of Venice. Economic and Social Issues*. Venice: Socrates Intensive Program.

van der Borg, J., Costa, P. and Gotti, G. (1996). Tourism in European heritage cities. *Annals of Tourism Research* 23(2): 306–321.

Chen, H. M. and Sheldon, P. (1997). Destination information systems: design issues and directions. *Journal of Management Information Systems* 14(2): 151–176.

Ebner, A. (1992). TIS – Das Tirol Information System. In Alt, R., Schmid, B. F. and Zbornik, S. E. M. *Electronic Markets* 2(1). Available at: http://www.electronicmarkets.org/modules/pub/view.php/electronicmarkets-408

Garrod, B. and Fyall, A. (2000). Managing heritage tourism. *Annals of Tourism Research* 27(3): 682–708.

Haimeyer, P. (1995). *Ist nachchaltige Regionalentwicklung mit Tourismus realistisch*. Berlin: Arbeitskreis Freizeit und Fremdenverkehrsgeographie, Institut für Tourismus der FU-Berlin, Berichte und Materialien, No. 14.

Jansen-Verbeke, M. (1998). Tourismification of historic cities. *Annals of Tourism Research* 25(3): 739–769.

Masters, D. S. and Barrow, G. (2002). Sustainable visitor management system. Discussion paper.

Moscardo, G. (1996). Mindful visitors: heritage and tourism. *Annals of Tourism Research* 23(2): 376–397.

Mourato, S. and Mazzanti, M. (2002). Economic valuation of cultural heritage: evidence and prospects. In De la Torre, M. (ed.) *Assessing the Values of Cultural Heritage*. Research Report. Los Angeles: Getty Conservation Institute.

Mullholland, P. and Collins, T. (2002). Using digital narratives to support the collaborative learning and exploration of cultural heritage. *Proceedings of the 13th International Workshop on Database and Expert Systems Applications (DEXA '02)*, 1529–4188/02.

Papathanasiou-Zuhrt, D. and Sakellaridis, O. (2003). Scio, urbs Nobilissima. Tourism uses of the fortified city. *Euromed Heritage II International Conference*, Mytilene, 6–8 November.

Poria, Y., Butler, R. and Airey, D. (2003). The core of heritage tourism. *Annals of Tourism Research* 30(1): 238–254.

Rachman, Z. M. and Buchanan, J. (1999). *Effective Tourism Web Sites, Part 1: Literature Review and Features Survey. Part 2: Expectation versus Delivery of Tourism Web Sites*. Hamilton, New Zealand: Department of Management Systems, University of Waikato.

Ritchie, J. R. B. (2002). A framework for an industry supported destination marketing information system. *Tourism Management* 23: 439–454.

Russo, A. P. (1999). Venice: coping with culture vultures. *UNESCO Courier* 56.

Russo, A. P. (2001). The vicious circle of tourism development in heritage cities. *Annals of Tourism Research* 29(1): 165–182.

Russo, A. P. and Caserta, S. (2002). More means worse: asymmetric information, spatial displacement and sustainable heritage tourism. *Journal of Cultural Economics* 26: 245–260.

Serageldin, I. (1999). *Very Special Places: The Architecture and Economics of Intervening in Historic Cities*. International Bank for Reconstruction and Development/World Bank No. 19255.

Steiner, T. (2000). Software agents in tourism industry – prototypes and prospects. *Zeitschrift der Schweizerischen Informatik Organisation/Revue des organisations suisses d'informatique* (1): 33–38.

Throsby, D. (2001). Conceptualizing heritage as cultural capital. In *Heritage Economics Challenges for Heritage Conservation and Sustainable Development in the 21st Century*. Conference

Proceedings 2000, Australian National University of Canberra, 07/2000. Australian Heritage Commission.

Throsby, D. (2002). Cultural capital and sustainability concepts in the economics of cultural heritage. In De la Torre, M. (ed.) *Assessing the Values of Cultural Heritage*. Research Report. Los Angeles, CA: Getty Conservation Institute.

Websites

CHIMER Digital Heritage Programme, www.chimer.org

Heritage Restoration and Conservation Programme, www. vitra.org

Conclusion

The future of the past: visions and trends for cultural tourism sector

Marianna Sigala and David Leslie

Cultural heritage is the essence of tourism in many destination areas worldwide. Every year, millions of people travel to view the Acropolis of Athens, the Colosseum in Rome and many other historic sites of international renown. These sites are of general interest to visitors, even though the visitors probably have no significant ties to the heritage sites that they visit. Although world heritage attractions draw large numbers of international and domestic tourists, for most foreign tourists these sites consist only a small part of a more extensive travel package. These attractions can evoke feelings of admiration, but they probably do not evoke feelings of personal attachment. Visits to historic sites are mostly motivated by the belief that such places (and the objects at these places) are linked to the remote past. In addition, millions of other people engage in travel to experience heritage of a more personal nature; most of the world's historic sites are not internationally known and only relatively few ever attract international tourists, except perhaps in combination with other relevant attractions. For every world-renowned cultural attraction, there are hundreds of other – not famous – sites that are appreciated at a more local basis.

This text aimed to analyse under one cover substantive management issues that transcend national boundaries facing the planning and development of cultural tourism. To further this aim a thematic approach was adopted based on four key areas, namely marketing, operations, environment and sustainable development, and new technologies applications management. Each of these sections comprised an overview chapter summarizing the major management issues and three related international case studies that aimed to provide practical and first-hand experience and knowledge on the management issue and subject. Throughout these sections, the writers have sought to stimulate further discussion and debate by identifying major trends and developments that would challenge the sector both now and in the future. In this vein and based also on previous discussions, this concluding chapter aims to present the major challenges facing the future of the cultural tourism sector as well as to provide some directions for future research.

This book also explored the many extant definitions of heritage and cultural tourism, and discussed the recent significant growth of the cultural and heritage tourism market. In addition, notions of post-modernism and its relevance to heritage-cultural tourism, both offline and online, were discussed to shed further light on this recent growth in heritage-cultural tourism. Recent research on heritage tourism research was also presented, including such issues as the different types of heritage visitors and the experiences that they seek at heritage sites or when visiting websites of online heritage-cultural operators. The present book also focused on the importance of planning at cultural and heritage sites. A review of the heritage-planning literature in this planning respect includes the relevant elements of interpretation, authenticity and sense of place, and the importance of these elements in the heritage experience. The importance of demand, motivation and segmentation in tourism research supports the need for further research in the heritage-tourism area. This is also necessary for better understanding of heritage tourists themselves. Finally, a review of the service operations management-marketing literature was included in this book, because of the necessity for quality service in the heritage-tourism industry, and its vital role in sustainable planning and development.

The book content clearly illustrates that nowadays the world's cultural institutions are facing very rapid and dramatic transformations. These transformations are due not only to the use of increasingly sophisticated technologies, which become obsolete more and more rapidly, but also to a re-examination of the role of modern public institutions in today's society, and the rising expectations and demands of visitors. These trends affect all aspects of the modern cultural institution, from the many facets of management to providing universal and dynamic access to their cultural resources, as well as creating new experiential values, motives and learning forms. Moreover, technological innovation plays a major role in the way cultural institutions develop strategies for valorizing and managing their collections and visitors, and the case studies compiled in this textbook clearly illustrate how new technologies can be exploited and managed to achieve the former.

However, the frequent assumption that the implementation of new technologies can serve as a motor for organizational change and transformation is more than questionable. In practice, such notions lead to short-sighted and unsuccessful technological projects. This is because the main prerequisites for the successful use of new media, such as skilled employees (networkers, information or knowledge workers), radical changes in the workflow, and the adoption of new media by cultural visitors and local communities are often neglected.

Indeed, analysis of Europe's cultural institutions from the viewpoint of their awareness of new technologies reveals a wide spectrum with regard to the adoption and exploitation of the benefits of information and communication technologies. At one end of the spectrum, there are the pioneer institutions and early adopters of information technologies. These institutions have a clear plan for digitizing their collections and creating enhanced digital visitors' learning experiences by thinking of innovative technological applications on the Internet or by integrating new technologies in their traditional settings. At the other end of the spectrum, there are very many small operators that are unaware of the new technologies and their possibilities, and do not possess the financial or human resources to participate in these new developments.

It is the challenge of national and regional governments as well as of cultural operators to increase the capacity and competence of small cultural heritage institutions and create the conditions that allow those under-resourced organizations to participate in the information society. Policy makers and researchers should have as a priority the development of a comprehensive cultural heritage policy that claims to provide cultural heritage for all would need to address the issue of how to strengthen small cultural operators and regions with valuable cultural resources. Such policy should be underpinned by research and findings identifying the facilitating and inhibiting factors of technology adoption with cultural institutions, but also by individuals. Research and discussion are required to identify ways in modernizing training programmes provided by cultural institutions. Technology training is a major factor enabling technology diffusion, but skills and competencies such as project management, digitization and life-cycle management of digital resources that need to be learned should be investigated. However, research is required not only to reveal the necessary technological skills, but also to identify the new roles, responsibilities and activities that cultural actors and stakeholders have to assume. Technological applications are transforming the role of cultural operators and actors (e.g. curators) and the latter should learn how to assume their new responsibilities and better manage the change.

In the longer term, there is a need for a shift in orientation in the management of cultural resources and the associated tourism potential, away from market-led to resource-based development. Thus, there is a need to promote awareness and understanding on the part of the community of their own cultural resources and to develop further on this basis. Furthermore, there is a need to foster in the community better awareness and understanding of the actual and potential benefits, particularly the indirect, of tourism, and to encourage participation and ownership. Thus, building on and developing a tripartite approach from the outset should lead to sustainability. In this, heritage interpretation and presentation has a key role not only in terms of access, but also through appropriate messages to increase respect for the cultural resources of others and recognition that some facets of such resources, even when presented as a cultural attraction, are not necessarily open to visitors. In this sense, visitors are outsiders. However, in the broader context of global society these outsiders are also stakeholders in terms of their support for sustaining the cultural heritage of others and thus arguably also when appearing as tourists. This stakeholder interest often appears to be absent from the management planning and development of cultural tourism, and it needs further investigation.

There is little doubt that every country, region or locale has viewed or is viewing its cultural resources in terms of tourism potential. This is markedly so in the post-industrialized nations of the Western world, especially in Western Europe, which has been losing the market share of international arrivals for well over a decade as traditional visitors go elsewhere. This increased competition, allied with innovation, information and communication technology, and dissemination of best practice, has led to improvements in the management planning, development and presentation of many cultural attractions. However, this has generated further challenges, as today's visitors are generally more demanding and have higher expectations than previous visitors. For many of these visitors, 'the past', in terms of practices and presentation, is not good enough. Therefore, it is essential that those involved in the management of cultural tourism not only get the fundamentals right but also adopt best practice in all aspects of planning, development and delivery, including the introduction of an environmental management system. Further, due consideration needs to be given to managing access and facilitating visitor needs by attending to the superstructure. But, for contemporary and new developments to be sustained it is not sufficient to be an example of best management practices; the cultural attraction itself must be founded on a secure base. It must not be a contrivance of a currently popular theme or overstated based on too few resources, for such attractions will be subject to the vagaries of fashion, soon to become the white elephants of what has been so poignantly described as 'the heritage industry'. We must also be wary of tiredness in the marketplace. Tourists consume places with increasing speed and the novelty of major cultural events and promotions, such as 'European City of Culture', begin to wear thin as tourists become blasé, tired of the same old thing, and search for the new and that which is different. Undoubtedly, this is one of the major challenges facing the management of international cultural tourism. Conversely, the real cultural icons will become more treasured for their substance, founded as they are on the cultural capital of their communities, their society. The challenge to management is to conserve these icons and capacity in a sustainable way while ensuring that the necessary resources are in place to maintain their future.

As the case studies have illustrated (particularly those related to the development of cultural tourism packages), in the networked and digital world, the demand for unique cultural heritage resources does not stop at the institutional walls, but highlights the need for co-operation and co-ordination among destination operators, community and stakeholders. Therefore, cultural operators need to enter into new relationships with their environment, other institutions across sectors, private businesses, intermediary organizations and new user groups. Cultural operators should exploit the innovation-driving role of digital technologies with the aim of extending their supply chains and creating cultural ecologies. Major objectives of these partnerships are to collaborate in the cost-effective creation of new services and cultural products, to collaborate for sustainable development strategies, to co-ordinate digitization programmes, to define standards and structures to provide seamless access, and to share resources. Networking with other institutions across sectors is an essential component of every organization, and cultural operators are no exception. The governing principle of such networks is not competition but partnership, and research investigating how institutions can develop and maintain quality partnerships with other firms is required. Collaborative quality is a new concept that needs further investigation and support from practical experiences.

The explosion of online cultural publishing is also 'democratizing' cultural access and expression, while also pressing the cultural operators. Indeed, digital cultural resources are not the property of a cultural élite, since, as Sigala showed in her case study, millions of people can use online technologies for creating their own collections as well as developing their own meaning of cultural artefacts. In this way, in the future, many different microcultures will demand to be present in society's cultural resources and collections with their own cultural record. In this society, the role and vision of the cultural institutions required by both visitors and policy makers need to be further developed and researched.

In this vein, research and debate into the new vision of cultural institutions could and should address the following issues. These are not exhaustive, but summarize the major issues introduced in previous discussions:

- the role and value of cultural heritage in the knowledge and digital society
- the role of cultural resources in fostering sustainable development
- the adoption of environmental management policy and practices
- enhancing the role of cultural operators and resources for driving innovation and development
- the criteria used for including or excluding resources from future cultural collections, such as issues of social inclusiveness, or the inclusion of new forms of cultural expressions and interpretation
- multilingual access as a means to communicate to an increasingly pluralistic society and the global community
- the changing role, objectives and scope of the activities of cultural institutions and their actors
- the positioning of the visitor, the tourist, as a stakeholder and implications of this in terms of the way in which cultural tourism is managed.

The book editors: Marianna Sigala, University of the Aegean and David Leslie, Glasgow Caledonian University.

Index